Ninety-Nine Newfies

Edited by

Pat Seawell

ISBN: 0-7596-6329-7

This book is printed on acid free paper.

1stBooks - rev. 10/24/01

Books for Young Readers by Pat Seawell

Canyon Secrets
Desert Whispers

In memory of
Charlotte, Emily, and Rose

Introduction

After having at least one, most often two, beloved Newfy girls underfoot for over fourteen years, our house seemed sadly empty when we lost Rose early in 1999. Although the time was not right for another puppy, I sat down at my computer, entered "Newfoundland dog," clicked "Search," found Newf-List, and discovered a new world. I didn't have a Newfy, but I had found hundreds of people willing to share their Newfies with me via e-mail.

Over the next few weeks I lurked and learned and wished I had found the Newf-L community sooner. Occasionally, amid the informative discussions of diet, health, exercise, and other Newf-related issues, someone would post a "story"—an account of an amusing incident or a tender moment or an unusual occurrence involving their dog. I loved the stories. I loved the echoes of our own three girls that I heard in the stories.

When Wendy Scheeres of Wyong Creek, New South Wales, Australia, posted an exceptionally amusing tale about her dogs, I was inspired. Wouldn't it be fun to read a whole *collection* of Newfy stories? Wouldn't it be fun to *compile* and *edit* a whole collection of Newfy stories? Thus, with more enthusiasm and confidence than knowledge, I proposed the idea of a Newfy story collection to the subscribers of Newf-L. With the help of contributing authors, I would compile, edit, and organize the Newfy stories into a book, publish it, and donate 90% of the profits to an organization that supported Newfoundland dogs. The idea was discussed on Newf-L. Many suggestions were offered. The consensus was that it would be a worthwhile project. So, in the summer of 1999, we began working on this book.

Pat Aheimer of Bay Village, Ohio, USA, was the first contributing author. She was generous with her time and her patience as we worked out a procedure for writing a book via e-mail. Sending the draft of the story back and forth to each other, we edited it and polished it until we had a story which pleased us both. Pat was thrilled at having found a way to honor her Sweet Kate, and I was thrilled at having found a way to help her do so.

A few months into the project, an invitation was issued to the members of Newf-L to join Ausnewf, an Australian Newfoundland dog list. I subscribed to Ausnewf and was soon asking the members of that jovial group to contribute their doggy tales to the book. Between the two lists, I had a constant and steady supply of stories.

The more stories I collected, the more delightful the project became. People throughout the world were sharing their lives, their families, and their adorable Newfies with me—and they were *thanking* me for allowing them to do so! Of course, it was I who should have been thanking them. The truth is, we were all having a fine time. Because of the cooperation of the contributing authors, compiling and editing this collection has been one of the most joyful celebrations of my long and happy life. To you contributing authors, each and every one, I am forever grateful. It has been an honor to work with you. Thank you.

Many, *many* people helped me with this project. I especially thank:

My husband and Grand Companion, John P. Seawell, for critiquing every story, for creating many of the titles, for serving as my postal consultant/assistant, and for being incredibly patient and supportive during the past two years while my focus has been "all Newfy, all the time."

Kathee Kiesselbach for creating the cover art and the wood engraving for the interior. Not only is Kathee an artist, she also has the specialized knowledge necessary to convert her art into CMYK color PSD and TIFF files with just the right number of pixels to satisfy our publishing company.

Larry Pratt (greyfuzz@eskimo.com) for bringing his Government Printing Office experience and proof-reading/editing expertise to this project. His ability to spot errors, as well as his suggestions for improving sentence structure, order, sense, wording and style, have been much appreciated. Larry gave me the grammar and editing rules, but was patient with the "special" rules I invented. Thus, having created my own rules, I accept the responsibility for any and all errors, glaring or otherwise.

Joanne Seabloom for helping write a document which described the project and requested permission from the contributing authors to include their stories in the book.

Cathy Comstock, Mary Runkel, and Susan Sundquist-Kelly for taking turns monitoring the lists for stories when I had to unsubscribe for short periods of time.

Cynthia and Mark Chatelain of Galactic Technologies in San Antonio for promising to "help with the book," and for coming to my rescue every time I got lost amid my computer's files, directories, and other intimidating mysteries.

Leo Abbot and Jenny Manning for giving advice and instructions every time I panicked over a virus scare—or the coming of a new millennium.

You Know Who You Are for sending calming words and reassurances when I panicked over other stuff; for cheering so loudly and having so much fun while writing your story; for locating contributing authors when they went missing; for working through difficult, unanticipated obstacles to complete your story; for sharing photos and jpegs of your precious Newfies; for correcting the accuracy of health-related info; for sending copies of your Newfy art; for sending Newfy mugs for my coffee breaks; for sending notes and newspaper clippings and videos and Newfy newsletters; for being patient when I insisted that you *hurry up, hurry up* while I moved at glacial speed.

And, You Know Who You Are, for becoming my friend for life.

About Newf-List

In December, 1994, while an employee at The University of Colorado, Jon Giltner created Newf-L. He had a Newf with health problems and was looking for information. The University ran a general-purpose e-mail list server for the campus community, so Jon used their platform to launch Newf-L.

Newf-L grew rapidly. Within six months it had approximately 300 subscribers. By the end of the first year, there were approximately 500 subscribers. For the past several years Newf-L has been fairly stable at approximately 1,200 subscribers.

Jon left the University in 1996, and it has been by the good graces of his colleagues there that Newf-L lives on in its original home. Mike Carter, in particular, has been sympathetic to Newf-L. He supervises the group that manages the University processing systems. He personally oversees the University e-mail lists, and Newf-L is one of the higher volume lists.

After Jon left the University, Newf-L began taking more time than he could devote to it. Ashley McLure had been one of the first subscribers and had begun responding to some issues on her own when Jon failed to get to them. Jon asked Ashley to officially become a co-owner of Newf-L. Ashley accepted the responsibility and has been ably managing Newf-L for the past five years.

Heartfelt thanks go to Jon, Ashley, and Mike. Their efforts are much appreciated.

Today Newf-L is a self-moderating list with some 1,200 subscribers who live throughout the world. Because of the knowledge and generosity of many of these subscribers, Newf-L has become an invaluable source of information pertaining to Newfoundland dogs.

You are invited to join Newf-L by sending an e-mail to listproc@lists.Colorado.EDU. In the body of your message write "subscribe Newf-L" followed by your e-mail address.

About Ausnewf

Ausnewf was born in February, 1998. Vicky Bartlette, Marnie Davidson, and Angela Cook met via Newf-L. They loved Newf-L, but thought they might be able to bring the Australian Newf community a bit closer if they started an Australian Newf list. They wanted a place that reflected their own sense of time and place. They also knew Aussies tend to be rather laidback, have a somewhat warped sense of humor, and have no trouble poking fun at themselves.

Angela was involved in an Internet Server Provider business at the time, and with the help of a friend with technical expertise, set up the list. The first posts to Ausnewf went through on February 20, 1998.

Within weeks subscribers were sharing information and funny stories, asking questions and getting answers, and generally creating a happy community for exchanging information.

In March, 2001, Angela, and Heather Hoogendorp (who had been the first subscriber to Ausnewf and is now second-in-command) switched Ausnewf from its original ISP to *Elists.com.au.*

Heartfelt thanks go to Angela and Heather for their efforts. Keeping all the rowdy list people in line is no easy task!

Today Ausnewf is a self-moderating list with approximately 100 subscribers. 85% of the subscribers live in Australia or New Zealand; 9% are in the UK; and 6% are in the USA and Europe.

You are invited to subscribe to Ausnewf by following this link: http://wombat.elists.com.au/cgi-bin/info.cgi?ausnewf or by sending an e-mail to Majordomo@elists.com.au. In the body of the message write "subscribe ausnewf".

The Ninety-Nine Newfies

(in the order in which they received their Story Completed titles)

Good Kate Sweet Kate

Ashley, our very first Newfoundland, was given to us when she was 7½ years old. She was the sweetest, warmest, most loving creature I had ever known. Over the next eight years, her cheerfulness and gentle dignity enriched our lives and endeared her to people throughout our whole community. She had a wonderful presence about her that seemed to bring out the best in everyone with whom she came in contact.

When I learned that Ashley's only daughter of breeding age was expecting a litter, there was nothing to ponder. All I wanted for Christmas that year was one of Ashley's grand-puppies! So, three days before Christmas, with Ashley in the back seat of our old Buick, my husband and I made the 1½ hour trip from Bay Village, Ohio, to Erie, Pennsylvania, to select my new three-month-old puppy.

As it turned out, the new puppy selected me. Joyfully, if somewhat clumsily, one big black fluff-ball repeatedly bounded over to me as I sat visiting with the puppies. With her smiles and kisses she completely stole my heart away. Her name was Benhill's Good Kate Sweet Kate. We called her Kate.

What had been a bad snowstorm on our way to Erie had turned into a blizzard by the time we headed home. But, on we drove through the storm, thirty-pound Baby Kate sitting happily in my lap and Grandmother Ashley leaning excitedly over my shoulder. Ashley seemed thrilled about the new puppy. She could hardly wait to mother her little granddaughter.

Three months later, our daughter and her two youngest children visited from Florida. One cold, snowy day during their visit, our other daughter and her family came over for a special family dinner. Afterward, the Florida grandchildren, the Ohio grandchildren, all of us adults, and Ashley and Kate spent the evening playing in the snow. As always, Kate knocked herself out trying to keep up with Ashley and the older children.

After our exuberant romp, we were all tired. Our daughter changed Jacob, her youngest, into some warm sleepers and the whole family gathered to relax in the living room where a warm, cozy fire crackled in the fireplace.

Kate was utterly exhausted. She lay at my feet on her back with her paws in the air. Little Jacob was the only one with any energy left. Unexpectedly, he began a fast crawl toward Kate and me. Since he was the youngest and just beginning to move about on his own, all eyes focused on him. We thought he was coming to see Kate and we wanted to watch the interaction between the baby and the puppy.

But to everyone's surprise and before anyone had time to react, Jacob scooted right past Kate and made a bee-line for the fireplace. Immediately Kate, though she was still a "child" herself, sensed that the baby was approaching danger. She forgot all about taking a rest and rushed to protect him.

She hurried right past Jacob and positioned herself squarely in front of the fireplace. Then, to our amazement, she turned, faced Jacob, and urgently began barking at him.

Startled by this unexpected sound, he stopped crawling. The minute he stopped, Kate walked to him and gently began "crowding" him with her head and body. She continued this gentle but persistent pushing and was not satisfied until she had caused him to retreat to the far side of the room.

All of us were astonished by what we had witnessed. We could almost see Kate's mind working as she decided what she should do next to keep the baby from harm. In an instant she went from being a big, silly puppy waving her paws in the air to a serious girl with a vital mission. And one of the vital missions of Newfoundlands is protecting the members of their families.

Of course she was praised and given treats by the awed adults, but she didn't understand all the fuss. As far as she was concerned, she had only done what her strong Newfy instincts told her she *should* do.

Now, six years later, Kate and Jacob are best buddies. He knows the story of how courageously she protected him on that frosty Ohio evening. He loves her and cheerfully accepts her huge and generous kisses. And so, Good Kate Sweet Kate, The Apple of My Eye Kate, do I.

Pat Aheimer
Bay Village, Ohio, USA

Not In My Back Yard!

My three children, ages nineteen through twenty-four, have a condition known as Fragile-X syndrome. Because of the fairly recent identification of this condition, it has only gained public attention within the past ten years. However, it is the most common inherited cause of mental retardation known to exist. About 80% of the boys and 30% of the girls who have Fragile-X syndrome have varying degrees of mental impairment.

Although my children have above average intelligence and can be socially engaging, they are frustrated by other symptoms of the condition such as short attention spans, hyperactivity, and motor delays. Happily, they have benefited from steadfast family support and individualized special education programs. Eventually, they will be able to live independently. It just seems to take them longer to sort everything out.

When our dog died about five years ago, we wanted another. Because of the Newfoundland's reputation as being good with children, I felt that it might be an appropriate breed for our family. My only stumbling block was size. I wasn't sure how I would cope with a 120-pound dog in the house. Fortunately, in the 4½ years since we've had Katy, I've learned that the only time size is an issue is when this gentle giant is sleeping stretched across a doorway and I have to step over her.

Katy came to live with us as a puppy, a wonderful little ball of fluff. From the very first day, she has been a superb addition to our family. When Katy and I are alone, she never leaves my side. However, as soon as the children come home, her demeanor changes. "Mama's baby" becomes "nanny." She takes this self-appointed job quite seriously, persistently staying attentive to the children and their activities.

It has been said that having one hyperactive child is like having six children, so with our three, we have quite a houseful! I am so thankful to have an extra pair of eyes and ears to help me. I can't think why we didn't get a Newfy earlier!

With her laidback, gentle nature, Katy seems to have a calming effect on the children. Often I have seen her sitting quietly beside one of them, just keeping them company. Just now as I write, my youngest son is relaxing with her on the patio. They are swinging together in our porch swing and both seem to be enjoying the movement.

We knew before bringing Katy into our home that the Newfoundland was renowned for protecting children. And we have seen her place herself between them and what she perceives as danger on several occasions. However, my favorite "Katy to the Rescue" story involves our middle son, Tim. However, it can't exactly be called "successful."

Tim is a bright, curious, and very headstrong young man. One of his intense, almost insatiable, fascinations is with fire. While we have allowed him to strike matches under our supervision, we have repeatedly warned him this is not an appropriate activity for him to engage in alone. Unfortunately, he does not always adhere to our wishes.

About a year ago, I came out onto our front porch one afternoon and was alarmed to find him not only striking matches, but also setting fire to little pieces of paper!

"Tim!" I cried, "Why are you playing with matches on the front porch?"

Tim looked at me calmly. Then he frowned, clearly annoyed.

"Katy wouldn't let me play in the back yard," he explained.

I was not pleased with Tim's behavior, but it made me smile to know Katy had attempted to save him from a dangerous situation. Unfortunately, Tim had created the dangerous situation anyway—but not in her back yard!

Catherine Smitha
Manhattan Beach, California, USA

Protecting the Peepers

The table had been cleared and the dishes washed. I was about to leave the kitchen when I heard panicked peeping just outside the back door. Since our fifteen hens with their many baby chicks spend most spring days roaming between the house and the barn, I am accustomed to "chicky chatter." However, the frantic pitch of this particular sound sent me scurrying to find its source.

I opened the door to find Brittania, our first and oldest Newf, sitting on the porch looking immensely proud of herself. Wobbling unsteadily at her feet, a tiny, wet, baby chick cried plaintively.

Since the Newfs are trained not to touch the chickens, I was exceedingly displeased with this development. Scolding Brittania soundly for picking up the chick and bringing it to the back door, I grabbed the terrified little creature and ran toward the barn in an effort to reunite it with its mother.

On the way I passed the children's wading pool from which the geese, the dogs, and sometimes the hens, all drink. Then I stopped short! More frantic peeping noises? What was going on here?

Inside the pool, struggling for their lives, were two additional baby chicks. Feverishly, they were trying and miserably failing to climb the eight-inch sides of the pool. They were exhausted and saturated with water. They could not have survived much longer.

I fished the chicks out of the pool, gently tried to dry them, and finally returned them to their mother, simultaneously humbly apologizing to ten-year-old Brittania as she monitored every step of the proceedings. I think she understood, as she is wise.

I call this a small, but symbolic, water rescue. This Newf's inherent instinct to save the drowning chicks overcame her training to leave them alone. But, as I already said, Brittania is wise. And, to me, she is clearly a heroine.

Suzanne Bidwell
Martingrove Newfoundlands
Shawnee, Kansas, USA

Baby Ben

In doing my research prior to purchasing our first Newfoundland, I had read much about the Newf lifesaving instinct. However, I imagined that this instinct developed over time and would only be exhibited in adult dogs. Since our Ben is only four months old, I wasn't expecting to see any evidence of the lifesaving instinct for awhile. Yet, today I was privileged to witness its emergence in my very own puppy!

I was getting my one-year-old son's bath ready. I tossed his tub toys into the empty bathtub, started the water, and went to get him undressed. Ben, always at the center of any family activity, was lumbering about in the area.

Just as I began undressing my son, the sound of Ben's loud barking came from the bathroom. This in itself was unusual because he is normally quiet and soft-spoken inside the house. However, the *tone* of his bark was even more unusual. Something of a cross between panic and urgency, it was different from any sound I had ever heard him make.

Extremely alarmed, I left my son and rushed back to the bathroom to see what had happened. As I ran into the room calling his name and asking what was wrong, I found him bouncing about at the side of the tub, his eyes never leaving the water.

By now his barking had reached a frenzied pitch. He seemed almost frantic. I looked over the rim of the tub and gasped in disbelief. There, floating face-down in the water, swirling lazily in the foam, was my son's large, lifelike doll.

Evidently Ben thought she was a real baby. Had she been, she would most definitely have been in need of rescue!

Immediately I pulled the "drowning victim" from the water. Ben stopped barking and began a thorough inspection of the doll. After carefully licking her face and sniffing her, he relaxed and seemed satisfied that she was all right. He may even have been a little surprised or embarrassed to see that she was only a toy.

Perhaps you think Ben is not so clever after all, since his victim was only a doll. But I was dazzled by his valiant rescue. Even though the doll was not a drowning infant, the incident taught us both a valuable lesson. I learned how Ben sounds when he calls for help. He learned that I will respond to his call. Thus we initiated a bond of trust that will grow ever stronger.

Ben and I are destined to do great water rescue training together. I am very proud of my "lifesaving" pup.

Rose Lamarre
Fall River, Massachusetts, USA

Night of the Rodent

In addition to my husband and myself, our pack includes two feisty Chihuahuas who weigh approximately six pounds each, an ever-alert Borzoi who weighs sixty-five pounds, and a remarkably calm Newfoundland who tops the scale at 150 pounds. Despite the size and temperament differences among the dogs, they cooperate as a harmonious team most of the time.

However, a break in the ranks occurred recently. I got up at 1:30 A.M. and let the dogs outside for a five-minute bathroom break. As soon as they all trooped back inside, I returned to bed and snuggled in for a long, peaceful sleep.

Then, before it even began, my rest was interrupted. Riley, the Newfy, suddenly appeared at my bedside. She thrust her big head in my direction and, with great enthusiasm, began panting in my face.

After several whispered "Go lay downs!" from me, Riley started pawing the bed. Recognizing this as her "I'm *really* serious" move, I reluctantly got up to see what was the matter.

Quickly she wheeled around and led me through the bedroom door. As I stepped into the hall, I glimpsed something white zooming along the floor. Flipping on the light, I saw my husband's pet rat racing down the hall. Right on her tiny pink heels thundered the two Chihuahuas and the Borzoi!

In the next second, the Borzoi, bred by czars to capture *wolves* on vast open steppes, zeroed in on little Miss Rat in the confined space of the hallway! To my horror, she was moving in for the kill!

"Leave it!" I managed to shout. "Jade! Leave it!"

Jade, being an exceptionally good girl, remembered her obedience training and instantly left the poor rat alone. My shouts had startled the Chihuahuas, and in the ensuing confusion, I was able to get all four dogs out the door and back into the yard.

Now I was faced—Egads!—with the challenge of getting Miss Rat back into her cage! Even though I had never picked her up before, it didn't seem fair to awaken my husband. You see, I had cleaned her cage that afternoon. Could I have left the top ajar? Was I responsible for her pre-dawn, near-death experience? I knew the answer was "yes."

Fortunately, after a short foot chase, I was able to get the rat to take a treat from me. I thought if she had food in her mouth she couldn't bite me while I scooped her back into her cage. Not that she had ever attempted to bite, but I feared the sight of big Borzoi teeth coming at her in the night might have rattled her a bit!

As soon as I let the dogs back inside, Riley checked to see that Miss Rat was safely in her cage. Then, confident that her work was done, she lay down and went to sleep.

I was sincerely grateful for Riley's help in saving Miss Rat. I know that lifesaving is an instinctive Newfy trait rather than something I taught her. However, I do plan to teach Riley an additional skill—one that *all* dogs would do well to learn. It will take some practice, but I know she'll be successful because she's a smart girl. In no time she will have learned that, henceforth, *daddy* is to be awakened in case of emergencies, not *mommy*!

Susan Sundquist-Kelly
Omaha, Nebraska, USA

The Newf and the Masseuse

Lord Byron has a new occupation! He has become a masseur! Of all the skills he has learned during the year he's been a member of our family, this one may become my personal favorite. What a fine contribution to my well-being he can make with this recently discovered vocation!

His therapeutic talents first blossomed late this evening. My back had been acting up a little and my daughter, Cassie, graciously offered to give me a back massage with my small wooden massager.

I lay down and she began her soothing treatment. Lord Byron, always available and anxious to participate in entertaining family activities, came in to see what he might be missing. The three-legged "spider massager" Cassie was moving across my back immediately got his attention. Aha! An intriguing, new, just-gotta-have-it toy!

He jumped on the bed and began pursuing the massager. As Cassie continued rubbing my back he followed her hand, attempting to capture the alluring plaything in his mouth. The excitement of the chase increased his already high-volume exhalations, thus adding some wonderful moist heat to the massage.

When the mouth method of securing the massager failed, he tried to nab it with his paw. However, despite his heroic efforts, he was always one strike behind Cassie as she moved her hand from point to point. His paw would whack my back just as she slid the massager away. In this way, he provided firm, invigorating, pat-pat-pat follow-up strokes to her rubdown.

Still determined to ensnare the massager, Lord Byron's next attempt was his most creative. He simply flopped his 145 pounds down on top of it! By draping his massive body over Cassie's hand and across my back, he successfully captured the prize!

Lord Byron's enormous puppy grin showed how delighted he was with his victory. I, too, was delighted with this solution. His big, hairy body gave the muscle-relaxing effect of a weighted, vibrating, warm blanket. Even after Cassie managed to wriggle her hand out from under him, he remained sprawled across my back for several minutes. This provided the perfect, peaceful ending to an unusually lively massage.

Afterward, I felt remarkably rejuvenated. Not only were the muscles of my back warm and relaxed, the muscles of my face had had a great workout as well. Laughter, after all, is said to be the *best* medicine, and Lord Byron had provided that in abundance.

Now I'm wondering about two things: first, can I get a repeat performance of this on a daily basis? And, second, how much can I charge clients for this *Newf* form of physical therapy?

Camille D. Mercurio
Babylon, New York, USA

Bailey-Aid For the Artist

From the first day we brought ten-week-old Bailey home, we suspected he was a genius. Our initial impression has not changed. Throughout the 2½ years he has been a member of our family, evidence of his exceptional mental abilities has continued to grow. From demonstrating a perfect "sit" the first time he heard us give the command to helping the whole family stay warm when the house temperature plunged dangerously low during a power outage, Bailey has confidently handled all challenges with intelligence and imagination.

Last Monday, I realized how truly lucky I am to have such a clever boy in my family. I was painting some silk scarves and blouses for a gallery show and was preoccupied with having my best pieces ready. I was also distracted about the travel arrangements I would have to make to get my work to the gallery. Indeed, taking care of business was all I had on my mind.

As I opened the door to go down to my basement studio, I gave my normal explanation, "I'm going to work now, Bailey. I'll be awhile." As usual, his reaction to this announcement was to flop his big, burly, 140-pound body across the doorway at the top of the stairs in preparation for his morning nap.

I usually leave the door to the basement open, but this particular morning I was working with hot wax. Since this material gives off strong fumes, I closed the door to keep the waxy odors from wafting into the kitchen.

In order to increase the air circulation in my studio, I was taking a large fan mounted on a heavy, four-foot stand down with me. Somehow while carrying this fan, I managed to fall down the last flight of stairs, hitting the concrete wall and the floor.

The fan's plunge to the bottom of the stairs took five seconds. Mine took six. But even before I came to rest on top of the fan, I was getting a frightening, fuzzy-headed feeling. Every bone in my body felt broken and I was certain I was going to faint.

Yet even in my dazed state, I realized Bailey was already on the job. I could hear his loud, booming voice barking at the top of the stairs. I could hear his big, powerful paw trying to open the closed door.

"Bailey, help me!" I called out, weakly.

His barking continued and then I heard him rush into the living room. A few seconds later he was back at the basement door. Back and forth he thundered. Back and forth. Barking all the while.

Then the basement door opened and Bailey came charging down the stairs. Tracy, my twenty-year-old daughter, was following right behind him.

"Mom! What happened?" she cried. "Mom, your lips are white!"

With my daughter's help and Bailey's supervision, I struggled up the stairs. We made it into the living room where I gingerly sat down on the couch and lowered my head to my knees.

At that point, Bailey pushed himself between Tracy and me and began administering his version of first aid. Totally focused on his task, he started licking my face. Vigorously. Over and over again.

When he completed that part of his treatment he sat so that his head was right under mine, as if to give me support. Finally I convinced Bailey I was okay and he lay down by my side. But, he continued to keep a close watch—ever ready to administer more first aid should I seem to require it.

Tracy and I have discussed Bailey's behavior during this incident. She had not heard me fall, but Bailey's barking and body language told her something was wrong. As soon as she stood up, he rushed her right to the basement door.

Fortunately, the only ill effects of my fall were extreme soreness and a generous collection of bruises. Two days later I was able to deliver my silk art to the gallery in New Jersey.

I am thrilled with how well my work has been received, but it is the behavior of my big, bright boy that I will always associate with this art show. He came to my aid when I was in trouble. This means more to me than a lifetime of successful shows. Bailey is my playmate, my pal, my very special Newf.

Sharon M. Nummer
River Forest, Illinois, USA

http://hometown.aol.com/silkart1/index.html

Saved By the Balli

My love affair with Newfoundlands began when I was seventeen. My mom and I were living in Maui, but we were planning to move to North Carolina. One of the most exciting aspects of returning to the mainland was knowing we would have room for a larger animal family.

Although we had always had family pets and had brought our two cats and our Giant Schnauzer, Shali, with us to Hawaii, I was already dreaming of the pets I would have on my own someday. I knew I wanted a dog, but beyond that, all I knew was that I wanted him to be BIG. In one of our discussions, my mom told me about a magnificent breed called the Gentle Giant, a.k.a., the Newfoundland.

From then on I was a woman with a mission. Over the next eight years I researched the breed. I read books. I attended dog shows. I questioned breeders. I consulted owners. And, best of all, I visited with *dozens* of Newfies!

I loved the Newf temperament and relaxed nature. I loved their rescue traits and their gentleness with children. I even liked their slobber and their fur! Without doubt, the Newfoundland was the right dog for me. Our "personalities" matched!

During those eight years of research, my living situation was never appropriate for becoming a Newfy mom. At first, I was just too young; then I was recuperating from a near-fatal auto accident; next I was going to vet tech school, and after that I was searching for the ideal place to settle. Yet, throughout this period, I never stopped wanting a Newf. So, I waited. . .and waited. . .and waited.

It wasn't until June, 1998, that conditions were right. I had found "home" and I had the economic resources to care for a Newf properly. Giddy with excitement, I began a search which ultimately led me to Suni-side's Bodacious Ballofur, a.k.a., Balli. He was brought into the world on November 19, 1998, and came to live with us when he was nine weeks old. I *finally* had my big boy!

Balli is all I had prayed for, and more. He somehow makes me whole and I just can't think of enough words to say why. He is curious and comical, and he cheers me up when I'm down. He gives me the best, most loving hugs I've ever had. From the very first day, he has been Mr. Personality—my *precious* Mr. Personality! And how can a pair of dark brown eyes in a jet-black face show so much expression?

His eyes say, "I'm not doing nothin', Mama," and, "You're *leaving* again?" and, "Mama, do something interesting! I'm bored!" and, "You're home! Where'd you go? Alaska? Can I go next time? *PLEASE*, Mama?"

By the time Balli came to live with us, my mom and I, helped by my fiancé, had been actively fulfilling our dream of surrounding ourselves with animals.

Our "zoo" included Shali (by now fourteen-years-young), five cats, two birds, two ferrets, and two horses.

Balli enjoyed his many brothers and sisters, but it was Shali that he loved the most. He quickly learned to respect her and her elder-dog needs, and she was very tolerant of the little guy and his exuberant puppy behavior.

She did what she could to appease him by participating in a game which utterly thrilled him and didn't require too much activity on her part. She would sit in the living room and pay attention to him as he tore around the coffee table. Each time he slid past her she would bark at him, and off he'd go for another exciting round!

We were so proud of him because he never tried to jump on Shali or attempt to play in rough ways. He was *very* good for a rambunctious young pup.

In the beginning of June, 1999, we learned that Shali had a type of cancer called fibrous sarcoma. We were told it was not too aggressive, but it would cause her some problems in the future. By now, she had begun sleeping a lot. We thought it was due to old age and maybe the cancer. Again, Balli was respectful of this. He seemed to understand that when she was asleep, she was not to be disturbed.

That's why on Thursday, June 24th, I was surprised to hear Balli barking in my mom's room where Shali most often slept. I assumed he was barking at her, attempting to get her to play. I called out "Leave it!" because I thought Shali was sleeping.

Although Balli usually obeys this command, he continued barking. By now his barks were unusually loud and had become non-stop. When I went into my mom's room to check, I found the problem immediately.

Shali lay next to a table that had an iron on it. The cord of the iron was dangling down off the table. She was lying on it. And the iron was inching off the table!

I caught the iron just in time! Once I had it in my hand, Balli stopped barking and lay down next to Shali. No nibbling at her paws, no trying to roll on her, no puppy exuberance—he just breathed a soft, little, Newfy sigh.

I don't know what would have happened if the heavy iron had fallen on Shali's fragile back and hind legs. She had bad arthritis and an old cruciate injury. Thanks to Balli, I never had to find out. I truly think he was trying to warn her, and me, of the danger she was in.

Sadly, only three days after this incident, Shali passed away. At 3:15 A.M. she laid her head on my mom's bed. She was telling her goodbye. Then she lay down and went to wait at the Rainbow Bridge.

Balli and I were not there that night, but somehow Balli seemed to have known she would be leaving us. After the iron incident, his attitude toward her changed. Rather than attempting to engage her in noisy puppy games, he began bringing her his toys. He would place them in front of her and then lie down, calmly and quietly, beside her. While Shali was preparing to say goodbye, he was comforting her by giving her what he could—his toys and his love.

All of us mourned Shali's death. For days Balli brought his toys to the place where she died, and he continues to sleep in my mom's room in Shali's spot.

He also seemed to be trying to comfort my mom. For many days, he wouldn't leave her side when she was home. He had always been "velcro dog" to me, but during those first few weeks after Shali passed away, he became "velcro dog" to her.

We still miss Shali very dearly and although life has continued for us, it will never be the same. Shali lived fourteen long, wonderful years and left us with many memories to laugh, cry, and smile about. One of our fondest memories is of the loving relationship she formed with a bouncy, little puppy named Balli. He enlivened her final months and saved her from a bad injury. I think her spirit will always live in his heart, just as it will always live in ours.

Keri King
Raleigh, North Carolina, USA

The Highway Nightmare

Another wonderful weekend of boating and swimming and visiting with our extended pack had come to an end. It was time to climb into the car for the trip home.

Usually I love riding in the car with the windows down. Usually I love sniffing the air and watching the world fly by. But on this particular evening, it was too hot and I was too tired. As soon as we reached the highway, I settled down next to my water bowl. For a few minutes I listened to Annie and Russell chatting quietly up front, then like any exhausted two-year-old, I drifted peacefully off to sleep.

Suddenly, with no warning, the nightmare began! Annie yelled out! Russell slammed on the brakes! Then came terrifying, crashing sounds and a huge, frightening jolt. Next the car filled with black smoke. After that, and for just a moment, everything was quiet. I was so scared. What had happened to Annie and Russell? Why had we stopped? How did we get into this corn field?

Then Russell began making strange sounds and Annie began calling out to him. I did not like the sounds he was making; I did not like the fear I could hear in her voice. Nothing like this had ever happened to us before. It was very frightening.

Finally Annie opened her door. I was so glad when she got out of the car and started around to the back. I knew she was coming to get me. When she opened my door I could see tears streaming down her face. Over and over she asked if I were okay. She took my face in her hands and hugged me tenderly and kissed my cheek. She felt me all over and whispered, “Everything will be all right, Cora. Everything will be all right.”

I just looked at her. Her voice was gentle and soothing but I was bewildered; everything was fuzzy and vague and my face was wet. The water from my bowl had splashed all over me. I didn’t like this! I wanted to go home!

Things began happening quickly then, confusing things. People I didn’t know were calling out and running around our car. Another car had run a stop sign. Russell’s arm was broken. Annie was making phone calls.

Everything in our car was in a jumble and Annie couldn’t find my leash. When she spied her measuring tape, she tied it to my collar and helped me out of the car. Slowly we walked over so Russell could look at me. When he saw I wasn’t hurt, he suggested Annie and I sit down and relax.

More people were coming and going. A man I didn’t even know come over and retied Annie’s tape measure to my collar. I was surprised when Grammy and Uncle Pete arrived. Grammy was crying. I didn’t like seeing everyone so upset. *Nothing* was the way it was supposed to be.

Next came sirens and flashing lights. Men wearing heavy yellow jackets and strange hats came up and spoke with Russell and Annie. After that Annie walked me over to Grammy's car and opened the back door. Then she told me to get in. I obeyed but I didn't want to leave her. I didn't want to leave Russell. Why did she want me to go with Grammy and Uncle Pete?

Annie hugged me and kissed my cheek and told me to be good. Then she closed the door. I watched anxiously as she walked back toward Russell. I saw some people help her onto a stretcher and lift her into an ambulance. Soon they put Russell into the ambulance with her. The last thing I saw were flashing lights growing dimmer in the distance as the ambulance took Annie and Russell farther and farther away.

After I waited at the lake house for a long time, Uncle Pete brought Annie home. I was so glad to see her! I checked her black eye and her scraped nose. I checked the bandage on her arm and the stitches under her knee. I could tell she was glad to see me, but she moved very slowly and seemed very tired.

But where was Russell? Why was Annie going to bed before Russell came home? I kept going to the door to watch for him. Finally, I lay down and fell to sleep. It had been a long, stressful evening. I couldn't stay awake any longer.

Right after my breakfast the next morning Annie took me next door to Grammy and Uncle Pete's house. She then got into the car and left with Uncle Pete. I couldn't imagine why.

I waited and waited and waited by the window. When Annie and Uncle Pete finally returned, they had brought Russell home! I was thrilled! I ran to greet him, frantic to see him.

His right arm was in a cast and a sling. He was very weak and in pain. As soon as he got settled in his chair, I sat as close to him as I could. Annie rested on the couch nearby. My pack was together again and I felt relieved and blissfully happy.

For some time after our accident, I had nightmares. Annie felt badly about this and was sorry I hadn't been riding in a crate. She said I would have been much safer. Our new car is big enough for my crate, and I'm content riding in it. As long as I still get to go to all the regular places, like festivals and flea markets, I'm happy.

Now our lives are almost back to normal. I watch over the house while Annie and Russell go to work. When they come home, we take our walks and our rides and go on our picnics. But ever since our accident, I think we enjoy our happy times even more than we did before. Often Annie hugs me and whispers, "Oh, Cora, we're all very lucky to be alive."

She's right. But I've *always* known this. So I just smile and wag my tail and give her a big, wet, slurpy, Newfy kiss.

Cora
&
Annie Milliron
Beavercreek, Ohio, USA

http://www.geocities.com/cora_newf/newf.html

A Simple Pleasure

When the treasured and rare opportunity to sleep in presents itself, I take full advantage of the occasion. I make plans. I delegate responsibilities. I seclude myself in the spare bedroom. I adjust the curtains so I won't be disturbed by the morning sun. I even turn on a fan for white noise. I *relish* this infrequent and valued event!

This morning was to be one of those lovely, lazy mornings. Last evening after making my preparations and reminding my husband he was in charge of the dogs, I tucked myself under a soft down comforter, piled pillows all around, and settled in for a wonderful sleep.

Peaceful slumber and sweet dreams followed until 5:00 A.M. That's when the thundering Newfy herd stampeded past my door and continued on down the hallway. Since our four Newfs usually have at least one episode per night of barking at who knows what, I turned over and pulled the covers over my ear. This was my sleeping-in morning and I was determined to enjoy it!

However, that was just a fleeting thought because suddenly pandemonium erupted! Led by our overly-excited cat, Tacki, four frenzied Newfs, Jericho, Jordan, Jazz, and Alice, skidded into my smallish room, thumping, bumping, and barking. The five of them then began careening into the furniture and each other in a frantic effort to capture a *bird* that was fluttering around near the ceiling.

Before I could even begin to imagine how a bird had gotten into our house, it swooped down between the bed and the wall. Tacki attempted to swoop down behind it and promptly got his fourteen-pound, yellow-striped, Maine Coon body stuck in the narrow opening. Meanwhile, Jazz and Jordan jumped up onto the bed and began bouncing around looking for the bird, while Alice and Jericho barked their exuberant encouragement from the sidelines.

As Tacki yowled and attempted to wriggle out of his tight space, the bird rose from behind the bed like the proverbial Phoenix and swooped across the room to the printer on top of my computer work station.

Instantly, all four dogs lunged at the computer desk and tried to squeeze under it. By then Tacki had extricated himself from the crack and leaped over onto the printer.

My early-morning daze and the speed with which this melee had begun and was unfolding, plus the fact that I had been pinned down by two cavorting Newfies, made my reaction time slower than usual. However, at this point I was able to leap out of bed and begin scrambling for falling objects.

By now the bird had returned to circling overhead and Jordan and Jazz were barking and leaping up at it. Jericho and Alice imagined it had gone behind the bed again so they were directing their frenzied efforts to that area.

Grandma's marbled-topped night table upon which sits the antique globe lamp was the next place the bird sought refuge. Jordan and Jazz, aided by Tacki, attempted to follow it. Jericho and Alice were still convinced the bird was behind the bed. I was still retrieving falling objects.

"Enough!" I finally shouted, grabbing the globe lamp just before it fell.

Firmly clutching Jordan and Jazz, I led them out of the room. Jericho and Alice, always the followers, trotted out behind us. I closed the door.

With the dogs out of the room, I could now deal with the cat and the bird. Thinking I would be able to capture the bird by tossing a cloth over it, I hurried down the hall to get a towel. As I returned, I glanced into the master bedroom. There was the human father, asleep with a pillow over his head. There were Alice and Jericho, on the foot of the bed with their heads hanging over the edge. And there were Jazz and Jordan, sitting parallel to the end of the bed, with *something* on the floor between them.

A toy? A brown, fluffy toy? Oh, no! Not another bird! Do I have a nest in the house? Has a whole family moved in?

Moving swiftly, I put the towel over the terrified bird, picked it up, and carried it outside. Then I returned to the small bedroom to tackle the problem posed by the original bird.

When I opened the door and stepped inside, all I found was a *very* annoyed Tacki prowling between the bed and the night table. The only evidence of the bird was one, small, delicate, brown feather on my pillow.

What actually happened this morning remains a pre-dawn mystery, but apparently one of the Newfs caught the one and only bird, hid it in her mouth, and carried it into the master bedroom. When I spotted it on the floor, the dogs were simply watching it. Maybe they were just waiting (and *hoping*?) it would begin flying around again so they could resume their wild chase game.

But all's well that ends well. The bird flew away, the dogs went back to sleep, the cat continued prowling, and I got back in bed. Ah, the luxury, the pleasure, the delight of it all! I dearly *love* sleeping in.

Elaina Kintgen
Bloomington, Indiana, USA

Swamp Girls

As the sun drops lower and lower toward the horizon, Honey Bear, Keely, and I anxiously scout around on an unfamiliar trail looking for a campsite. It is late spring and very hot for the Newfs. They are panting.

We pass a big, smelly, slimy swamp. Keely looks at it wistfully. Knowing I'll be sharing a small tent with her, I yell, "Keely, no!" We move on.

We find a suitable site and double-back to get my friend. He was last seen standing on the trail rearranging items in his pack.

We pass the same big, smelly, slimy swamp. Keely, now *really* panting, gives me another look. A *decisive* look. I know what is coming. I yell, "Keely, no!"

She starts toward the swamp. I know Keely will never listen to me unless I manage to speak in a reasonable, pleasant tone. But I cannot help myself. I scream as if someone has a gun to my head, "NOOOOO!" Keely keeps walking.

Gleefully, Honey decides to follow Keely. I'm still thinking, "Bedtime. Small tent." I yell even louder.

Keely looks back over her shoulder at me. Then, she steps into the swamp.

I think I hear her go, "Ahhhhhhhh!" I keep yelling, "NOOOOO!" She wades in up to her chest. She sits down. Only her head and shoulders are visible above the vile goop. By now Honey has joined her. Both of my girls are jubilant.

I am utterly beaten. My two dogs are covered in slime and my friend surely thinks by my cries that I'm being mauled by a bear. I'm thinking I may not be *too* fond of camping.

It is four hours later. It is midnight. We are in the middle of an abandoned road a mile and a half from the trailhead. It is the only level ground we could find before night fell. It has gotten much cooler.

The Swamp Girls are sharing my tent. I have put my knapsack on the floor between us. I have *standards*. Their stink and slime will not get on me as long as I maintain this knapsack boundary. We all fall asleep. Contentedly. This is our very first camping trip ever.

It is three hours later. It is *much* cooler. Cold! And extraordinarily damp. I am freezing. My idea that I wouldn't need a sleeping bag begins to seem. . .well, ridiculous. My down coat and fleece pants aren't warm enough. My space blanket is not reflecting back ninety percent of my body heat.

Across the tent floor, on the other side of my knapsack, I can see the Swamp Girls. They are stretched out blissfully in the chill. Keely is lying on her back with her legs in the air. She is smiling in her sleep. In her dream somebody has finally fixed the air conditioner!

I wonder if I should wake my friend and ask if I can share his sleeping bag. I reject the idea because I know he will not let the stinky dogs into his tent. He has actual standards. I cannot stand the idea of my girls being left outside. I would rather freeze.

Suddenly I remember the phrase "two-dog night" from someone's Newf-L post. I wonder where the expression came from. I wonder about the actual mechanics of a two-dog night. My two dogs are just too disgustingly swampy. I have *standards*.

I am getting colder. I cannot feel my nose anymore.

Five minutes later Honey emits a noxious smell unrelated to, and surpassing, the swamp odor. I sit up, unzip the tent door, and let Honey out to powder her nose. I remain sitting up on the drop cloth that I knew would be lighter than, and I thought would be just as insulating as, a mattress. I am totally, *totally*, freezing.

Honey comes back in. I zip the door closed and try to lie back down. Someone has crossed the Knapsack Boundary while my back was turned. The intruder is now curled up on my side of the tent. She grins at me and joyously pounds her huge, slimy tail on the drop cloth. Where my head should be.

It is Keely Swamp! Her big, stinking, wet, foul self has destroyed the inviolate cleanliness of my side of the drop cloth. But her insouciance and her merrily-thumping tail delay my scolding long enough for me to realize: THIS IS GOOD!

Keely is warm. I am excruciatingly cold. I lie down. Keely moves over a little to the tent wall. I inch toward her. Soon I am pressing tightly against her. A little warmth begins to creep into my body.

Twenty minutes later, I am still too cold to sleep. I start eyeing Honey Swamp. Odor and slime are no longer factors in my equation. I am now calculating how to get the biggest percentage of my body surrounded by dog.

Keely is pinned against the tent wall by my body. She can't move. Will Honey agree to cuddle against me on my other side? I seriously consider leashing her to my body. But, on being invited, she is as obliging as Keely.

Surrounded by my sweet swamp things, I begin to warm up. It is 4:30 A.M. Pitch black. Silent. Just me and my magnanimous Newfs. I feel better now. I am getting *warm.*

Way off in the distance, a siren goes off. A police siren. I wonder how I can hear it all the way up here in the woods. A lot of trail and a small mountain are between us and the road. I hear it again. It seems closer.

The siren goes off for the third time. I feel irritated now. This is like being back in Manhattan! Then I relax. It doesn't really matter because, *warm in the embrace of my Newfs,* I am *finally* beginning to drift off.

Then I hear the siren again. I'm sure it's nearer. Suddenly, I remember that I have pitched my tent in a road. But it's an *old* road, probably some by-way from the Revolutionary War. It begins and ends deep in the woods.

I drift away. Then I'm dragged back by an undeniably *close* sound of a siren. Out here in the middle of nature! Has a bad guy off-roaded it to this by-way? Is he barreling down on us? Are the police in pursuit? Will they both run us over? Will cars somehow appear in the deep woods? I realize I am crazy and tell myself to go to sleep.

But soon my far-fetched fears overwhelm me. I should get us off this road! I should get us out of this tent and move us into the woods until it quiets down.

I call out to my friend. I tell him I'm getting up. I tell him I'm cold. He announces he's warm. He has been ever since he zipped up the side of his sleeping bag. I feel annoyed.

I don't mention that the real reason I'm getting up is that I'm afraid a car will run over us. A car. Deep, deep, deep in the woods of Harriman State Park. It's just *too* embarrassing. Like my *standards*, I also have to maintain *appearances*.

Honey and Keely and I get up and move off the road, well into the safety of the trees.

The intermittent siren sounds are extremely loud now. Inconceivable, a *spotlight* pops on down in the middle of the "abandoned" road. I can make out a single vehicle. It is moving closer. This is exactly the content of my crazy musings of a few minutes ago.

I yell to my friend. He is snug in his tent. He is warm in his sleeping bag. He sleeps on.

Now a *power saw* starts up near the car. Behind the glare of the spotlight.

THIS IS TOO MUCH! I am trapped inside some sort of cheesy horror movie like the ones I used to laugh at with my friends! But I'm not laughing now. Whoever is sawing the fallen trees blocking the "abandoned" road we are camping on is doing it to get to *us!* The Swamp Girls and I have awakened to something between Close Encounters and The Texas Chainsaw Massacre.

Above all else, I am terrified that my Newfs will get hurt. Their leashes are inside the tent. I am crouching off to the side of the road, hanging onto them with my arms around their necks. My hands are holding hanks of their long hair. Tightly. My girls are exceptionally strong. I am afraid they will slip out of my grip.

The vehicle arrives and stops right in front of us. A pick-up truck. My tent is blocking its way. Without warning the Newfs and I are *directly* in the spotlight.

I feel very weird and very scared and, bizarrely, I think, "Gee, my hair must look a mess."

I'm wondering if I did something wrong. Was I supposed to get a permit?

Honey Bear and Keely begin barking. Ferociously.

A park ranger yells from the truck. He says he should write us up a "mess of tickets" for camping outside the designated areas.

"Huh?" I'm thinking. "Sirens and chainsaws for *that*?"

He says he'd give us the tickets if he had time. But he's in a rush. He's searching for a hiker. She's been missing since sundown.

The Newfs continue barking at him. He yells, "You better have a good grip on those dogs!"

A good grip. That—now, and in general—is a concept I would *definitely* like to know better.

My friend and I move our tents. The park ranger drives on.

For two adults dogs, ages three and five, Honey and Keely are now in an absurdly playful mood. They're celebrating their success. They saved us! From a park ranger!

I was petrified. I still feel shaky. It is still dark and cold.

Then I put myself in the shoes of that missing woman, lost in the woods on such a cold night. I feel very, very grateful that I will always have Honey Bear and Keely with me when I hike. Brave and true. Swampy and loving. And, above all, always toasty warm.

Dawn finally breaks over our very first camping trip ever. I am bleary-eyed, irritable, and hungry.

But. . .I realize. . .despite getting covered in second-hand swamp goo, freezing half to death, and nearly getting run over by a park ranger. . .I realize. . .I *love* camping! The Swamp Girls and I are even kind of *good* at it.

As I share my last Power Bar with my delighted Newfies, I'm already planning our next trip.

Elizabeth S. Potter
New York, USA

Our Perfect Reward

Our Brigid cannot tell us about her early years, but the clues she brought with her to the Albuquerque shelter where I volunteered suggest she had been kept in a small, muddy pen for at least two shedding seasons. She had been underfed, ungroomed, neglected, and, ultimately, abandoned in the nearby hills.

Hungry, thirsty, and driven to seek help, she had approached a mountain biker and loped along beside him down the canyon. Despite her unkempt appearance and revolting smell, her gentle, friendly manner caused him to take pity on her. He leashed her and brought her to the shelter.

Because there was no Newf rescue group in New Mexico, I had been acting as the local Newf rescue contact. Although I had been checking all three Albuquerque shelters weekly for eighteen months, as well as checking numerous reportings of Newfs in shelters in other cities, Brigid was the only Newf to come through during this time.

Since she arrived at the shelter near my birthday and near the time when we were to leave New Mexico, I felt almost as if she were my reward for the hours I'd spent attempting to help her kind. As soon as I saw her I went straight to the front desk and adopted her on the spot.

During the mandatory waiting period before we could take Brigid home, my husband, Mike, and I began the daunting task of cleaning her. For three days in a row we removed dead gray hair, leaves, sticks, and even baling wire from her coat. She was matted from head to toe and smelled of mildew and excrement.

Happily, once she was bathed and groomed, we discovered a black Newf who had actually been spayed. But at ninety-five pounds, she was very thin. She had so little muscle tone she was swaybacked, and her teeth were so bad she appeared to be at least six years old.

Four weeks later, we moved to Chicago where we continued building her muscle strength with a good diet and three walks a day. Mike and I introduced her to chew toys and house trained her. Willingly and gratefully she made the transition from an unkempt, outdoor, country dog who slept in the mud to a leash-trained, indoor city slicker who sleeps on her own futon.

Now, one year later, she has become a lovely 129-pound beauty who runs like the wind, appears to be only three or four years old, is in excellent health, and is no longer swaybacked. A calm, relaxed, sweetheart of a girl, she loves our three smaller dogs and has a pacifying effect on their rambunctious behavior. She clearly appreciates being a member of this pack.

Brigid is also curious, remarkably intelligent, and has a *serious* yen for all foods flavored with garlic. A few weeks ago she proved this point quite dramatically. I should have thought about her fondness for garlic before I hid the unwashed pans from the garlic chicken in the oven. But, it had been a long evening. I was tired. I would get to them later.

When I came home from work the next day and walked into the kitchen, I was horrified! My heart skipped a few beats! I almost fainted! For there, lying face down in what seemed like the *middle* of the floor, was the stove! The big, white, Magic Chef, four-burner, gas *stove*! And there, scattered all around the stove were the garlic chicken pans—meticulously licked to a sparkling shine!

Since I could see that the gas line had actually been pulled away from the wall and I could smell gas in the room, I was convinced we had a gas leak. In a panic, I called Mike and insisted he come home from work immediately to check it.

After he turned off the gas and determined that the gas smell was just the result of the pilot lights going out, the two of us set the stove upright again and moved it back to its original location.

By then we had pieced together what had happened in our kitchen that day. Brigid had successfully opened the oven door, removed the pans, and licked them clean. When she returned to search for more garlic goodies, she had stood on the opened door while sticking her head inside for a thorough look. Fortunately, she had been agile enough to get out of the way when the stove crashed to the floor.

Although I had learned my lesson about leaving unwashed pans in the oven, Brigid couldn't resist checking for more treats the next day. Once again, I came home to find the stove face down on the kitchen floor! However, this second crash had broken the oven heating element. Since we had been needing a new stove anyway, this seemed like the right time to get it.

Of course I will never again leave garlic-flavored treats in the oven, but for Brigid's safety and our own peace of mind, we have taken an extra precaution. We have securely *bolted* our new stove to the floor.

Brigid, however, has moved on to a new challenge. She now focuses her problem-solving skills on Mike's satchel. Discreetly and without a trace of drool, she unzips it and removes the sandwiches he puts inside to take with him to work. Even though he never makes garlic-flavored sandwiches, she seems completely satisfied with his culinary efforts. Indeed, the "missing sandwich syndrome" is becoming a regular part of his working day.

But whether we are bolting down stoves or Brigid is bolting down sandwiches, all we can do is laugh and *love* this wonderful Newf. She has been our *perfect* reward.

Melissa & Michael Collins
Chicago, Illinois, USA

Crashes In the Night

After reading many stories about Newfies coming to the aid of their humans, we became curious about our own seven-month-old Newf, Shadow. We wondered about his instinctive nature. We wondered if he would try to help us if we were ever in danger.

Our questions about Shadow's concern for our safety have now been answered. When I had an accident recently, we were grateful to see that he did his part to help save my life.

On this occasion, my wife, Iz, needed to go in to work much earlier than usual the next morning. Since she didn't want to wake me before it was necessary, she decided to sleep in our front bedroom rather than in the master bedroom.

Shadow took this change in routine in stride, however, rather than sleep in the master bedroom as he usually does, he slept in the hallway so he could patrol between the two bedrooms.

At about 4:15 in the morning, Iz was awakened by loud barking in her doorway. Shadow makes many different noises and we have almost become master translators of his vocabulary. Even though this was a bark Iz had heard on only one previous occasion, she immediately recognized it as his "danger" signal.

Just as she made that assessment, she heard a loud crash in the master bedroom.

She got up quickly, and with Shadow running beside her, she rushed in to see what had caused the noise.

The 3'x4' mirror on the ceiling of our custom-made bed had dislodged and fallen, breaking and shattering as it hit me. Although it had not knocked me unconscious, it had startled me and severely cut the back of my left hand. Iz and Shadow found me bleeding, surrounded by broken glass, and somewhat shaken.

Grabbing a towel, Iz wrapped my hand, and with me attempting to apply pressure to the wound, we rushed to the nearest hospital emergency room approximately fifteen minutes away.

It took eighteen stitches to close the wound in my hand. When we returned home about an hour later, Shadow seemed very concerned about me. He inspected my bandaged hand several times and stayed right by my side.

While I recuperated at home for the next two days, Shadow would not let me out of his sight. He seemed to think my life might still be in danger and, evidently, he wanted to protect me against future threats.

I have wondered how Shadow knew the mirror was about to fall. My only explanation is that with his superior hearing, he heard the mirror as it began pulling away from the ceiling of the bed. I know he didn't realize the consequences of the mirror falling. Rather, he recognized the sound as "foreign" and unusual enough to warrant waking Iz. In other words, he wasn't sure how to handle the situation, but he knew there was a problem and he knew he should make his human companion aware of it.

This incident has shown us that Shadow is eager to protect not only his house, but also his human mom and dad. Some Newfs might not be watch dogs; however, we know our Shadow is—he's definitely a keeper!

Frank Merklee
Oro Valley, Arizona, USA

Guarding the Girls

Part 1

Sammy wasn't allowed in the house. He *drooled.* His drool was *nasty*. Offensive. Unclean. He kept growing. The drooling kept getting worse.

The husband loved Sammy and cared for him, but his clothes got dirty when he played with him. They got *slimed.* His wife *hated* this. She always insisted he take his dirty clothes off in the laundry room before he came into the house.

And Sammy kept growing. And things kept getting worse. For 2½ years the husband's clothes kept getting dirty. Sammy kept getting dirty. The yard kept getting dirty. Enough! This was not the right family for a Newf!

I wasn't surprised when the wife called. She had called before with questions and with complaints about the drool. But this time she asked me to find a new home for Sammy.

I gave her two choices: 1) If she wanted to sell Sammy, I would refer people to her and she could screen them. 2) If she wanted to give him away, I would pick him up, she would sign over his registration, and I would find him a good home.

Fifteen minutes later, the wife called back. "Can you come get him tomorrow?"

The husband was grief-laden the next day as I loaded the muddy Newf into my Toyota. He had been outside playing with Sammy. He couldn't remember if their contract had a "return to breeder" clause. He couldn't remember where they had put their contract. As I drove away, the wife was complaining about the husband's dirty clothes. And the husband was crying.

I called Sammy's breeder. She wasn't interested in coming to get him. She wasn't interested in helping to re-home him. She asked me to place Sammy.

I knew of a family that was looking for a Newf. But I was a bit concerned. Sammy hadn't had much training. He was a little wild. But the wife in the interested family was dedicated, the husband was supportive, the little daughters were wonderful with dogs, and Hobbes, their seven-year-old retriever mix, was accepting. I relaxed. I knew I had found a good home for Sammy.

Part 2

Although Sammy demonstrated a genuine fondness for our two young daughters from the first week he joined our family, we were especially touched last summer when he appointed himself their chief guardian. By then he had been with us for almost a year. He was 3½ years old, Carys was four, and Sarah was six.

We were enjoying a vacation at our family cabin in Montana and had taken Sammy and Hobbes with us. One afternoon I took our daughters down to the little river that runs through the property. Sammy was delighted to be included in this excursion. He jumped right into the water and found a deep hole where he could swim.

Carys, Sarah, and I continued a little way upstream until we found a quiet, shallow stretch. We began playing a little game in which, one at a time, the girls would walk a short way along the river bank to a designated spot, then wade into the water and float down to me. I would catch them, stand them up, and help them get out of the water so they could walk back upstream for another turn.

Sammy stayed in his chosen swimming area as long as both girls were by my side, but as soon as he saw Sarah wade into the water upstream from me, his manner changed. Initially, he seem a bit shocked. Then he became very alert and focused his full attention on her.

Sizing up the situation quickly, and noting that I was allowing the children to take turns leaving my side, Sammy decided a safety monitor was needed. He left his swimming hole and splashed over to provide his services.

As each child entered the water at the designated spot, Sammy would carefully position himself in front of her. He made it obvious that she was supposed to hold on to him, thus using his strength to steady herself in the current.

While each daughter stood in the water waiting her turn, Sammy would look first at her, then at me, then back at her. Only when he was satisfied that both of us were ready would he step out of the way and let her float down to me.

Thus we spent a memorable afternoon. Our two little daughters had a delightful time playing in the river, and Sammy obviously took great pleasure in his role as lifeguard.

A few weeks later, Sammy once again felt compelled to take care of his girls. On this occasion, Sarah and Carys had talked their dad into setting up a tent and joining them in a backyard campout. When it was time to go to sleep, I brought both dogs inside so they wouldn't bother Bill and the girls during the night.

I lay down in our bedroom and attempted to go to sleep only to have an insistent Sammy repeatedly poking his nose into my back. When I couldn't get him to stop, I finally let him into the back yard.

He stepped outside, then turned back and looked at me expectantly. His message was unmistakable.

"Well, aren't *you* coming? Your *kids* are out here!"

When I didn't follow him outside, he gave me an exasperated look. Then, completely disappointed with my lack of motherly concern, he sauntered over to the door of the tent and lay down with a loud, insinuating sigh. The amusing thing is that he *almost* succeeded in making me feel guilty!

When I got up the next morning, Sammy was still on duty at the door of the tent. He continued his vigil until Bill and the girls woke up some time later. We feel sure he stayed awake guarding them all night long because once they got up, he went to sleep and could not be roused for the rest of the day.

Once he committed himself to the responsibility, Sammy has never relinquished his role as chief protector of the girls. Occasionally he still seems somewhat critical of my child-care decisions, but more and more often he trusts my judgment. As with any effective team, Sammy and I have learned to work together. Although we sometimes disagree on exactly how much protection the children need, their safety is our common goal. Sometimes his zeal makes me smile, but I will always accept his help gratefully. He has become a treasured and valuable member of our family.

Wendy Pangle
Briggsbay Newfoundlands
Bend, Oregon, USA
(Part 1)

&

Marjorie Gilbert
Harrisburg, North Carolina, USA
(Part 2)

Newf Nanny

When Lucy came to live with us at nine weeks old, she was our smallest Newf and our only Landseer. She was also something of an outsider since our other three Newfs are a close-knit, mum, dad, and son family. Perhaps that is why she felt it necessary to throw her weight around. Even though Nash is eight weeks older and at the time was some thirty-five pounds heavier than Lucy, she was undaunted. She attempted to play with him in such a brash, rambunctious, body-slamming fashion that his mum, Katie, had to step in and teach her some manners.

Katie used the same training techniques with Lucy that she had used with her own son. These included stopping her if she began running too fast, and standing over her with a growl if she started playing too roughly. Gentle though these warnings were, and always accompanied by tail-wagging, Lucy understood the lessons and quickly learned the finer points of acceptable puppy behavior.

Although she acquired good manners, Lucy has remained high spirited and eager for adventure. She is an extremely intelligent girl, always curious and inquisitive.

Among her many fascinations are our twenty horses. She enjoyed accompanying me to the barn, so she made friends with them when she was still quite young. Although the horses have always been friendly with our Newfies, they have never quite known what to make of Lucy. She is the only Newf who has ever greeted them with enthusiastic nose licks! Yet even though they often react with astonishment, they consistently put their heads down to accept her warm, moist greetings.

During her first year with us, our elderly pony, Buddy Boy, became Lucy's special companion. He had lost his best friend, an amazing, 17½-year-old Newfoundland named Henry,* just before she arrived, and Lucy seemed to sense his sadness. Every morning she would hurry over to greet him first. She would lick his nose and then carefully lead him to his breakfast bowl. This was a help to me as well as to him because our Buddy Boy had become blind. Instinctively, Lucy understood his need for assistance.

Although she continued to maintain her close bond with Buddy Boy, it was with the arrival of Trinket that Lucy's nurturing nature truly blossomed.

Lucy was just days away from her first birthday when Spirit, my thirty-one-inch tall Miniature mare, foaled. Unfortunately, her tiny, little, 15½-inch filly had very weak legs and needed help standing. For the first two nights of Trinket's life, I stayed in the stall, milking her mum and bottle feeding her.

On her third day, Trinket took a sudden turn for the worse so we rushed her to the vet's office. It was determined that she was suffering from hypothermia and low blood sugar. After a day on an IV in our kitchen she recovered nicely, but since it was early spring and still cold outside, we decided to keep her in the house for awhile longer. I began feeding her milk from her mum, supplemented with milk replacer, every hour and a half around the clock.

Lucy was beside herself with excitement when we brought Trinket into the house. She simply adored the little filly and immediately become her foster mum. She stayed right by the baby's side, covering her with warm Newfy kisses at every opportunity.

At first, Lucy thought Maxzi, our eight-inch high Toy Poodle, was a danger to Trinket. Perhaps she was right! On the first day Trinket was in the house I was shocked when Maxzi took one of her tiny hooves in her mouth and attempted to drag it away. For several days after that Lucy would lie between Maxzi and Trinket. This was her non-aggressive, yet completely effective way of keeping the small dog at a distance. Since Trinket lived in the house for over three months, Lucy gradually allowed Maxzi near her, but only with close supervision.

When I set up an X-pen in the kitchen for Trinket, Lucy was visibly disappointed. She even gave me a few dirty looks! She didn't like being separated from her baby. However, every time I put the little filly in the pen on her blankets and her hot water bottle, Lucy used the occasion as an opportunity to entertain her. She brought squeaky toys into the room and would lie beside the pen squeaking them for Trinket's amusement. I think this constant Newfy attention helped keep the little filly's spirits up during her first days when she was unable to stand without support.

As Trinket gained strength and become steadier on her feet, I would put little training pants and rubber pants on her and take her into our carpeted living room so she would have an easy surface on which to practice walking. Like all youngsters, she loved to play and would crow-hop around the room. I had to watch her carefully because she was still very frail. I didn't want her bumping into the furniture or tumbling down the stairs.

On the day Trinket took her first trot across the living room, Lucy was ecstatic! Trinket was *playing* with her! Lucy lay down and rolled over onto her back as the baby danced nearby. Excitedly, she waved a big paw in the air and gave Trinket a little nudge. For an instant the tiny filly was airborne, but fortunately, I was able to catch her before she fell. Of course, Lucy meant no harm. She was just thrilled to see Trinket prancing around and she was trying to encourage her.

It was when I began having trouble waking up throughout the night to feed Trinket that I discovered Lucy knew my schedule. If I were a few minutes late, she would be in my face squeaking her toy! Groggily, I would climb out of bed and she would hurry me to the kitchen. There I would find Trinket "tap dancing" while she anxiously awaited her bottle.

Incredibly, Lucy finally taught Trinket to squeak a toy to call me. When she saw the filly couldn't get her little mouth around the toy, she somehow taught her to stomp on it with her foot. They both seem pleased at how well I responded to their squeaker training program!

As the weeks passed and we continued the practice sessions on the carpet, Lucy understood that Trinket was to stay in the living room. If she headed toward the stairs, Lucy would lie across the door to the hallway. If she changed directions and headed toward the slippery kitchen floor, Lucy would be there to block her way.

Finally Trinket was strong enough and the weather was warm enough for her to move back to the barn to live with the other horses. But, predictably, the puppy-filly bond has remained strong. Trinket accepts Lucy as her mum and doesn't seem to care at all for horses.

Lucy, of course, remains convinced that Trinket is her puppy. Every morning she thoroughly washes the little filly's face and recently she has begun passing on to Trinket two of the lessons she learned from Katie—no dangerous running and no body-slamming. Trinket bucks and kicks and plays, but Lucy won't allow her either to run too fast or to get too close to the other horses. It's amusing to know that my little filly is learning canine etiquette!

I suppose knowing proper dog manners is to Trinket's advantage since she must surely think she's a Newf. Each morning when I walk her from the barn to her kennel in front of the house, all four Newfs accompany me. They surround Trinket and march confidently along as if they are her body guards! Trinket, assuming her doggy persona, puts her nose to the ground and appears to be sniffing out a trail. She has also become interested in investigating dog chew bones.

Although we are still struggling to find exactly the right diet for her, Trinket is doing well out in the barn now. I know Lucy would like it very much if Trinket still lived in the house, but she needs room in which to grow and to exercise.

However, I humor Lucy on cold nights. If she looks out the living room window and lets out a little whine, I know she is thinking about her "puppy." If she brings me her squeaky Mickey Mouse, I know she is really *worried.* That's when I grab my jacket and we go out together to check on Trinket and make sure all is well.

Lucy is a wonderful girl with many good qualities, but the trait at which she excels is helpfulness. Beginning with Buddy Boy and continuing with Trinket, Lucy looks for ways in which she can be of service. She has even found a way to help me. Every morning, after I finish feeding the horses, she happily carries the grain bucket back to the house for me. She is truly everything I could wish for in a Newf nanny.

Joanne Seabloom
Seabloom Newfoundlands
Lone Butte, British Columbia, Canada

http://seabloom.freeyellow.com

*Read more about Henry in *Henry Forever: The Gift of Life*
by Claire Carr & Joanne Seabloom
Wynship Arts, 4119 Legends Way, Maryville, TN 37801

Ah, But Do They Do Windows?

Although my recent return to work has required some adjustments for me and my family, our transition has been going fairly smoothly. Even our five "free-ranging" house dogs have been coping well with the new routine. Other than rumpling my bed and indulging in the occasional paper towel feast, the dogs have been model citizens during the day. I've been finding everything in order, just as it should be, when I come home in the early afternoon.

In an effort to keep the dogs from getting lonesome, I've been leaving the bedroom TV on while I'm gone. I thought perhaps it would act as a sort of electronic human for them.

When I came home from work Friday, my son asked if I had also left the living room TV on for the dogs.

"Nope!"

"*Somebody* did!"

"Okay, well. . .maybe I did."

Perhaps I had forgotten to turn it off. I didn't really remember. I do have a few senior moments.

Saturday everyone was home, but Sunday we all went out at the same time. My daughter and I went to the supermarket to get groceries, and my husband and son went to the service station to gas up the truck.

When Brittany and I got home, the living room TV was on. Again?

"Darn! Hubby left the TV on!" I thought to myself (or words to that effect!).

But upon being questioned about it later, my husband denied having been so forgetful.

"Okay, sure. Right, Dear," I thought to myself (or words to that effect!).

Today is Monday. I came home early. I could hear the living room TV *blaring* when I came up the driveway!

"What is going on?" I gasped. "What is this craziness with the TV?"

Cautiously, I crept to the front window and peered into the living room. I was greeted by the most tranquil of scenes. Gracie, the almost two-year-old puppy-mill rescue black Newf, was stretched out on the love seat. Admiral, the almost two-year-old Hubba Bubba good ole boy Landseer, was lounging on the couch. The other three were lying on the floor. All five dogs were staring at the TV. MTV to be exact!

"Okay, that proves it! *I* didn't do it! *I* wouldn't have chosen MTV for the dogs!"

I went back to the driveway and slammed the car door to announce my arrival. I heard Gracie and Admiral's feet hitting the tile floor.

I walked into the house and was greeted with the usual, "MOMMY! You're back from Phoenix!" chorus. (This is a joke in our house. Every time the dogs don't see us for thirty seconds we believe they think we've left the state!)

Of course there were no guilty looks. Of course none of them had done anything naughty. All I got was that beguiling Newfy innocence and those happy doggy faces.

I'm thinking, "Poltergeists? Newfiegeists?"

I turned off the TV and pretended I was leaving. But instead of driving away, I waited for a couple of minutes at the side of the house. Then I crept back and peered in through the living room window again.

In front of the TV stood Admiral and Gracie. To my absolute amazement, that big, bright, *goofy* Admiral, was poking at the TV control panel with his paw! To make the scene even more bizarre, after a few more Newfy swats, the TV came on!

Then, most contentedly, Admiral and Gracie took their seats on the couch and the love seat, respectively, and got comfortable. The other three dogs stretched out happily on the floor. Finally, just like any normal teenagers, all five dogs directed their attentive gazes at the TV.

Now, if only I could get them to do windows. . .

Carol Watt
Browns Mills, New Jersey, USA

Jake, the Rescue, Comes to the Rescue

Our peaceful winter evening shifted to an adrenaline rush hour as soon as I answered the phone. Our vet identified herself, then said quickly, "Gidget, I need a *huge* favor from Jake!"

"Jake? A favor from Jake?"

I was baffled. I had been waiting to hear from Dr. Clarke, but it was in reference to our fifteen-month-old puppy. Why was she asking about Jake? What possible favor could she want from Jake?

"We just finished an emergency C-section on a Doxie," she explained, hurriedly. "We delivered her five breech puppies successfully, but she lost a lot of blood during the surgery. She's in dire need of a transfusion. Can Jake help?"

"Of course!" I exclaimed.

Clutching the phone tightly, I was dancing around the room in a daze of compassion laced with fear. I *wanted* to help. I *wanted* Jake to save the Doxie. But what was I agreeing to do? What was the procedure? What was I asking of our dear, old boy?

But even as these questions flooded my mind, I heard myself saying, "We're on our way!"

Rushing to put on my shoes, I interrupted my husband's shower with, "Daryl! Dr. Clarke needs Jake!"

"Jake? I thought Ariel was the sick one."

"She is! But they need a blood donor! They need Jake!"

"They need *what?*"

I realized I was leaving Daryl completely confused, but I couldn't stop to explain. I'd call him from the clinic. Our boy was needed *immediately*.

Rushing Jake through the kitchen door, I got him into the van, and quickly backed out of the driveway. As I drove toward the clinic, more questions were running through my head. "What am I *doing*? Is Jake going to be okay? Did I make the right decision?" Should I be doing this alone?" My heart was overflowing with the unknown, and my fear of the unknown was great.

Then, somewhere amidst all my questions, an image took shape and remained steady and clear: it's four months ago; it's Labor Day. Daryl and I are in our local animal shelter. We're responding to a rescue call. We're being greeted by a very thin, black Newf. He is dirty and smelly and matted. But he greets us with dignity. He greets us with gentleness. And he greets us with a hopeful wag of his tail. He's seven or eight years old. We're falling in love with him. We're adopting him. We're naming him. . .Jake.

As we approached the vet's office, Jake was *thrilled* to see Dr. Clarke and some of his tech friends waiting for him at the door. He wagged his tail furiously and accepted pats all around as they hurried us through the reception area and into the surgery.

Other techs were waiting with their supplies in hand. After asking me to have Jake "sit," they drew a small blood sample from his foreleg.

On a slide, they combined Jake's sample with a sample from the Dachshund. If the blood clotted, the Doxie would need a different donor. If it didn't, she could use Jake.

My heart was beating very hard and very fast. Although still fearful of the unknown, I was doing my best to stay calm for Jake. I'm not good with blood or medical procedures or pain, but I was not leaving his side—we were in this together.

As we waited for the results of the test, Dr. Clarke explained that cross-matching blood prior to a transfusion, or more accurately blood typing, is considered proper protocol prior to a transfusion, *if time allows*. But in this case, the Doxie was almost out of time. Dr. Clarke told me that a dog can get blood from any other dog one time, and one time only, without the two being compatible. However if that dog should ever need blood again, it would reject anything except a perfect "match."

We seemed to wait forever, but in reality, it took only a minute. Jake was an appropriate donor. Jake was a "match." I *think* I was happy. I *know* I was scared.

Without wasting a second, Dr. Clarke pulled out a vial about ten inches in length and three-quarters of an inch in diameter. I felt faint when I saw the size of that tube. It looked *huge*! I must have gasped, and I'm sure I turned white, because Dr. Clarke asked me if I were okay.

As Jake sat calmly, I knelt beside him with my arms around his shoulders. I whispered in his ear, thanking him, telling him what a brave boy he was, reassuring him that everything was going to be okay. In truth, I needed to hear the reassurances more than he did.

The tube filled amazingly fast from the vein in his foreleg. The whole process took less than a minute. Although it was a terribly difficult minute for me, Jake didn't seem to mind at all. He just sat there patiently waiting for the procedure to be over.

Throughout the entire time we had been in the surgery, I could see the poor, little Doxie lying on the operating table just a few feet away. The anesthesia had worn off, but she was weak and listless. My heart broke into a million pieces when Dr. Clarke described her as "a very sick little girl." I feared her life was ebbing away.

While one of the techs removed the tourniquet from Jake's leg and put pressure on his vein, Dr. Clarke immediately began transferring his blood to the Doxie through her IV. I watched it move, drop by drop, ever so slowly.

Within a few minutes we could see a positive change in the little dog. At the end of fifteen minutes, she began lifting her head to look at her babies. In a few more minutes she began squirming in an effort to get to those babies.

Incredibly, two hours later, the Doxie mom and her five puppies were strong enough to go home. Jake and I had waited with them. We walked out of the vet's office right behind them.

This was a proud and happy moment for both of us. Jake seemed to understand that he had done something *wonderful*, and I was truly grateful we had been given an opportunity to help. Thanks to Jake, the rescue who came to the rescue, the evening had been a beautiful success.

Daryl & Gidget Hayworth
Greenwood, Indiana, USA

This story was published in the May, 2000, newsletter of the
South Central Newfoundland Club,
Newf Tales,
with permission.

Baby Buddies—Parker and Sam

Having two babies in our lives at the same time was not the original plan, but life is filled with lovely surprises. During the two years in which we began our Newfy research; got approved by members of the local and then the regional kennel clubs; were put in touch with breeders; chose the line we wanted; put our names on the waiting list, and were notified that the puppies had arrived; our son, Parker, was born.

We had been absolutely thrilled when we learned our first child was on his way. But as we planned for his arrival, we began wondering whether we should postpone getting a puppy. We knew Newfs were good family dogs, but we didn't know how a Newfy puppy would react to a young baby.

When we discussed this with our breeder, she was confident the puppy would be fine with the baby. Her only concern was whether or not we would be able to manage two babies at once. Since I was going to be a stay-at-home mother with plenty of outside support, we were sure we could handle the challenge.

Thus is was with much excitement a few months later that we began the twelve-hour trip from our home in Mackenzie to a rendezvous point in Edmonton to pick up our puppy. Dropping three-month-old Parker off to stay with his grandmother in Prince George, we traveled on to collect eight-week-old Sam.

Sam's breeder is in Saskatchewan, but we had made arrangements with the new owner of one of his littermates to bring him as far west as Edmonton. Since this would be our first visit to Alberta's capital city, we were somewhat apprehensive about making our connections. It had taken many worried phone calls to reassure ourselves we would be able to find our way to the designated meeting place. Then, in our rush to arrive on time, we were issued not one, but *two*, speeding tickets! However, all our troubles were forgotten when we finally met our little bundle of black joy! Within the hour, with Sam securely in my arms, we were heading home.

We drove all night, arriving in Prince George in the morning. We picked Parker up and, after another two hours on the road, finally completed our journey. It had been a long trip, but Parker and Sam had slept most of the way home.

Quite tired and weary, we walked through our doorway and placed Parker in his play pen so he would be safe while we unpacked the truck. Soon he began crying, and Sam, who had been wandering about exploring his new home, immediately hurried to his side. While Parker continued to fret, Sam lay down as close to him as was possible.

I was so amazed at Sam's response to Parker's distress that I called my husband to come see what had happened. As we watched the young dog show his concern for the young human, we knew we had made two good choices. We had chosen both the right breed of dog for our family and the right time in Parker's life to get a puppy!

When I called a breeder friend of ours and told her about this incident she asked, "Do you realize what just happened? You just lost your puppy! He's Parker's dog now!"

Although we laughed at the time, more than two years have passed since that day and the bond between these two "babies" had grown ever stronger. From the beginning, we made it possible for Parker and Sam to have an abundance of supervised interaction. We renovated our house so Sam could have a large kennel in our family room with a gate he could put his head over.

Before Parker could sit up on his own, Sam would lie on the floor in a "stay" position while we leaned Parker against his side. The only time Sam would move a muscle was when, much to Parker's delight, he would reach his head around to give the baby a kiss. As soon as Parker was able, he would pull himself up to stand at the kennel gate and merrily accept Sam's kisses. From their early beginnings as a forty-pound puppy and a thirteen-pound baby, these two little boys became best friends.

The strength of this friendship and the patience of the puppy became even more evident after Parker began crawling. He would spy Sam chewing on a favourite toy and scoot across the room to sit in front of him. Then he would reach out, take the toy from Sam's mouth, and place it in his own. Sam would wait, watching carefully, while Parker had his chew. Once Parker got tired of the toy and removed it from his mouth, Sam would pick it up again and take another turn. This sharing could go on for quite awhile, the baby and the puppy trading the toy back and forth, drool and all. I figured if this were the worst thing Parker ever put in his mouth, we'd have it made.

Because they have each other for entertainment, our two boys have rarely gotten bored. In our Toyota 4-Runner Sam rides in the back cargo area and Parker rides in the back seat. Always cooperative and within reach, Sam is Parker's greatest plaything in the truck. Once when I glanced back to see why Parker was giggling, he was gleefully holding onto Sam's big, slimy, wet tongue and moving it from left to right. Another time, when I checked to see why things had gotten so quiet, Sam was resting his head on top of Parker's, his jowls covering over half of our little boy's head. In this peaceful, comforting position, they had both fallen fast asleep.

As Parker grew older and started to walk, he used Sam as a support to hold himself up. When the puppy had had enough of Parker's climbing and hugging, he would simply walk away.

It did not come as a surprise to us that among the first things Parker learned to say were:

"Sam, sit!"

"Sam, down!"

"Sam, come!"

But what was a surprise, and what still continues to amuse us, is that Sam cheerfully responds to these commands! He also responds with big grins and tail wags to my favourite of Parker's comments:

"GOOD BOY, SAM!"

I know this is Sam's favourite of Parker's comments, also.

Now, as our boys move toward their third birthdays, their bond is steadfast and unwavering. They spend enormous amounts of time playing together. When they finally tire and need a rest, Parker sometimes uses Sam for a pillow. More often, Parker gets a pillow and a blanket for the two of them to share. As cuddling buddies, they are unequaled.

Having a young son and a Newfy who is three months younger has added much joy and pleasure to our lives. We are immensely proud of our two boys. Getting Sam when he was so close in age to Parker was the best thing we could ever have done.

Lesley Florell
Mackenzie, British Columbia, Canada

http://www.geocities.com/newfysam/index.html

Amazing Gracie

Mid-summer had arrived, and my garden was thriving. Most mornings would find me weeding, or hoeing, or staking the pole beans. Since my gardening activities were always of great interest to my Newf, Gracie, she usually accompanied me while I worked.

Gracie was just a bit over a year old, so I was used to having her poking around in her inquisitive, puppy manner. That's why I was a bit surprised the morning she lay down at the edge of a flower bed and spent over an hour, silent and still, staring intently at the sunflowers.

I assumed she had spied a bug or something and didn't give it too much thought. But the next morning she immediately returned to the same spot and resumed her intensive surveillance. Imagining she might be developing some sort of neurotic fixation, I decided I'd better investigate.

At first I didn't see anything unusual among the sunflowers. But upon looking carefully at the back of the flower bed, along the edge where it borders the garden shed, I finally spotted a three-inch hole in the ground. It appeared to be the mouth of a little burrow that was hidden beneath the shed.

I wasn't sure what had made the burrow, but I had my suspicions. We had had cottontail rabbit nests in our yard in previous summers, and our Beagle, Keeper, had even caught and destroyed a few bunnies in the past.

When ten-week-old Gracie arrived to live with us, Keeper had adopted her as her own puppy. I knew she had taught Gracie many of her Beagle ways, and I was concerned about this present situation. I feared Gracie might be attempting to practice the noble Beagle art of rabbit routing! So, during the next few days, my gardening routine included watching Gracie watch the hole.

On the fifth or sixth day of Gracie's vigil, I glanced over to check on her and did a double-take! Gracie lay motionless, her neck and chin tight to the ground. Crawling around on her muzzle were two tiny bunnies!

"Be careful, Gracie," I whispered. "They're babies. Be careful."

This is the same command I give when we visit a friend who has a Chihuahua and a Papillon. I had also taught Gracie to stay in a "down" position when the little dogs were nearby because I didn't want her to step on one of them by accident. The little dogs would run around her and, yes, sometimes climb on her head, just as the little cottontails were doing.

I pretended to go back to my weeding, but I kept watch as this amazing interaction between Gracie and the bunnies continued.

These babies were so small Gracie could have swallowed them both in one gulp. Instead, she stayed perfectly still as they poked their tiny noses here and there into the hair on her face. Then, standing on their little hind legs, they stretched up to examine the top of her head.

Since they showed no fear whatsoever, I suppose the bunnies thought this huge black nose at their front door was a normal part of life. They had probably been seeing it there from the first moment they opened their eyes!

The bunnies' investigation continued for about two minutes before Gracie, without moving another muscle, began wagging her tail. The thumping tail startled the bunnies and sent them scampering back into their burrow.

Gracie then began whining in an attempt to call them back out to play! She must have bonded with them because beginning that night, she started taking a toy out to their burrow every night during her final bathroom call.

The first time it happened, I just thought she had dropped her toy in the yard and forgotten about it. However, when I found it the next morning, placed carefully in front of the rabbit hole, I wondered if she might actually have intended to leave it with her new friends. I became more convinced of this when, from that night forth, until the bunnies left for greener pastures, Gracie always dropped a toy at the entrance to their burrow.

As the bunnies got bigger and started coming out often and hopping around, I had to keep a closer eye on Gracie because she seemed to want to round them up and herd them back to their home. She was either displaying a herding instinct or she and the bunnies had invented a inter-species game of hide-and-seek!

The excitement would begin when a bunny came out, made a dash for the garden, then hid in the pole bean patch. Gracie would gleefully search for it by poking her nose among the bean vines. After a few minutes the bunny would dart out, and with Gracie loping behind it, take a couple of laps around the bean pole. Finally it would zoom back to the burrow. Then, just when everything got quiet and settled again, the whole process would start over!

When both bunnies dashed for the bean patch at the same time, Gracie's excitement intensified. Grinning and bouncing and panting away, she searched for her elusive playmates. Of course I had to re-stake the bean poles on a regular basis due to this exuberant game.

Occasionally Gracie would get close enough to touch one of the bunnies. She would just give it a little nudge with her nose, as if encouraging it to move a little faster. I was happy and relieved to see that she could be so gentle. Even when she was extremely excited, her friendly Newf nature prevailed.

After a few days, the bunnies began hopping through our fence into the neighbor's yard. Still wanting to engage them in play, Gracie started pushing her toys through the fence. When our neighbor found the toys and handed them back to me, he was completely puzzled. It wasn't easy describing Gracie and her many playthings, which included a stuffed talking pig and two live bunnies, to someone who informed me that *most* dogs are quite satisfied to play with a stick!

Finally the bunnies stopped returning to their burrow, but Gracie continued checking their hole often. Spotting them in the neighbor's yard a few days later, she was ecstatic. With her tail wagging wildly, she grabbed a toy, rushed to the fence, and went into a deep play bow.

But, try as she did to attract their attention, the bunnies ignored her. Eventually she seemed to understand they would not be coming back. I must say, I felt a bit sorry for poor Gracie.

However, she never gave up or forgot about the bunnies. For the rest of that summer she grinned and wagged her tail every time she spotted a rabbit. Feeling confident she was thinking "playmate" rather than "prey," this behavior always made me smile. I was very proud of my gentle, friendly girl.

During the twenty years before Gracie arrived, I had read about Newfs and longed for one. The breed characteristic that most attracted me, yet most *puzzled* me, was the Newfs' ability to totally engulf their owners' daily lives. Now I have a Newf. Now I understand this engulfing ability completely. Gracie is intelligent and entertaining. She is amusing, warm-hearted, and loving. She fascinates me. She intrigues me.

Amazing Gracie. How sweet she is.

Mary Runkel
Ashland, Wisconsin, USA

Gentle Grace

There was a dog named Grace,

she had a beautiful face.

She was as big as a house

and as gentle as a mouse.

I would like to have a dog named Grace

because she would always love me and lick my face.

Tony Ledin
(Gracie's 13-year-old neighbor)
Ashland, Wisconsin, USA

Tony's poem was published in the Summer 2000 newsletter of the South Eastern Ontario Region,
Gentle Giant News
and is reprinted with permission.

Breaking the Chain

Among my most cherished childhood memories are the summers we spent with my grandparents in Newfoundland. Next door to them lived Chip, the gentlest, most beautiful dog my four sisters and I had ever met. He was the first and only Newf we knew during those years, and we all loved him dearly.

Although Chip was kept chained outside, we were forbidden from entering his yard. On the day the temptation was just too great for an eight-year-old, I did, in fact, visit him. And on that day, I did, in fact, get a spanking for my transgression! So, even though we were all immensely fond of Chip and eager for his company, we had to wait for him to come to us.

But come to us he did! For one of the many joys of those Newfoundland summers was being able to walk to the bay for a swim. Whenever we felt the urge, the five of us would don our swimsuits and head down to the water. And whenever we headed down to the water, Chip would *break his chain* and bound down to the bay to "rescue" us.

As strange as it seems now, we children often went to the beach with no parental supervision. When the adults saw Chip heading out, they would either take their time showing up, or not bother coming at all. I suppose they had seen him in action so many times they knew he would take care of us.

The minute this remarkable Newf reached the bay, the game would begin! Our goal was to stay in the water! His goal was to keep us on the shore!

If we hadn't reached the bay before he arrived, he attempted to block our progress into the water. If we were already in the water when he got there, he would come splashing in and get us out!

Chip's water rescue strategy consisted of methodically swimming around and around the five of us in tighter and tighter circles until he had organized us into a small, shrieking cluster. Once he had us together he would begin herding us toward the shore by swimming back and forth on our outward side, pushing nearer and nearer to us with each pass.

Naturally, we tried to foil him by heading out in all directions, but our repeated attempts to escape never seemed to distress him. Patiently and tirelessly, he simply kept forcing us back into a group and kept moving the group toward the shore until he had accomplished his goal.

Although we would sometimes get annoyed with him, he never let our shouts of displeasure interfere with his determination to get us to safety. Chip just didn't like the idea of five little girls splashing about in Bonavista Bay by themselves! We could never swim for any distance without meeting up with him. His perseverance was extraordinary, and the size of the chain he had to break to rescue us was impressive. Occasionally he even showed up with several big links of the chain trailing behind him!

As soon as he got us out of the water and headed home, Chip felt his day's work was done. He would return to his yard, go back to his dog house, and wait calmly for his owners to come out and fix his chain.

I don't think Chip's family ever punished him for breaking his chain. I think they just repaired and reinforced it to prevent his wandering off and getting shot. When we children were visiting and he was missing, his family always knew where he had gone. He never allowed us to be unattended at the beach!

Chip was a working Newf. Wood was the only source of heat for the families in my grandparents' town. As soon as the water froze over in the fall, Chip was used to haul wood in from across the bay. Throughout the long Newfoundland winters he had work to do, but we children were his only diversion during his summer rest periods.

I think Chip enjoyed rescuing us almost as much as we enjoyed being rescued. My sisters and I will never forget this faithful, devoted boy. He lives in our memories amidst much laughter and love.

Glenda Baker
Sheet Harbor, Nova Scotia, Canada

Pat Seawell

On Becoming Celebrities

Early in our marriage, some twenty-plus years ago, my husband and I were employed by a London-based company and were offered a stint in Papua New Guinea. We had no children at the time, but we did have our beloved Newfies. Monty, a black dog, was three years old and Hugga Bear and Cindar Bear, the Landseer bitches, were 4½.

Before we agreed to the assignment, we made certain our dogs could accompany us. We checked the "importation of animals" regulations (No German Shepherds! No Dobermans!). We studied the temperature and humidity ranges, and we even spent a week in country, without the dogs, getting "the lay of the land." Finally, confident that we would be able to keep the dogs healthy and comfortable, we accepted the assignment.

Departure day arrived. In high spirits and ready for adventure, we crated the dogs in Sydney. We assured them we'd be reunited soon, and saw them through onto the aircraft. Robert and I were relatively unconcerned. These guys had done well on previous flights so we had no reason to think this one would be any different.

Five hours later, our flight arrived without incident at Jackson Airport, PNG. We left the aircraft hoping our dogs would be unloaded quickly. For the next twenty minutes there ensued much activity and excitement on the tarmac. Native PNG airport personnel kept rushing back and forth from the plane to the terminal. However, despite much shouting and animated exchanges on their part, we saw no apparent progress in the opening of the hatches and the removal of luggage. We'd experienced other airports that were slow at this process, but it seemed that Jackson was going to become the record holder.

As more and more time passed, grumbles from fellow passengers waiting for their luggage grew increasingly louder while Robert and I, waiting for our Newfies, grew increasingly more concerned. We were not happy that the dogs were still sitting inside the closed aircraft in the tropical sun.

Suddenly a command boomed out over the intercom demanding that my husband or I present ourself at the quarantine inspection office *immediately*!

Obviously something had happened to our dogs! Obviously something had gone dreadfully wrong!

Our initial alarm turned to panic when we were met by the overwrought quarantine inspection officer. Our Pidgin was not all that good, but his English was even worse as, close to hysteria, he tried to impart his message. With the exception of "big dog" which he kept repeating with eyes the size of saucers, we could not understand a *thing* the man was saying! By now, near hysteria myself, I was convinced that at least one of the dogs was dead!

In desperation, the inspector, realizing he was getting nowhere in his attempt to *tell* us his news, rushed us out of his office and onto the tarmac so he could *show* us what he was talking about.

Shouting to the baggage trolley driver to follow us, the inspector hurried us to the aircraft. Then he yelled some instructions to the trolley driver, and literally sprinted away.

When the trolley driver reached the plane, he climbed onto the trolley and cautiously opened the baggage hatch. Then, off he sprinted to join the inspection officer!

What was wrong? What was causing the terror? Were *all* the dogs dead? Did we have a bomb on board? What? WHAT?

Filled with dread and foreboding, I peered into the baggage compartment. As my eyes adjusted to the gloom, I finally spotted what had caused the mayhem.

There, in all her glory, sat Hugga Bear, my beautiful, alpha, Landseer bitch. She was completely calm and completely unharmed. And she was completely free of her crate!

Hugga Bear was the smallest of our trio. Usually the quietest, and definitely the most dignified of the three, she was rarely given to frivolity (and then only in private!). However, one of the names we had for her was "Houdini." This bitch could open drawers, cupboards, gates, and doors with consummate ease. She could even scale fences. Running away was never her goal. She simply seemed to feel that being enclosed was beneath her dignity.

On this occasion she had chewed her way out of the crate and was waiting for me to come get her. She gave me the most disdainful look as if to say, "Mum, I really don't belong in one of those boxes, you know!"

I tried explaining that she would not bite, but the airport personnel refused to come within twenty feet of her. It had never occurred to me that some people might be frightened by Newfoundlands just because of their size. I guess the arrogance of youth is my excuse. *I* knew Newfies were exceptionally gentle and friendly. Didn't the rest of the world know this?

I put Hugga Bear's lead on her collar and led her onto the trolley. Realising we had caused enough hysteria for one day, we left the other two dogs in their crates, off loaded them onto the trolley, and, since the trolley driver had completely disappeared, Robert drove us to the quarantine area.

At that point, things suddenly began moving very quickly! The requisite pieces of paper were signed, our luggage magically appeared, and I was told, "Na Missus, mipela na laik lookim bilum bilong ui, uipela go tasol." ("No, Madam, we do not wish to examine your baggage! Just go!")

During our stay in Papua New Guinea, Robert and I traveled extensively, both internally and internationally. Initially embarrassed that news of our dogs had spread throughout the airport communities, we soon realised our good fortune. Everyone wanted to be our friend and we always got great allocations.

Even though flights would often be triple booked, we never, ever, got bumped. Evidently, getting us and our terrifying "cargo" out of their territory had become the personal goal of each and every PNG airport employee!

Throughout our stay and until the day we left, three years later with Newfies in tow, we were known as "Masta and missus who nau garim bigpela dok." ("White man and his wife who have the big dogs.")

We still chuckle fondly at our memories of those years and those adorable, big, dogs. Monty, Cindar Bear, and Hugga Bear were, among other things, the Newfies who made us infamous.

Wendy Scheeres
Bossnan Kennels
Wyong Creek, New South Wales, Australia

We'll Cross That Bridge When We Come To It... Or Not!

Our dilemma unfolded on the farm lane, just after the three of us crossed the cattle grid. My six-year-old Newf, Piglet, my partner, Patrick, and I were returning from our usual two-mile, round-trip walk to the quarry lake. Patrick and I had been chatting quietly. Piglet had been happily bumbling along in his normal, carefree manner. All was peaceful and calm.

As we approached the bridge which borders one side of our orchard, Piglet suddenly, and most determinedly, capsized onto the track. The deliberate manner of this abrupt and total collapse suggested he would be moving his 140-pound frame for no man and no thing in the foreseeable future.

Since this sit-down strike was completely atypical, unprecedented Piglet behavior, I immediately entered a state of panicky conjecture. Was he suffering from a stroke or a total memory wipe-out? Had he experienced heart failure or sudden-onset arthritis? Fearfully, I raced through my mind's index of dreadful possibilities.

Piglet came to me at age two after my four-year-old Zack died of a ghastly and mysterious auto-immune disease. Zack's long struggle had left me devastated. Now, with Piglet slumped on the ground, I recalled Zack's illness and imagined a terrifying genetic connection. Piglet is Zack's nephew!

However, after a while it became obvious that Piglet had not sustained an injury of any sort, nor was he suffering any apparent illness. Once I had calmed down, I could appreciate the beauty of his display: it was the most determined of lying downs I have ever been privileged to witness. He behaved as if an acting teacher had called upon him to impersonate a mountain, and he was after the best grade in the class.

After several minutes of increasingly desperate coaxing, Patrick and I realized that our forward thinking was getting us nowhere. Therefore, we attempted to work backward: turning ourselves around, we marched back along the track toward the quarry lake. Up popped a rather eager Piglet, and was quickly trundling between us, full-speed-ahead, back from whence we'd come!

After ascertaining that Piglet could walk perfectly well in the *opposite* direction, away from the bridge, we were certain he wasn't in the throes of some life-threatening medical emergency. Although this knowledge was reassuring, we remained completely mystified by his behavior.

Why this refusal to cross the bridge? It is a perfectly fine, wide, wooden bridge with steel girders underneath. It spans a relatively small stream and is only five feet above the stream bed. There was absolutely nothing alarming about this bridge! To make the situation even more baffling, Piglet had been crossing this bridge for over three years with nary a hesitant footstep!

I should point out that this bridge is also the only means by which my Newf has *ever* crossed this stream! Sweet Piglet takes a rather dim view of water sports in general, and on manoeuvres down at the quarry lake with the regional Newf water-rescue group, has been known to feign complete indifference as I flounder about in the chilly water in my purple wetsuit.

This behavior may be rooted in embarrassment on his part, or in the conviction that I'm perfectly able to swim and he must take a firmer line with me, but he does display a determined reluctance towards even getting his toes damp. Faced with the most insignificant of puddles, Piglet always takes the option to detour.

Eventually, having determined that there was no physical problem with Piglet, and having been exposed to several more "down-stay" displays on approaching the bridge, Patrick and I assumed we were engaged in some sort of power struggle over who determines the end of the walk.

At last, Patrick staying with the unrelentingly prone Piglet, I crossed the bridge, fetched the car, and backed it down the driveway and across the bridge.

After a fair amount of heaving and ho-ing, we hoisted the still-mountainous Piglet into the back of the Subaru. Without further incident, we transported him across that most feared of bridges to his home sweet home.

The next morning, hoping Piglet had forgotten the stand-off, yet determined to give him an opportunity to overcome his anxiety and face down the bridge, I leashed him, and with great fanfare, announced we were going for walkies. He was eager and cooperative, and, in fact, particularly enthusiastic, as he is exceptionally fond of leash-wearing activities.

All went well as we sauntered across the garden. All went normally as we ambled through the orchard. Then we approached the bridge. Down went Piglet! Once again he demonstrated a very decisive "down-stay." If yesterday he had been Everest-Dog, today he was Mount Kilimanjaro, lording it over all of East Africa, and winning an Oscar or two en route.

After an hour-long coaxing session involving favorite toys and treats, including raspberries and a much beloved and greatly admired squeaky carrot, Piglet remained firmly planted on our side of the bridge. No amount of my joyful bouncing about on the wide wooden span changed his judgment. My boy was *not* crossing the bridge!

Pertinent to this dilemma is the fact that our home is completely surrounded by rivers and streams. Our cottage is a converted warehouse dating from the late 1700's, the heyday of inland waterway transport in England. It stands at the junction of the rivers Thames and Coln, near the last lock on the Severn Canal. Water is the property's defining characteristic. This bridge is the *only* way out to civilization on foot, thus the urgency of reacquainting Piglet with the notion of crossing it!

By late afternoon, having had several more futile sessions out at the bridge, my guilt level was running high. I had begun thinking that Piglet's refusal to cross the bridge was my fault.

The day preceding Piglet's strange behavior had been the anniversary of a very sad time in my life. Because of this, I had been feeling rather distressed. To calm myself and put things into perspective, I'd gone out to sit for a time on the bridge. While dangling my legs off the side, I'd shed a fair number of tears into the trout stream beneath me.

My emotional black cloud blew past soon enough, and my tears were nothing too terrible to behold, but Piglet was out in the orchard at the time. He must have heard me crying and worked out that setting foot on the bridge caused me to make distressing noises. Then, in his determination to save me from sadness and/or to prevent the same miserable affliction from befalling him, he made the decision never again to set foot on that most nefarious of wooden structures.

It mystifies me that he managed to make it across the bridge the following morning on our way to the quarry lake, but I can only surmise that his enthusiasm for walkies outweighed his fear of the bridge on our outward journey. He may well have hesitated on that trip across; I just wasn't aware of any change in his behavior at that time.

It seemed a break in the cycle would be helpful, so for the next several days I didn't ask Piglet to cross the bridge under his own steam. Instead of taking our usual stroll to the quarry lake, we went out by car to the beech woods where we frequently walk.

These woods are atop a neolithic hill fort, with a fine view out across the valley of the Thames as it meanders through the eastern Cotswolds. However, the most attractive feature about this area in Piglet's opinion are the many fellow canines we usually encounter there. Since he finds visiting with these other dogs exceedingly entertaining, this is by no means a second-best experience to the quarry lake.

After a week of commuting to walkies, we braved the bridge again. Although there was initial reluctance, Piglet did eventually position himself midway between the sides, far from the edges where my musing on sad times past had occurred, and rather gingerly, but at great speed, beetled himself across and off the other side! This courageous feat was followed by much praise and heartfelt congratulations by Patrick and myself.

Although Piglet carried on this hot-footed approach to crossing the bridge for the better part of two weeks, he eventually resumed his normal, lackadaisical approach to getting across the river. Several seasons of the year on, his days of bridge trauma seem long forgotten.

His only problem with the bridge these days involves being denied access by his adolescent sidekick, Zeke the Pyrenean, who joined our family last summer. At every opportunity, Zeke scuttles back and forth attempting to keep Piglet from stepping onto the bridge. However, Piglet, cheerfully and with great confidence, simply barrels past Zeke's defenses.

It makes me happy to see the bridge incorporated into playtime rather than remaining the stuff of Piglet nightmares. In retrospect, I'm convinced that my boy was upset because I was, such is our empathic bond.

Often, when I'm saying good night to Piglet, he looks up at me as if to say, "Day is done; all's well in our world, isn't it?" This gives me a strong and reassuring reminder of our intuitive connection.

I wish I could protect Piglet from being too sensitive to my sadder emotions. If only I could explain to him that the internal landscape isn't always reflected in the external!

One saving grace is that happy emotions are equally contagious to Piglet, and his reactions are just as demonstrative. Though he shares my occasional sorrow, he rejoices in my frequent bliss. We're with one another through the vicissitudes of life, and there's great comfort in that time-tested knowledge.

Margaret Notley
Lechlade, the Cotswolds, England, United Kingdom

Wake Up And Smell the Coffee!

After several weeks of working ten-hour days, waking up and getting ready for work was becoming increasingly difficult for my husband, John. As he stood searching for his comb on one particularly "foggy" morning, Morgan shoved the bathroom door open and barged in.

She began pushing at John's leg, seeking his immediate attention. She was so insistent and *demanding* that even in his sleep-deprived state, John realized something was wrong. Something was amiss. Something was funny. This was definitely not Morgan's normal behavior.

As soon as John looked down at her and questioned her, she wheeled around and headed down the hall toward the kitchen. He knew he was expected to follow.

Entering the kitchen, John immediately saw the cause of Morgan's alarm. *Coffee!* Coffee was everywhere! It was flooding over the breadbox, running across the counter, cascading down the front of the dishwasher, and splashing onto the floor.

Morgan was right! This was a problem! This was an emergency! This was a genuine kitchen catastrophe! John needed to *do* something. Quickly!

Between my forgetting to set the pot in place when I put the under-the-cabinet coffee maker together the night before, and my husband's not noticing my mistake before turning it on, we'd made a real mess! But it could have been worse. Fortunately, Morgan had sounded the alarm before all twelve cups had splattered onto the floor.

Morgan watched as John snapped off the coffee maker and began sopping up the brown brew. Then, convinced he had the problem under control, she trotted down the hall and snuggled in with me for a few more winks.

We were still thanking Morgan for saving the day when she found another situation in which her human parent had neglected to follow the proper procedure.

This incident occurred early one evening as I went about lighting my large Christmas candles. First, I lit the bedroom candle and the candle in the bathroom. Next, I lit the candle in the living room.

Just as I moved on to light the kitchen candle, I heard Morgan. She was down at the other end of the house barking and growling. She was kicking up a *terrible* fuss.

When I went to check, I found her standing in the bedroom doorway barking at the candle. At first I was puzzled. Everything looked normal. Everything seemed all right. The candle was flickering its soft, warm light onto the walls and ceiling.

Whoops! I'd forgotten something! Something *important*! Because we have an overly curious Himalayan cat with a huge, fluffy tail and long, luxurious whiskers, all my candle holders are topped with ceramic or metal shades. Thus, the candle flames are always covered and contained.

But I'd forgotten to put the shade back on the bedroom candle holder after lighting it! My mistake had left Morgan worried and none too pleased. Thanking her for noticing the problem, I quickly corrected my error.

For the next couple of minutes Morgan carefully observed the new patterns that illuminated the walls and ceiling. Finally, satisfied that the candle was properly covered, she relaxed. With everything right in her world again, she calmly trotted down the hall to resume her full-time job as keeper of the living room carpet.

We find Morgan's attention to detail extraordinary. Her sensitivity to her environment both amazes and reassures us. She notices when things aren't as they should be, and she knows how to get help. Since she can spot small problems such as coffee spills and missing candle shades, we're confident she will alert us should other, more serious, situations occur.

When I think of this two-year-old, Newfy girl's background and the complications she suffered during her first ten months of life, I marvel at the secure, confident girl she has become. For at the age of five months, she was returned to her breeder. Her family had been unable to house train her. She needed a new home.

After my first conversation with the breeder, I was convinced we could give her a good home. The next day was Mother's Day and Morgan was the gift I wanted! So, at 2:30 the following morning, John and I loaded our three-year-old Newf, Murphy, into the Explorer. Then, with high hopes, we began the thirteen-hour round trip through horrendous pouring rain and fog to pick up our new pup.

We were definitely not prepared for the sight we saw on arrival. Morgan was out back in the mud with the other dogs, and although she had been given a bath, she smelled like something akin to urine-soaked burned rubber. It was a terrible odor.

When she was brought into the house, she wouldn't stand up or make eye contact with anyone. Instead, she cowered on her stomach with her head out flat, like a bearskin rug. The poor little girl was terrified.

Holding back the tears, we lifted our new puppy into the truck next to Murphy, our *Grande Dame*, for the ride home. Murphy seemed appalled. She showed her disdain at being stuck in the back with this smelly creature by refusing to look at her.

The next few days were spent determining that this pup didn't have a house training problem. She had a physical problem. Her condition, called ectopic urethra, occurs when the urethra enters the bladder in the wrong place. No amount of house training could have prevented her from having accidents. Our vet, a close friend, assured us that her condition was correctable and could be repaired when we had her spayed.

Meanwhile, we attempted to minimize Morgan's odor by bathing her every day. As she got a bit older, she gained some control over her muscles during the day, but she continued to have accidents when she slept.

Morgan's medical condition had so traumatized her that it was weeks before she would stand erect. Yet even though she was insecure and unsure of herself, we felt it important to treat her as much like a normal puppy as possible. We began taking our timid, painfully shy, little girl to socialization classes and obedience training even though her odor was a constant problem. I ached for her when she began feeling secure enough to go to people who held their friendly hands out to her. They would begin petting her, then grimace and recoil in horror when her awful smell reached them.

Because of serious complications during her spaying, it was not possible to do the urethral repair at that time. Morgan was ten months old before she could finally undergo her corrective surgery.

When we brought her home after the urethral repair, she slept for eight hours. When she awoke, the comforter under her was wet. Our vet had told us that the surgery might not completely solve the problem since the muscles had never received continual use. He had cautioned us not to expect too much change for at least two weeks. Despite his warnings, I looked at the wet comforter, and my hopes were dashed. My heart broke. My eyes filled with tears. But, happily, blissfully, *joyfully*, that was Morgan's last accident! From that day forth, she never left another puddle.

Morgan seemed to realize her nightmare was over. On the second day after her surgery, she hopped up on the love seat for the very first time. It was as if she understood she no longer smelled bad, so sitting on furniture wouldn't create problems. At last she was normal and was able to begin the process of becoming a happy puppy. A cheerful, new personality began emerging, and within days she had the confidence to look us in the eye.

Morgan has more than repaid us for all the paper towels, baby wipes, shampoo, baking soda, hot water, back aches, and distress of her first five months in our home. She fills our hearts and lives with her gratitude. Without the hard work of helping her get physically and emotionally well, we would never have known the delight and joy of her devotion and sweetness. . .and we would never have had a big Newfy girl insisting that we wake up and smell the coffee!

Carol & John Campbell
Southington, Connecticut, USA

Joy To The World

Bringing joy to the world is not an easy job, but *some* dog's got to do it, and for the past eight years our Newfy has devoted himself to the task. He is a dedicated working dog, and making people happy is the work he does best.

Thor seems to believe that joy, like charity, begins at home. He adopted us when he was only nine weeks old, and he has been doing his best to entertain and amuse us ever since. Always the prankster, one of his favorite tricks involves hiding things from my husband, John.

"Cathy, where's my little bag of M&M's?"

"Don't look at me! I don't even like M&M's!"

"Thor, do you know anything about my bag of M&M's?"

Thor cocks his head to one side. He attempts to look serious. He attempts to look concerned. But his eyes are twinkling. They give him away.

"You have it! I *know* you have it!"

Then the game begins! Thor, all helpfulness and innocence, prowls around the house. John follows. And follows. And follows. Finally, at that perfect moment, that moment just before teasing changes to tedium, Thor saunters over to the couch and flips up one of the cushions.

Surprise! There's the bag of M&M's! He *found* it!

I laugh. John laughs. Thor is thrilled. He knows he has saved the day. All of us are happy.

Thor also knows how to bring joy to the neighborhood. I put on his harness, attach it to his thirty-foot chain, and the two of us go out into the front yard.

Adults in jogging shoes stop and talk to him. Little kids on bicycles stop and pet him. Teenagers on skateboards stop and ask him about his day. Thor generously gives them his gifts of tail wags and kisses, and he graciously accepts their gifts of laughter and smiles.

Thor's additional joy-bringing responsibilities include our wonderful next-door neighbors, Herbie and Sheila. He has known them for as long as he has known us and considers them part of his extended pack. John and I are convinced they love him as much as we do, and Thor definitely thinks they are wonderful.

When we are away from home, Herbie and Sheila invite him over, and when they see him in the yard, they never pass up an opportunity to receive his hugs and sloppy kisses.

Occasionally, Thor evidently feels the need to check on Herbie and Sheila. First he asks to go outside, then I hear him barking. If I go out to see what's going on, I find him at the fence, facing Herbie and Sheila's kitchen window. He gives me an "I'm not calling you, Mom!" glance and continues summoning his special friends. It's never long before their front door opens and out they come!

They bring him a biscuit, give him a hug, and, of course, thank him for his concern regarding their welfare.

Since Herbie enjoys playing practical jokes almost as much as Thor does, they sometimes team up to conspire against unsuspecting souls. Last weekend the young daughters of visiting friends were fooled by one of their games.

John and I were to be gone all day Saturday so we had asked Herbie and Sheila to let Thor out during the day. When their friends stopped by, Herbie asked their two little girls if they would like to see his dog. He explained that Thor was so big he had to have a regular house for his dog house.

The girls thought Herbie was teasing until he got out the key. They were just old enough to read "Thor's house" on the key chain. For them, the written word was completely convincing. The youngest child was so impressed that a dog would be given such a fine house she commented, "I didn't know Daddy had any rich friends."

Naturally, Thor went along with the joke. At 130 pounds, he was definitely the biggest dog the little girls had ever seen so it seemed possible to them that he would require a house of his own. Besides, he greeted them as warmly and as enthusiastically as any good host would have done and made them feel welcome in his home. They shared many laughs, a fair amount of slime, and dozens of kisses. From all reports, a good time was had by all!

Yet, even as much fun as all these neighborhood events can be, in Thor's opinion, *nothing* compares to the thrill of Halloween. Trick-or-treat Night is the highlight of his year. Children come! To *his* house! To visit *him!* The excitement is almost more than he can bear. Ecstatically he kisses each and every child, and he refuses to call it quits until the streets are completely quiet and the last little gremlin has gone home. He dispenses so much joy during this one evening that he has to sleep the whole next day away. We call it his Halloween Hangover.

To say that Thor has changed our lives would be an understatement. He has enchanted us and enriched us. How could it be otherwise? Pure devotion pours from his big, brown eyes and his beautiful, soft face. We call him our human kid in a fur suit, and we are consumed by his love and affection. We *cherish* our Newfy boy. He is the best thing that has ever happened to us. He brings joy to us, and joy to our neighborhood.

Cathy & John King
Colonia, New Jersey, USA

Unplanned Parenthood

"Newfoundland," it read, "free to good home."

The ad made my skin crawl. What kind of family would give away their Newfoundland? What kind of *villains* would dump their pup?

I did not want another dog. I already had a rambunctious, candle-eating Labrador puppy. Anyway, I didn't know anything about Newfs. I had never even seen one. Oh, I had seen *pictures* of them. I had heard people talk about how *wonderful* they were. But. . .I had never actually met one in person. . .and. . .I had always wanted to.

I dialed the number.

It was a sad, distressing story: people buy pup; pup has horrible hips; people's hopes of showing and breeding are dashed; pup is replaced; "damaged" pup is disposed of.

A few hours later I was introduced to the sweetest, most gentle soul I had ever met. Although he was only about two years old, he was already *huge*.

But I had only come to satisfy my curiosity. I had no intention of leaving with this dog. And, in fact, I did not. But a few days later, I received an unanticipated phone call.

"We've completed our interviews. Congratulations! We've chosen you!"

This wasn't what I was expecting! This wasn't what I'd planned! I tried to speak. I tried to *think*!

Clutching the phone tighter, I glanced around my small house. I had recently erected a large run for my Lab outside in my small garden, and we had established a nice, simple routine: outside when I leave; inside when I come home. Somehow, the idea of two dogs was *scary*!

Yet, hadn't I felt protective of this pup from the minute I read the ad? And didn't I now feel that someone was leaving a baby on my doorstep? Within three seconds all my compassionate instincts kicked in. I would take that puppy! And I would love him and care for him as if he were my very own child!

Fortunately, when I brought Zeke home, Zack was thrilled. He acted as if he'd *always* wanted a big brother! Within minutes, the two boys had become best friends. I smiled with relief. Who said having two dogs was scary?

With hardly a hitch, we continued our routine: two dogs outside when I left; two dogs inside when I came home. Like many people who must regularly leave their dogs alone during part of the day, I wondered how they entertained themselves when I was away. I had already had some experience with Zack. I knew he was always busy, always on the move, always into something, but I was curious about Zeke.

It wasn't long before my curiosity was satisfied. I was sick one day and had to stay home. Because Zack could behave indoors while I was home, and Zeke still wasn't trained, I separated the two dogs. I let Zack stay inside, but I didn't feel well enough to watch Zeke so I put him outside. As usual, I left him with a nice snack in his bowl and lots of water.

In late morning when I got up to get a drink, I peeked out the kitchen window. In all my imaginings about what Zeke did while I was at work, I'd never even come close to the scene I witnessed in the dog run!

There lay Zeke, two feet from the food dish, his muzzle to the ground, and there, running right in front of his muzzle on its way to the food dish, was a tiny mouse! Fascinated, I stood watching as, one by one, a whole *family* of tiny mice ran past his muzzle to the food dish. Each mouse would grab a morsel and race back to a hole under the concrete. I could hardly believe Zeke's level of tolerance. Not only were the mice running back and forth just inches from his nose, their path took them right over first one big, black paw and then the other.

During the entire time I watched, Zeke did not move a muscle. He must have lain motionless for hours because the mice's food procurement was still going on when I woke up in the afternoon. I wondered how many days this scenario had been repeated, and tried to envision the opulence and abundance of this particular mouse family's pantry.

But then I remembered that Zeke was rarely in the run alone, and Zack could *never* have been this calm! Both my boys were sweethearts, but they were very, very different.

Almost twenty-five years have passed since that happy day Zeke suddenly became my boy. He was with me for over nine years. During that time the only visible sign of a hip problem occurred when he ran. He never appeared to be in pain, but his rear legs seemed to be fused together. His hopping gait resembled that of a rabbit.

Zeke was sweet, caring, alert, protective, and wonderful to the end. When he died unexpectedly in his sleep, I was heartbroken. But I knew he had had a life full of playtimes, long walks, enjoyable swims, devoted companionship, and true love. And I knew there would be another Newf in my future.

Kathee Kiesselbach
Niles, Michigan, USA

www.biggieboy.com

Look What the Bear Dragged In!

Blame it on the fact that I'm a first-time mom, but I'm finding my big bear of a puppy absolutely *fascinating*. Evidently Berry finds me rather fascinating as well because even though he can come and go through his dog door as he pleases, he spends most of his time inside watching my every move. I attempt to meet his expectations by providing us with a variety of amusing activities, but it's Berry himself who creates much of our entertainment. During our six months together, he has given me many giggles and a few gasps. But last night he had me giggling and gasping at the same time.

The weather had been stormy much of the day so Berry and I were spending a nice, cozy evening at home. He came in from the yard and flopped his soggy self down on the floor next to the sofa where I was sitting. Since this is normal Berry behavior, I didn't really pay too much attention to him.

Then I heard a big Newf sigh. Since this is also normal Berry behavior, I still didn't pay too much attention. However, a few seconds later, the first big sigh was followed by a second big sigh.

Something about the second sigh caused me to look over the arm of the sofa at my big, damp furball. He gazed up at me, then put his chin on the floor and stared at the slobber puddle he had created there. Comically, without raising his chin from the floor, he looked back up at me and heaved a third big sigh.

At last all this sighing achieved its desired effect. Berry had finally captured my full, undivided attention. With growing curiosity, I peered at him over the arm of the sofa.

Suddenly I realized the slobber in front of his chin was *moving*. Though at times it seems as if his slobber has a life of its own, this was definitely out of the ordinary. I got up and knelt down on the floor next to Berry. This particular puddle warranted a closer look.

It was at this point that my simultaneous gasps and giggles began because there, mired in the muck, deadlocked in the drool, I spied a tiny, little frog. Not more than an inch long, it was struggling unsuccessfully to get out of Berry's sticky slime. Not too surprisingly, a tuft of black fuzz stuck to its small green body.

I watched in wonder as the frog pushed its tiny back legs against Berry's muzzle. It was making a gallant effort to free itself from the goo. Berry, meanwhile, seemed pleased with his own gallant effort. He had successfully gotten my attention and I was showing appropriate excitement over his prize.

Amazingly, the little frog seemed completely unharmed. When I scooped it up with a piece of paper and set it free, it quickly hopped away from its canine encounter. For obvious reasons, I released the little creature *outside* my big bear's fence.

It was astonishing to me that Berry, all 90-ish pounds of him, did not hurt this little frog while catching it or bringing it inside. He is a very clumsy guy, with ungainly limbs, huge feet, and a long lizard tongue that darts out to kiss unsuspecting bystanders. Yet with all his goofiness, he was ever so gentle with this tiny amphibious creature. I have never seen anything like it. But then again, as I've already mentioned, I'm a first-time mom. Berry is my very first Newf.

Kira Attwood
Chapel Hill, North Carolina, USA

Miss Maggie Measures Up

Fifteen-month-old Maggie cheerfully holds her "down-stay" as almost a hundred first and second graders and Special Education students crowd into my classroom and begin taking turns measuring her. And measuring her. And measuring her. These children have been studying measurement all week. My puppy is providing today's lesson.

Maggie grins and happily thumps her tail against the floor as the children compile extensive amounts of length-related data. Her eye, they announce, is one teddy bear counter long, her back is fifty-six link cubes, and her tail is 3½ pencils. Her front leg, they discover, is fourteen inches long, her mouth six oblong pink erasers, and her back foot is three-fourths of a brand new, unused, yellow crayon.

Although Maggie is not a stranger to school visits, she seems unusually delighted at being the central player in this amusing new game. She understands she's been chosen "it," and adds her own twist to this position by planting a few juicy kisses whenever a little face hovers tantalizingly near.

By the end of the afternoon, almost every part of my little girl has been measured. And, as usual, and in flying colors, Miss Maggie has measured up. She gets a treat and an extra cuddle on our way home. I'm so proud of this exceptionally cooperative young Newf!

Maggie came to live with us and our eight adult Newfs when she was four months old. Although we weren't sure how the adults would handle a new puppy who was not related to any of them, they graciously accepted her into their pack the same day she arrived.

Like most healthy puppies, Maggie immediately brought new action and excitement into our lives. She is a high-spirited, high-energy pup. When she's not playing with her soccer ball, she's bouncing her Boomer Ball off the fence, or hanging onto one of the adult dogs' ears, or inviting me with a tug rope or a fetch toy for an impromptu game.

Despite this non-stop puppy exuberance at home, when Maggie goes to school or *anywhere* in public, she's a perfect lady. This has been true since her very first school visit. She was only five months old at that time and had never before encountered a large group of young children. Yet, instinctively, she demonstrated impeccable manners.

Our school district has a summer program for children who speak English as their second language. Many of these children have not been exposed to dogs in their native countries so the summer program teachers asked if I would bring some of our Newfs and present my dog safety lesson for their classes.

When I told my husband, Marty, I was taking Maggie, along with our ten-year-old Harvey, he wasn't sure that was a good idea. She was at the "snapigator" stage—constantly nipping at us, constantly untying our shoes. But, somehow I knew she'd be okay.

I was right! Any worries vanished when the first group of children came through the door. Maggie's tail began wagging and never stopped as she meandered among them, nudging and licking.

After the third or fourth group visited, Maggie abruptly crashed. She was still a baby, after all, and it was *long* past her nap time! As she snored away on the cool tile floor, one little boy had a sudden burst of curiosity. Before I realized what was happening, he picked up her head and began rooting through the puppy fuzz searching for her ear! Fortunately, Maggie just cracked open an eye, gave him a quick kiss, and went back to sleep.

For more than twenty-five years our Newfs have been coming to school with me every Halloween. After all the classes of the grade level I'm teaching that year and all the Special Ed classes in our school gather in my room and participate in our dog safety lesson, the dogs and I visit the children's individual classrooms delivering treats the Newfs carry in their backpacks.

That this tradition has created many fond memories is confirmed by former students who return as adults to visit. Always, *always*, they ask about the Halloween dogs by name.

Last fall, Maggie made her first Halloween visit. Although surrounded by large groups of giggling children, each on a sugar high, each wearing a strange, flapping costume, she seemed completely at ease. Interestingly, she did what our twelve-year-old, Gussie, always did—*immediately* zeroed in on the neediest children in the room! Maggie headed straight for these special youngsters and spent most of the visit draped on their laps, leaving Harvey to mix and mingle with all the other children. Her intuitiveness prompted our guidance counselor and resource teacher to ask if they could hire a Newfoundland for their Child Study Team!

After teaching first, second, or third grade for thirty-three years, I plan to retire at the end of this school year. However, I've already chosen my retirement career. Maggie and I have been invited to continue coming to school for the dog safety lessons. With my additional free time, I plan to branch out to other schools in our area, and it is my hope that Maggie and I can eventually assist the administrators of a large, nearby animal shelter in their efforts to establish a statewide dog-safety program.

For many years I have defined a Newfoundland as a dog who is big enough to protect me, sound enough to rescue me, with a face that says "I love you," and, of course, the temperament to go with that face. Maggie is, as have been most of the other twenty-one Newfs who have shared our home over the past thirty years, all of these things.

And that is it! That is the reason I love Newfs! I didn't have to teach Maggie to be kind and gentle with children. I didn't have to teach her to be patient and calm with their unpredictable behaviors. She just *knew* to be.

When I watch a frightened child reach out and gingerly touch her soft fur, then slowly get brave enough to touch her ear, then beam with pride and sit down to *really* pet her, I know why I've spent all these years grooming and trimming, pooper-scooping and bathing, vacuuming and de-sliming. It's because of the laughter. It's because of the joy. It's because Newfs spread happiness everywhere they go.

Next school year we will go *many* places. *Hundreds* of children will be smiling. Sweet, mellow Miss Maggie will be smiling with them. And so will I.

Lynne & Marty Rutenberg
Ferromont Newfoundlands
Newton, New Jersey, USA

A Special Kind of Perfect

My name is Magnificent Grace, but my family calls me Maggie Mae. I am a beautiful, three-year-old, black Newfoundland. But, wait! I should start from the beginning!

My human mom and dad have always loved dogs and each of them had several mixed breeds while they were growing up. My mom even volunteered at the local animal shelter for several years when she was a teenager.

When Mom and Dad got married they lived in an apartment, then moved to a small house. They both worked. They were happy. Life was good. But dogs were not allowed.

Ten years passed. During this time Mom and Dad had two children. When the prospect of buying their own home became a reality, Mom had two goals. First, she would find the *perfect* house. Second, she would find the *perfect* dog.

It didn't take her long to find the *perfect* house. It had all the rooms she needed, plus a wonderful, shady, fenced, back yard.

Then she began her search for the *perfect* dog. She wanted a big dog that would love children. She wanted a well-tempered dog that would enjoy walks and outings with the family. She began reading every book she could find about dogs. After all her research, she decided the Newfoundland was the *perfect* dog.

After talking on the phone with a few breeders, Mom visited my birth home. I was eight weeks old. I was a little black fuzzball. I was cuddly! I was cute!

It was love at first sight! Mom was ecstatic! She had waited so long for me, and here I was! Within the hour I was sitting in her lap on my way to my new life. I was excited, and even though I threw up on the front seat, Mom didn't mind. It didn't matter. She had *me*, and I was her *perfect* puppy.

Now Mom had a new goal. She would become the *perfect* dog mom. She wanted to do everything right. She got me my shots, and lots of toys, and a pretty pink collar with a pink bow. She got me a cozy bed, and a nice water dish, and for mealtime, she got me nothing but the best.

For about four months everything was wonderful. *Perfect.* Then Mom began noticing how easily I got tired. She began noticing how oddly I carried my tail when I tried to run. She had read about hip dysplasia, but she didn't want to think about it. Anyway, *I* couldn't have it! I didn't have any problems! I was *perfect*.

But the trainers at the puppy kindergarten noticed right away that something was wrong. I was different. I had a hard time changing positions. I had a hard time getting up after I had been lying down. One night in class, I just couldn't stand up and squat to pee. I remained sitting and wet myself. The trainers told Mom this was not normal. They said I seemed to have a problem. They urged Mom to have my hips checked.

Mom didn't want to hear it. She didn't want to believe it. I was her precious, *perfect,* little girl. Yet she made an appointment. Just as a precaution. Just to be sure. But after the exams and the X-rays, the news was bad. My diagnosis was confirmed.

I have hip dysplasia, a malformation of the hip joint which causes the head of the femur to rub the edges of the joint. This causes arthritis and degeneration of the joint. It is a very painful condition.

My poor, poor mom. I had never seen her cry so much. Wasn't hip dysplasia a "death sentence"? Wouldn't my options be limited by finances? Wouldn't the rest of my life be wracked with pain? All Mom's hopes and dreams for me were shattered. Her warm tears were falling on my ruff. I tried, but I couldn't kiss them from her face. She was hugging me too close.

When the breeder heard about my hips, she offered to exchange me for one of my brothers. Mom told her she wouldn't exchange one of her two-legged children if they weren't perfect, and she wouldn't exchange me. I knew she would say that! My mom *loves* me!

After getting second and third opinions, Mom chose one of the best orthopedic vets in the country to perform triple pelvic osteotomy (TPO) surgery on my right hip and pelvic area. Thankfully, his hospital is only forty-five minutes away. But for a working family with two young children and a new home, major orthopedic surgery was not going to be easy financially. Mom looked around our home and gathered up some of her cherished possessions. Then she sold them. To help me. She's my sweet, sweet mom.

During my long recovery period, Mom would hold my head and gently massage my hip. She would talk to me, and often ask me if she had done the right thing. This was a hard time for her, and a hard time for our whole family. But, gradually, I became stronger and began to move much easier. I returned to being a fairly rambunctious puppy. But because of the weakness in my hips, I never did naughty things like dig holes in the yard or jump on people. I was a very well-mannered puppy. I was *almost* perfect.

After I recovered, Mom thought I might make a good therapy dog. One day she took me to the nursing home where she is a nurse. I was so excited I slipped on the tile floor and fell. My poor mom! My fall hurt her more than it hurt me. The looks on the people's faces broke her heart. She couldn't bear seeing pity for me in their eyes. She decided I would not become a therapy dog.

For a long time Mom felt sad about the things I will never be able to do. I will never be able to pull a cart, for example, or become a water rescue dog. But then I showed her there are *other* things I can do. I can open new doors for her. I can inspire her to do amazing things she never even imagined she could do.

I began by lying around in my wading pool all day and getting my coat in a mess. When Mom wasn't able to comb through the mats I'd made, she called on the help of my kindergarten trainers. In addition to being trainers, they are also professional groomers. When Mom saw what they did for my coat, she was very impressed with their skill. Suddenly, she knew she wanted that skill. She wanted to learn from them. She became their apprentice and began learning training, as well as grooming.

After adding grooming and training skills to her nursing skills and her love for dogs, Mom was ready to volunteer for the Humane Society. She became the *perfect* foster parent and I became her *perfect* helper. We have already had four foster dogs, and after grooming them and training them, we placed all of them in *perfect* homes.

Not so long ago, Mom was having a conversation with a good friend whose dog has cancer and was about to be euthanized. They talked about quality of life and Mom wondered when it would be time to think about quality of life for me.

Her friend said, "Maggie will let you know when it is time. Trust her."

When Mom got home, I immediately jumped up on her. This is something I don't usually do, but I wanted to let her know it is not time yet. I will let her know when life is no longer fun, but, for now, I am happy. I am spoiled. I am loved. And, yes, in my own very special way, I am *perfect.*

Maggie Mae
&
Cathy Dobbs
New Castle, Indiana, USA

She Dreams

In the cover of darkness she dreams.
No longer held captive by an uncooperative body,
her legs twitch and move with ease.

She is swimming to rescue a victim,
or pulling a cart of happy children.
She frolics in the fresh snow attempting to catch
snowflakes that dance out of reach.

In her dreams she is free.
Free to run and jump,
to move as she pleases.

But it is not to be, for by a cruel twist of nature
she was given a pair of dysplastic hips.

How could this girl,
so loving, so gentle, so kind,
be dealt such a hand?
It is not fair.

As she awakens, I stroke her dark fur,
knowing that her life will be tragically cut short.
With a heart of gold and a spirit that soars,
she deserves a life full of joy.
Instead, she endures the discomfort
of an uncooperative body,
limited in every step of her day.

The struggles she faces without complaint
bring a tear to my eye.

When weariness takes over and her body gives out,
she lies by my bedside and closes her eyes.

In the cover of darkness,
she dreams.

Cathy Dobbs
New Castle, Indiana, USA

A Spoon-Fed Champion

"Leave it down for awhile," people used to say. "If he doesn't eat it, take it away. He'll get hungry! He'll begin eating soon!"

Wrong! Not Greedy! Not that picky eater! The only result of following that advice was a Newf who grew distressingly thin.

Greedy was six months old and had just won Best Baby in Show at the Victorian Specialty when he came to live with us. But he had been a sickly puppy. While suffering some mysterious infection before he was four weeks old, he had even "died" and been resuscitated. After that illness, he wasn't fond of food. He became a very finicky, overly particular, extremely skinny pup.

Our little black boy had actually been named for Greedy Smith, a member of the Aussie band, Mental As Anything. But we also hoped calling him "Greedy" might inspire him to eat. We longed to see him gobbling and gulping, smacking and slurping, belching and burping. But it never happened. Our reverse psychology did not work.

Greedy's poor eating habits caused Mum and me a lot of worry. In an effort to stimulate his appetite, we consulted his breeder, we tried different foods, we even took him to a naturopath who normally saw humans rather than puppies. But nothing helped.

Although he was interested enough to pester us at mealtime, when we approached with his food bowl, he would step onto the carpeted floor just off the kitchen, drop into a "down-stay," and wait. When we put his bowl down in front of him, he would smile up at us—expectantly. And wait. And *wait.*

Mum finally discovered that by sitting on the floor in front of him and feeding him by hand, she could coax him to eat. But no one believed that was a proper, long-term solution.

In an effort to help us, his breeder took him back and tried to "reprogram" his eating pattern. But at the end of Greedy's third day of fasting, she gave up and gave in. A few days later, merrily un-reprogrammed, he was back with us.

Mum was happy enough to hand feed our picky puppy, but the feel of gooey food mixed with slimy slobber was abhorrent to a squeamish teenager. I *hated* it! After a few days, I tried feeding him with a spoon.

Curiously, Greedy seemed completely comfortable and even rather pleased with this new plan. He cooperated immediately. But spoon feeding was still a messy business, so I added another step to the ritual. By placing a towel over his legs to catch the "overflow," the post-meal clean-up became more efficient.

From that day on, Greedy absolutely refused to begin eating, not even by spoon, until his *towel* had been put in place. At this point Mum and I realized he had become delightfully cunning! He knew his every mealtime wish had become our command. The struggle was over. Our capitulation was complete. But what else were we to do? We loved him too much to see him wasting away!

So, for the next nine years—*nine years!*—Greedy amused us and regaled our visitors with his fastidious eating habits. By adulthood he weighed in at approximately seventy kilograms (150 pounds), and the sight of this huge boy, sitting with a towel daintily covering his legs, eating carefully from his silver spoon, brought laughter to even the most somber of guests.

Although Greedy always insisted that his main course be hand served, he happily ate treats on his own. He relished his "bikkies" and savored his Good O's, meticulously chewing them slowly, one by one.

When he was three years old, Newfangled Greedy Smith, our pampered boy, completed his Australian Championship. He was then retired from the show ring to become a working dog, pulling carts and swimming.

Sadly, six years later, Greedy was diagnosed with cancer. The first tumor was successfully removed and he had several more good months. However, additional, inoperable tumors formed, and the medications available were not effective. Eventually, we had to have him put to sleep.

Greedy has been gone for almost a year now, and how we miss him! How we always will! But we can't help smiling when we think of our funny boy. He will remain our favorite, spoon-fed champion. Forever.

Megan Boundy
Paddlepaws Newfs
Emerald, Victoria, Australia

www.geocities.com/paddlepaws_au

A Lesson and A Legacy

During the eleven years of learning about, living with, and loving Newfs, not one of them has been more fascinating or intelligent than Tugboat Timkas Harbour Grace, the girl we called "Maggie."

Maggie was a vivacious character with a mind of her own. She was one of my first Newfs and from her I learned many things. When she was 2½-years-old, she taught me the single, most significant, of her lessons.

The six-foot privacy fence around our back yard had a gate that opened into our unfenced front yard. The latch on the gate was too high for our young children to reach conveniently, so they overcame this obstacle by propping the gate open with a large rock when they were playing outside. Of course they were supposed to remove the rock and close the gate when they finished playing, but we worried that we might someday forget to check the gate before letting the dogs out. Finally we worked out a compromise.

My husband drilled a small hole in the gate, attached a length of clothes line cord to the latch, and threaded the cord through the hole. By pulling the cord, the children could lift the latch and open the gate whenever they wanted. This made it easy for them to come and go at will, successfully eliminating their need to prop the gate open.

After the latch cord arrangement had been working effectively for several days, I confidently put Maggie out into the back yard without checking the gate. Glancing out a window as I walked through the living room a few minutes later, I was surprised to see her sitting at the front door.

"Oh, those kids! They must be propping the gate open again!" I thought.

After letting a somewhat indignant Maggie in, I marched out into the back yard to close the gate. However, it was securely closed with the latch cord hanging innocently in place. I was baffled.

I became even more bewildered when this scenario was repeated several times. Even though I'd check to be sure the gate was closed, within minutes of being let out the back door, Maggie would be asking to come in at the front! Mysteriously, the gate would still be closed!

Something else about this situation puzzled me. Throughout the time Maggie was staging her Miss Houdini escapes, the front door was her only destination. Although I was happy about this, I found her decision to remain at home hard to understand. We lived only three houses up from a lake and she *loved* the water. Yet, despite numerous opportunities for unauthorized swims, she never left the front yard. Getting back into the house through the front door was her only goal.

Finally my curiosity overcame my bewilderment and I decided to set up a sting operation and spy on Maggie. As soon as I let her outside, she trotted to the gate, pulled the latch cord with her mouth, put her front paw between the gate and the gate post, released the cord, poked her muzzle into the opening, and gave a nudge. *Voila*! Freedom! Then around to the front door she raced!

It was easy enough to put an end to the escapes by shortening the latch cord. The children could still reach it, but it was too high for Maggie. Yet, even though we had solved the problem, I hadn't learned the lesson. That compelled Miss Maggie to find another venue and try a new teaching method.

It is said that when one door closes, another opens. This is precisely what happened in Maggie's case! As soon as escaping to the front door was no longer an option, resourceful little girl that she was, Maggie simply learned how to open the back screen door and let herself in.

She did this by tearing a small hole in the screen, reaching in with a dexterous paw, hitting the lever-type handle, then nudging the door open with her muzzle.

The first time she got inside through the back door she bounded into the house, found me, and bounced around smiling from ear to ear. She was beside herself with joy!

At that point, I got it. I finally understood what Maggie had been trying so hard to teach me. It was a simple, yet immensely profound idea: I don't want ten minutes of fresh air! I only wanna be with you, Mom! I only wanna be with you!

Now, eleven years and seven Newfs later, I still respect the lesson Maggie taught me. With very few exceptions, Newfs are happiest when they are as near as possible to their human family members—preferably directly underfoot! For that reason, directly underfoot is where our big boys and girls usually stay.

However, as much as Maggie relished being inside with her people, she considered being outside with us even more wonderful. She simply *adored* outings, and family adventures at the lake were among her favorite activities.

Typically, she felt it was her responsibility to save anything she saw floating in the water—twigs, leaves, buoys, ducks. She was especially conscientious about saving kids, particularly our youngest child. He had a little raft he liked to lie on, but Maggie would never allow him to stay in the water. Every time he got comfortably settled for a nice float, she would splash over to him, grab his raft by one corner, and pull him to shore. At six years old, he was neither impressed nor amused by her efforts. Rather, he found her constant attention immensely frustrating. Often we would end up taking Maggie home early so he could swim!

Although we had gotten Maggie with intentions of showing her, I got so busy with three young sons and school that her show career never began. But during those busy years I made time to learn more about the breed. I studied the Newf standard. I studied pedigrees. I attended dog shows. I participated on the board of my Newf club. I also, shamelessly, asked my breeder a zillion questions.

As a result of this learning, I came to realize what a nice girl Maggie was. She was conformationally correct and had an impeccable pedigree. She was sound in mind and body, as well as intelligent and full of spirit. She loved children and possessed a very strong water instinct.

Eventually, our children grew up, life settled down, and I was finally ready to begin showing. For my first show dog, I knew I wanted one of Maggie's pups. With Maggie's breeder as my mentor, I chose a stud, helped Maggie with the whelping, cared for the puppies, and screened the puppy referrals. With her first litter, our kennel, Moonsail Newfs, was born.

Although I was unable to give Maggie the formal opportunity to become a champ, she has shown she was more than just a pretty face through her offspring. JJ, a son from her first litter, now has seven points toward his championship and will be ready to test for his water titles this year. Moonsails Stormy Weather, a daughter from her second litter, completed her championship a year ago. Two more of her offspring will begin their show careers this year.

Our sweet Maggie has been gone for two years now, yet not a day goes by that I don't think of her—usually with a smile, occasionally with a tear. She was a very special girl and a very special friend. I honor her by sharing her offspring and her memory with others.

Kathy Morris
Moonsail Newfs
Hebron, Illinois, USA

Caveat Emptor

Spring. A beautiful New York morning. It was early, but we were up, dressed, and on our way. With fifteen-month-old Loki in tow, we were off to the New Pen Del Fun Fest in Elkins Park, Pennsylvania.

My wife, Teresa, and I were excited because this would be our first Newf event. It would, in fact, be our first dog show of any kind. Loki was excited because this was an auto excursion, and auto excursions top his list of desirable adventures.

Teresa and I were going to the Fun Fest with the sole intention of being educated and entertained. We wanted to see a large group of Newfs. We wanted to see a confirmation and an obedience trial. We were also looking forward to seeing some of the fellow Newf-Listers we had met previously, and we were hoping to meet several more.

However, when we arrived at the park, we were greeted with some *electrifying* news! It wasn't too late to register our Loki! It wasn't too late to play!

"What do you think, Teresa?"

"I'm not making a fool of myself. It's all you."

"It's only five bucks! What the heck!"

"Whatever. But—it's all you!"

And just that quickly, the focus changed, the paradigm shifted, and a career was launched! Our beloved Loki became a *show* dog!

The activities began with a group of amazingly exuberant puppies. They were lunging on their leads; jumping on their owners; bumping into each other, and kissing the judge. By the time they careened out of the ring, everyone was laughing, and Teresa was trying to convince me Loki needed a little Newfy brother!

Next came the twelve-to-eighteen-month class. Loki and I lined up with the three other contestants in our group. When our turn came, we made an attempt at walking, stacking, and generally strutting our stuff. We were doing our best, but this wasn't exactly our finest hour. Loki wasn't prepared. *I* wasn't prepared. But, courageously, we struggled on.

At last it was time for the four dogs to make their final lap. Since Loki didn't have a show collar, the judge kindly helped me fix his regular collar so he would walk better.

From what I could see, a show collar looks like a thin choke collar. When the handler lifts it toward the front of the dog's head and begins to walk forward, the collar gets tighter. When I lifted Loki's somewhat loose regular collar toward the front of his head and began to walk forward, he took the opportunity to put himself in reverse.

Suddenly, I was watching my show dog sprint out of the ring! While listening to the judge award first, second, and third places to the remaining dogs, I was running after my dog; pulling his head out of the crotch of one of the ringside dogs; slipping the collar back on his head, and trotting him back into the ring.

During this entire episode, I was hearing Teresa. She was laughing! She couldn't *stop* laughing! But neither could I. And when I looked down at my show dog, he seemed exceptionally happy, as well.

Loki came in fourth. He made his debut and retired from the show ring on the same day. However, his participation in the Fun Fest hadn't ended. The show ring events were followed by a luncheon. It was a cool day so we all left our dogs in our cars; some were crated; some were belted; and a few, including Loki, were left loose inside the vehicles.

Even though he had never been left in the car for more than ten minutes at a time, we weren't concerned. We believed he was so tired from the excitement of the morning he'd fall asleep. We opened the sunroof, cracked the windows several inches, and went into the church for lunch. Every time we came out to check him, he was okay. He was fine. He was just a little agitated with all the dogs around.

In the church, people chatted as we waited for the awards that were to be given out before lunch. Along with most everyone else, Teresa and I had just taken our seats at one of the tables when we heard the emcee give the most unexpected greeting.

"Oh! Hi, Loki!"

At that point all chatting ceased and everyone's attention was drawn to the front of the room as Loki came sprinting in and began running around the tables like a madman. Before I could even assimilate the fact that my dog had crashed the luncheon party, I heard Teresa insisting, "Glenn, go get him *NOW*!"

With a sheepish grin, I jumped out of my chair as Teresa hid her face, and everyone else began laughing. By the time I had grabbed Loki, Teresa was laughing, I was laughing, and, as usual, Loki was looking extremely pleased with himself.

Apparently, we had left our windows open a little too much for a determined Newf really committed to his escape. Yet, even with all the dogs around, he came into the church in search of us. Luckily, Loki taught us a lesson through amusement rather than tragedy. Next time he will be one of the dogs safely secured in a crate!

Although we were tired by the time we got home, the Fun Fest surpassed our expectations. We met many fine people, and appreciated their patience while Loki was honoring his namesake, the Norse god of chaos and mischief. Additionally, we learned more about Newfs. Although Loki remains the apple of our eyes, we were humbled by the beauty of some of the other dogs we saw. Loki is a wonderful boy, our first Newf. But, he came from a less-than-stellar background. Seeing the other Newfs reminded us of the lessons we've learned about acquiring pets.

For years Teresa and I had known that once we had a place that allowed dogs, we'd get one. We both grew up with big dogs, and knew we wanted a large breed. We just weren't sure which one.

At a parade three years ago, we saw a huge, black, stunningly handsome dog strolling along with two little toddlers on its back. The beauty of this animal was overwhelming, and it made a powerful impression on everyone who saw it. Teresa and I were hooked! We wanted *that* kind! We just had to have one of *those*! The owner told us it was a Newfoundland.

I went home, typed "Newfoundland" on the computer, and up came the Newfoundland Club of America website. I subscribed to Newf-L, bought some Newf books, and began a two-year learning project.

I did most of the research on the breed. By one look, Teresa knew that the Newf was the dog for her. Although she did a bit of reading and a lot of listening to me talk about their positive qualities and negative aspects, she wasn't steeping herself in information about Newf health issues, or the fine points of recognizing a good breeder, or the tell-tale warning signs of an inferior breeder.

We visited a breeder with whom we had communicated on Newf-L. Although we felt as if we were attempting to adopt a human baby from the strictest of agencies, we were not offended by the thorough way in which this breeder interrogated us. Her devotion to her dogs and her interest in their well-being was awe inspiring.

The more we played with her six dogs and were rewarded with their slobbery kisses, the more we were convinced that we had to have a Newf. And we wanted him *yesterday*!

But these dogs were hers and were not for sale. It would be several months before this caring, careful, conscientious breeder would have puppies available. It wouldn't be easy, but we prepared to wait.

Yet, just a few weeks later, despite all my careful research, and against my better judgment, we responded to an ad for Newf puppies we found in a newspaper. And, yes, one phone call confirmed that all the signs of backyard breeding were present. And, yes, I told Teresa of my reservations.

I droned on about the health issues since neither of the parents were Orthopedic Foundation for Animals (OFA) certified or cardiology cleared. I criticized the selling of these particular puppies on full registration. I pointed out that we hadn't been asked one thing about our family or our work hours or the size of our house. I explained that owning both the sire and the dam, neither of whom were show dogs, was not a good thing. I even mentioned that good breeders don't have to advertise in newspapers.

But not having done all the reading and lurking on Newf-L herself, Teresa didn't quite understand. Besides, we were only going to visit these puppies, just to take a look. We had absolutely *no* intention of buying one!

But when we got there, all Teresa could see were the six-week-old puppies. And they were for sale. And they were *adorable*! She was totally smitten. And, to be honest, so was I. Looking back on it now, we shake our heads in disbelief. We were completely puppy crazed, too far gone to be deterred. We just *had* to have our Newf! A week and a half later we went back to the backyard breeder and picked up our beautiful baby boy.

Having Loki in our lives has been wonderful on the one hand, and heartbreaking on the other. While his exuberant personality has brought us great joy, his health problems have caused us almost inconsolable grief.

When he was diagnosed with Osteochondritis Dissecans (OCD), our relationship with his breeder went from fair, to worse, to non-existent. What can one say to a Newf breeder who says she has never heard of this type of elbow dysplasia? While not the most common ailment in Newfs, it is clearly one every Newf breeder should have heard about.

In retrospect, we remember the limps in her dogs that she said were injuries. But at the time, we were blind. Now, one OCD surgery later, and surgery on the other shoulder as a future possibility, we know things should have been better. However, we also realize they could have been worse. Loki could have had additional problems common to the breed such as Hip Dysplasia (HD) or Sub-valvular Aortic Stenosis (SAS). And it wouldn't have mattered. We would have bought him anyway.

If our story has a moral, it is this: Please listen to those experienced, "fanatical" people who stress the importance of finding a reputable breeder. Don't buy a puppy on impulse, no matter how cuddly, no matter how cute.

Not for one minute do we regret having Loki. How could we regret owning a dog we absolutely love? But watching him struggle through surgery and pain has been heartwrenching. Supporting backyard breeders only increases the odds of more puppies being produced with serious health problems. In buying from Loki's breeder we made a grave mistake, but we will *never* make a mistake like that again.

Glenn & Teresa Maguire
Flushing, New York, USA

Ebony, An Equine Expert

Three times a week my Newfoundland, Ebony, and I leave the noise and confusion of the city and make the twenty kilometer drive to the tranquil countryside where I stable my horse, Aga.

Ebony has been accompanying me on these trips since she was a ten-week-old puppy. From the very beginning, I taught her how to behave around my horse. At first the three of us walked together very slowly; Ebony on her lead on my left, Aga on his lead on my right. After a few weeks, Ebony learned to walk on my left without her lead, and a bit later, she learned to stay on my left when I rode Aga.

During the almost four years Ebony has been coming with me to the stable, she and twelve-year-old Aga have become very good friends. We usually begin our routine with the three of us walking to the dressage arena together. Then Ebony lies in the shade just outside the fence and watches with great interest while I train Aga.

After I finish working with Aga, I ride him for awhile outside the arena and Ebony accompanies us. At the end of the riding session, Ebony always walks in front of us, leading us back into the stable. As soon as I put Aga into his stall, I give Ebony a carrot or an apple with the order to take it to her friend. Aga is always waiting for this reward, and Ebony always takes great pleasure in giving it to him.

One beautiful, sunny day, I decided to spend the whole afternoon riding rather than training. Ebony happily accompanied Aga and me as we meandered along the riding paths through the lovely meadows and woods that surround the stable. When Ebony is with us, I only walk Aga or put him into a little trot. I never gallop because I do not want Aga to kick Ebony by accident.

After a two-hour ride, we returned to the stable. The day had become hot and sultry, and even though we had not run fast, Aga had worked up a sweat. I washed him and walked him to his paddock to dry.

Ebony was tired after her long walk so I left her napping in the shade while I went back into the stable. I had plenty of work to do. I cleaned Aga's stall, and I cleaned and polished my saddle. My jobs kept me in the stable for quite a long time.

When I finished my chores, I went out to get Aga and return him to his stall. I was horrified when I saw the gate to his paddock was open! The paddock was empty! Aga was missing!

With my heart pounding, I called loudly to Aga. And far away in the distance, my good horse answered! But where? Where was he?

Near the paddock was the top of a hill so I rushed to the summit to get a good view of the countryside. At the bottom of the far side of the hill is a pond and beyond the pond is a meadow. There, peacefully grazing on the wonderful green grass in the meadow, was Aga!

I called my horse over and over without result. Occasionally he would look up toward me, but he would not budge from the meadow. He just continued grazing. The grass was too green and too delicious. He was not ready to return to the stable.

I looked for a way I could climb down the hill, but the hillside was like a primeval forest covered with trees and bushes. It was in a completely natural state—no human had ever disturbed one branch of this forest!

When I heard the rumble of thunder and looked up at the sky, I become even more alarmed. The sunny day was over! Dark clouds were rolling in. A thunderstorm was coming. If I were going to do something to get my horse back to the stable, I would have to do it in a hurry!

I ran back to the stable and grabbed a handful of carrots, then returned to the top of the hill. Of course, Ebony had been right by my side throughout this time. She had sized up the situation and seemed as concerned about Aga as I was.

With my faithful girl right behind me, I started down the hill. But it was awful! It was impossible! The brush was so thick and so tangled, I could hardly find a place to put my feet! With the sky growing ever darker, I struggled through the undergrowth. I was making very little progress, and I was frightened that I would not reach Aga before the storm.

Suddenly Ebony snatched the carrots from my hand and began bounding through the brush. She had to make many twists and turns, but after a few minutes she reached the bottom of the hill and began running toward the pond. Into the water she splashed and was soon swimming toward Aga.

By now Aga had become curious and began staring at Ebony. Then he saw what she carried in her mouth. Carrots! A treat even nicer than green grass! Without a pause, he trotted across the meadow toward the pond and began wading out to her.

With both Ebony and Aga in the water, I became more anxious than ever! The pond was deep enough that Ebony had to swim, but it was not so deep for Aga. I didn't know what might happen! I was afraid my horse might accidentally hurt my dog. Frantically, I called to Ebony to come back, come back!

She heard me and obeyed. She began swimming back toward me with Aga splashing along right behind her. When Ebony reached the shore, she did not try to run back up the steep hill where I was waiting. Instead, she cleverly took the footpath that circled around the bottom of the hill.

I watched as Ebony ran around the hill and up the gentle slope toward the stable. The carrots were still swinging from her mouth. Aga followed behind her, never overtaking her.

In a short time, both my good horse and my wise dog were trotting up to meet me near the stable door. Only when she knew Aga was in my control did

Ebony finally give him the cherished and long awaited carrots. As he eagerly munched his prize, I led him into his stall.

We were not a minute too soon! Outside the stable, the thunderstorm began in all its drama. Lightning flashed, thunder crashed, and the rain came down in buckets. But, thanks to my clever Newfy, we were safe and we were dry.

I turned and looked down at my Ebony, my sweet friend and companion for almost four years. I took her head in my hands and smiled into her gentle face. Then I kissed her above her loyal, loving eyes and whispered,

"Thank you, my wonderful, dear friend. What would I have done without you?"

Karin Trauhsnig-Payer
Black Pearls of Carinthia
Klagenfurt, Carinthia, Austria

The Quadruped Conspiracy

My suspicions have been confirmed! The adolescents are ganging up on me! In addition to being out-numbered and out-flanked, I am also being out-thought!

The pattern began emerging on Monday, but the participants did a masterful job of pulling the wool over my eyes. It wasn't until Friday night that all the pieces fell into place and I realized the magnitude of my dilemma.

Kahlan, the eleven-month-old cat, and Alley, the eleven-month-old Newfy, have joined forces. As long as their pact holds, I may be unable to regain control of my household!

Their arrangement was brought to my attention during a routine play-chase session. The two girls had been tearing around for awhile when I realized everything had suddenly gotten quiet. Past experience with these two has taught me that silence is not a good thing, so down the hall I went to check on them.

By some gift of fortune, I managed to get to my bedroom doorway and flip on the light without alerting the conspirators. Kahlan was in the middle of the bed. Alley was leaning across the side of the bed with one paw draped over her feline pal.

The culprits looked at me in the doorway and froze. Was that *guilt* I saw on their faces? Then the scene exploded into motion with Kahlan dashing toward me and out the door and Alley jumping after her and landing in the middle of the bed.

"Alley, no! Get off!"

Alley is *not* allowed on the bed and has *never* been on the bed before. I figured this blunder was due to an uncontrollable urge set off by the running cat. What fools these mortals be! It is only now that I see the *truth*.

I didn't know it at the time, but I had just witnessed the actual paw shake that sealed the Alliance Against Dad. All the subsequent action was just a clever ruse to distract me from putting the pieces together.

Alley and Kahlan were not in my bedroom playing. No! They were in there *planning*. "If you scratch my back," one conspirator was whispering to the other, "I'll scratch yours."

I'm certain, in retrospect, that their plot had its roots in a recent conversation I had had with a friend. I had mentioned that I needed to dog-proof the basement because Alley had learned to do stairs while chasing Kahlan. Ha! Now I realize the stair-climbing sessions were, in reality, actual training exercises for the guerrilla tactics to come!

A couple of days after the dog-proofing conversation, Alley strutted into the living room with cat litter on her muzzle! Darn! I waited too long to block off the door to the utility half of the basement where Kahlan's litter box is!

Downstairs I rushed to check the damages. Fortunately, satisfied with the cat litter (gross!), Alley hadn't discovered the cat food dish, or the bags of dog and cat food stored in the utility room.

After fixing up a length of rope and tying the door handle so there was only enough clearance for a cat and *not* a Newf, I went back upstairs. Pleased at how handily I had taken care of the problem, I settled into a smug, albeit *false*, sense of security.

To further keep me off guard, the girls went along with the new house rules for a couple of days. But then came the evening that the phone rang just as I spooned Alley's canned food into her dish. I left the kitchen to take the call. Thirty seconds into the conversation I heard the rattle of the dog dish on the counter.

I rushed down the hall calling to Alley. Merrily, she came out of the kitchen and returned with me to wait in a very cooperative "sit-stay" while I continued the phone conversation. A good dog, you say? Wrong! This charade of cheerful willingness was actually only a cunning tactic to make me relax my guard!

While I continued talking and my clever dog continued "sit-staying," Kahlan was on the kitchen counter enjoying the dog food I had spooned into Alley's bowl. I know this only because at the end of the phone call, I followed Alley's mad dash down the hall as she tried to warn her co-conspirator. I reached the kitchen just in time to see Kahlan leap down from the counter and streak downstairs.

The speed with which this operation was planned and executed shows the quality of my opponents! Although I wasn't sure just what Alley had gotten out of this little covert action, that question was answered later in the evening.

Still unaware of the comprehensive nature of the conspiracy, I nonchalantly went downstairs after dinner to take care of my laundry. Innocently, Alley followed me. As I went through the door to the utility area, I looked back to make sure she didn't follow me and get into the cat litter again. She feigned total fascination in checking out the other part of the basement, so I put her out of my mind.

As I put the clothes in the dryer, I caught sight of Kahlan sitting expectantly beside her empty dish. Being the sucker that I am, even after being the victim of her earlier food stealing operation, I went over and put a scoop of food in the dish. Then I turned on the dryer and left the room, carefully latching the door behind me so she could finish her meal undisturbed.

Alley was no longer in the basement, so I assumed she had already gone upstairs. However, a quick tour of the ground floor sent me scurrying back to the basement.

But I was catching on now! I realized that while Kahlan had distracted me, Alley must have squeezed past me without making a sound. Somehow she had slipped through a space less than twelve inches wide between my precariously stacked laundry baskets and disappeared into the darkness down near the litter box.

Of course I had heard stories of the "Stealth Newf" mode, but this was my first experience with it. Clearly, Kahlan, being a cat and excelling in stealth, had been fine-tuning Alley for this moment.

Basing what was left of my ego on the assumption that the flu bug I'd been battling all week had severely affected my faculties, I opened the door that I had recently latched so securely.

Surprise, surprise! There stood Alley happily waiting for me with a disgusting cat litter mustache! Suckered again! Twice in the same evening!

I knew it was time for a full retreat and regrouping. I may have lost this battle but the war wages on!

And on! As I was entering my conclusions about these two episodes into my operations log, Kahlan began scratching at the carpet. Ever ready for such displays of misbehavior, I grabbed the squirt bottle and pulled the trigger. Water dribbled out the nozzle and trickled onto my fingers. I pulled again. More water dribbled.

Looking at the nozzle, I suddenly recalled the strange little plastic cap I had found under the couch a couple of days ago—the one that had "Twist-Open" and an arrow on it. Although I couldn't figure it out then, I now know exactly where it came from!

"Okay, Alley! How did that nozzle get unscrewed? Who sabotaged my weapon?"

It's a conspiracy, I tell ya! I'm living in the Twilight Zone! And just because I'm paranoid doesn't mean they're not out to get me!

Paul Bohn
Belleville, Michigan, USA

A Rose By Any Other Name. . .

Early one evening several years ago, my old dog, Zeus, and I were enjoying our customary stroll along the Delaware River canal towpath. It was twilight—that quiet, peaceful time when dark begins to fall. I thought we were all alone.

As we rounded a bend, I saw a noisy group of six teenage boys coming toward us. They were laughing, shouting, swearing, telling dirty jokes, punching each other, and exhibiting the "show-off" behavior typical of fourteen-year-olds traveling in packs.

Normally, I wouldn't have given them a second glance. However, something seemed odd about this situation, and I didn't like it. Zeus didn't like it, either. He suddenly stopped short, and, standing between me and the approaching boys, stared at them. Just stared.

"C'mon, Sweetie," I murmured softly to him, "Let's go. Pay them no mind. They're just making noise."

Zeus heard me, but he didn't "c'mon." He didn't move a muscle.

As the kids approached, I began to make out what they were actually saying. As they continued to cut up and shove each other, I heard things like:

"Hey, big dog, Lady!"

"Bet he bites!"

"Bet he's got a big. . .!"

You get the idea. This was followed by more rude comments and obscenities in a similar vein, with uproarious laughter all around.

I was starting not to like this at all.

"Come *on*, Zeus," I muttered, wishing I could get home as quickly as possible.

Zeus remained firmly planted to the ground and continued to fix the boys with an unblinking stare. By this time the towpath was almost dark. Growing more uneasy by the minute, I stood behind Zeus and began staring at the kids with him, hoping they would pass us by and let us go home unmolested. When they were almost upon us, I saw that one of them had something in his hand. A rock? A brick?

"Oh, God, he's gonna hit us!" I thought.

But Zeus still stood his ground, unflinching.

"Hey, Lady, what kind of dog is that, anyway?" yelled another one of the boys.

Normally, when I'm out with my dogs and people ask me about them, I reply with a long speech about the virtues of Newfs. I wax on about their gentleness, their dignity, their beauty, their benevolence. But I realized none of these things was what I wanted at that particular moment. I think Zeus realized it, too. He continued to stand staunchly, holding his silent stare. Never before had my placid, indolent, old dog done anything that made him seem so formidable.

"What is he?" the boy yelled again. "He looks like a pony. I think I'll ride him! Bring him here!"

"That's it, I've had enough of this," I thought.

Pulling myself up straight to my full height of five feet, two inches, I replied slowly, enunciating every word with as much dignity and authority as I could muster, "He's a Rough-coated Canadian Pit Bull."

Silence. Six pairs of eyes simultaneously locked onto Zeus. No one spoke. Then, without another word and without taking their eyes off Zeus, the boys quickly stumbled past us, giving us as wide a berth as possible.

Zeus watched after them as they quickly disappeared into the gloom. Then, when we were alone again, he looked up at me and slowly wagged his tail.

"Good boy," I whispered as I knelt and hugged him. "My good boy."

We live in a small town, and I still occasionally see the boys we met that evening. None of them have ever bothered me, my family, or my dogs again. Evidently a single encounter with a silent, flinty-eyed, Rough-coated Canadian Pit Bull on a dark, narrow, towpath, provided a sufficient lesson in good manners.

What made this incident so surprising was that Zeus had never exhibited any guarding behavior before, nor did he ever do so again. When this incident took place he had been with us for three years and was about eight years old. He originally came to us as a rescue at age five.

After beginning life as a puppy from an upscale pet shop in New York City, Zeus had been in and out of rescue several times, including being removed from an abusive/neglectful home. Yet, despite all of the ill treatment he had suffered early in life, he was still sweet, loving, patient, and mellow. He possessed the archetypical Newf temperament that, amazingly, had held up in the face of all the mistreatment he had experienced. I simply have never understood why this gentle dog had had such an unfortunate life.

When we become Zeus's third family, I promised him that our home would be the last home he'd ever have. I kept that promise.

Zeus had an easy, low-key existence with us. He was not interested in competitive activities like water work, carting, or agility. He preferred to be a watcher instead of a doer, and was content to enjoy life from the sidelines. His favorite things were our long, shambling walks along the towpath and our Sunday-evening rides to get vanilla ice cream. He was a quiet, reassuring presence in our lives, spending hours lying at my feet as I worked at my computer; even when he wasn't in the room, a shuffle and a sigh as he shifted positions let me know he was nearby.

As Zeus grew older his disposition remained unchanged, but his 125-pound body gradually weakened. Finally, at age eleven, after years of medication and treatment for increasing joint pain, my old friend finally became worn out. When nothing we could do for him could help anymore, we made our final visit to our vet's office. I held my sweet boy in my arms, with my face buried in his fur as he left us—quickly, easily, without struggle or fear.

I miss my Zeus keenly to this day, but I cherish my memories of him, and I am content in the knowledge that he spent the best years of his life with us. He gave us so much. Thank you for everything, my sweet one.

Zeau Modig
Riegelsville, Pennsylvania, USA

Be It Ever So Humbling, There's Nothing Like A Newf

In the old, pre-Newf days, I could have been called a "normal" person. I went about my business in a quiet, unobtrusive way. I adhered to social customs. I practiced good judgment. One might even say I was dignified.

But with the arrival of our first Newf, my life began to change. My stately demeanor began fraying about the edges. Then, eight years ago when Mac was one year old, the last vestiges of decorum faded from my life completely.

At that time, Mac developed an acute case of rubbish bin terror. What began as a slight apprehension quickly developed into a full-blown phobia. Thereafter, being taken for neighborhood walks on our Friday rubbish day became a frightful ordeal for our young Newf.

Finally it came down to two choices. I could either stop walking Mac on Fridays, or I could help him overcome his great fear of rubbish bins.

For reasons I can only wonder at today, I chose the latter. I would re-train my dog. I would teach him coping strategies. It wouldn't take me long. It wouldn't be difficult. Besides, didn't I love Mac, and wouldn't I do *anything* to help him? This would be a genuine act of kindness.

The following Friday, amidst much animated happy talk, I leashed Mac, stepped out onto our street, and began our rubbish bin exercises.

I had devised a wise and simple plan. At least it had seemed wise and simple in the privacy of my home. Yet, somehow, when I put the plan into action on a public street, I began having second thoughts.

Isn't there something inherently absurd about a woman sitting on a curb patting a neighbor's rubbish bin? Isn't it somewhat alarming if she's also directing cheerful platitudes to the rubbish bin? No wonder her big, black dog is pulling as far away from her as possible!

And, oh, look! Now she's moving on to the next house! Now she's talking to *their* rubbish bin! She's putting her arm around it! Is she actually hugging it? Poor dog. He looks embarrassed. He's *really* tugging now! Perhaps we should call someone.

Not many Fridays passed before people began coming out of their houses to watch this bizarre rubbish bin show. Finally I explained the situation to some of my neighbors and they passed the news on to the others.

The neighbors seemed fascinated by our dilemma. Soon, I had met most everyone on our street, and Mac had acquired a fan club. When he finally overcame his fear and began sitting down with me beside the rubbish bins, he had many people clapping and cheering for him.

After Mac made friends with the rubbish bins, he would rush ahead of me on Fridays, plop himself down beside each one, and wag his tail proudly as I congratulated him and assured him he was an unusually brave and courageous fellow. At that point, there remained only one minor problem. Mac flatly refused to move on until I, myself, greeted the rubbish bin and gave it a good pat.

When our next-door neighbor bought a new rubbish bin, he actually invited Mac and me over to give it a hug before he began using it! Believe me, it was years before the rubbish bin jokes died down in our neighborhood.

Not to be outdone in keeping me humble, Scooby, our big Landseer, chose an even more public place in which to encircle me with dubious attention. His skylarking occurred at Westbury, in the Aussie island state of Tasmania, on a lovely sunny day in early summer.

That year we had combined a Newf mini-specialty show within the larger all-breeds champion show. We had our own judge, just for the Newfs. It was the first time we had ever done anything like this in Tassy and it was a big thing for us. Ordinarily we only have about four Newfs being shown in our state, but over twenty Newfs had been registered for this special event. That is to say, anyone and everyone who had a Newf was there to participate that day.

Scooby was four years old at the time, but he was then, as he continues to be to this day, very much a mum's big baby. I had already been in the ring with him for Best Aussie Male Newf, and my teenage son, David, was holding him at ringside while I was showing Mac for Open Dog. Just as I had finished stacking Mac and the judge was about to go over him, Scooby came bounding back into the ring and pushed between me and Mac. He gave Mac a big happy kiss across the face, looked up at me and gave a cheerful "woof," then proudly stood up in his best show stand and waited, tail wagging serenely, for the judge to go over him again.

This all happened in an instant! Before anyone could react, the four black dogs in the ring had suddenly been joined by an exceptionally large, exceptionally friendly, exceptionally *conspicuous,* Landseer.

David rushed in and tried to take Scooby out of the ring, but Scooby would have none of that! He was determined to stay with Mac and me. The ring steward came in to help, but Scooby continued to resist—turning both David and the ring steward in circles and barking all the way out of the ring.

By now the spectators were rolling with laughter and the judge was so amused tears were streaming down his face. I had to laugh, too. If there had been any nervousness or tension among the handlers, it had vanished. My comical boy's unorthodox and unexpected performance had put us all at ease. Big smiles became the order of the day.

And it is because of the big smiles that I have been sharing my life with Newfs for over seventeen years. Among other thing, these sweet, kind, gentle, loving dogs have taught me to see the funny side of life and expect the unexpected. Joy and good humor are contagious and my Newfs seem to start epidemics wherever they go.

Sue Gray
Yesallaw Newfoundlands
Westbury, Tasmania, Australia

http://yesallaw-newfoundlands.8m.com

Priceless Morning Moments

This morning my husband and I began our normal workday routine. We got up at six and I immediately took Suzy, our eight-month-old Newf, outside. While she did her business and got some fresh air and exercise, I fed the horses and the outside cat.

Meanwhile, the hubby dragged himself out of bed, made it into the bathroom, and began shaving. Several minutes later, Suzy and I came back inside. I fixed breakfast for her and the indoor cats, then went in to take my shower. The hubby was still in the bathroom, but by that time, he had finished shaving and was doing his business.

I got out of the shower and began dressing. Suzy, having finished her kibble, came in to see how we were progressing. She sat down just outside the open bathroom door where she could keep an eye on us.

I finished dressing. Had hubby nodded off? How could he stay there so long?

I finished brushing my teeth. Had he forgotten this was a workday? Is the toilet seat that comfortable?

I finished combing my hair. At that point, I became somewhat annoyed with the hubby. Trying to hurry him, I began asking how he manages at work without fifteen minute bathroom breaks.

In the midst of my cajoling, Suzy suddenly bolted up and trotted out of the bedroom. I thought she had to go outside again, so I began putting on my shoes. But within seconds, she came trotting back. I looked at her in disbelief. What was she thinking? What was her plan? In her big Newfy mouth she carried a large, white roll of toilet paper!

Brushing past me, she hurried over to the hubby and presented the roll to him. Then she sat down right in front of him, expectantly. It was perfectly obvious that she wanted him to use it and *finally* get off the toilet.

Suzy has known since she came to live with us at eight weeks old that she isn't supposed to play with the toilet paper. However, she must have thought this situation warranted breaking the rule. She had carefully detached the roll from the other bathroom and brought it in. Apparently, after six months of carefully observing the same routine five mornings a week, she realized the hubby was taking much too long at this particular phase. Wanting to get him back on schedule, she called on the problem-solving skills for which her breed is famous. Knowing that after the toilet paper is used, the interval on the toilet is over, she tactfully reminded him that it was time to move along.

His reaction was to laugh and comply with Suzy's not-so-subtle suggestion. I think deeper inside he may have felt a bit sheepish, yet he was probably just as amazed at her ingenuity as I was.

As for me, I saved my chuckles for the other room. I'm saving a few more of them for the next time I hear him urging Suzy to "hurry up, hurry up." We'll both laugh when I remind him of this incident.

After growing up a few houses down from two very gentle, well-behaved Newfs, I knew someday I'd have a Newf of my own. Someday—when I grew up. Someday—when *I* got to choose. Suzy is that Newf I wanted for twenty years. I just never knew she would have such a good sense of humor—or be so intelligent.

Yvonne Niesen
Bluffdale, Utah, USA

Why We Do This

This summer I've been preparing my two-year-old Sequoia for his Water Rescue Dog test. When I take him to the lake for practice, five-year-old Yogi always comes along to get a good swim in and, since he already has his WRD and has requalified once, to show the "youngster" how it's done.

By the time we got to the lake today, the other members of the Northern California Newfoundland Club who train at this site had already finished and gone home. So, for awhile, the dogs and I had the area to ourselves.

Sequoia and I got right to work. It didn't seem long before we had finished the directed retrieve, including practicing redirection. With his turn over, I tied Sequoia to the boat ramp and began working with Yogi.

Yogi retrieved and retrieved until we had water work items strewn along the beach like wreckage. He had just delivered to hand the Toss and Tug (a floating, fluffy, yellow ball) and was eagerly waiting for my next command when the peace and tranquillity of the afternoon was abruptly shattered.

Looking toward the source of a noisy commotion, I saw three teenage boys approaching the boat ramp. The NCNC has a special permit to train Newfs at this site, and no other dogs, swimming, or water activities are allowed in the area. Although this regulation is clearly posted, the restriction does not include the boat ramp which borders the training area.

The boys lurched noisily down the ramp with the canoe on their shoulders. Life vests, fishing poles, paddles, and additional assorted items were dropping and dragging behind them.

This was a fine distraction for the dogs, and while Sequoia wagged his tail with delight at the boys, Yogi continued working, going into the lake to get the bumper for the fifth time.

Meanwhile, the three boys began loading their gear into the canoe and, after much argument and discussion over who was to sit where, they settled themselves into the rocking craft. After more noisy talk and a great deal of laughter, they finally succeeded in launching the canoe out into the lake.

These boisterous boys hadn't gotten much more than 100 feet from the shore when they tipped the canoe over and all three fell overboard. They were dressed in jeans, T-shirts, and big, fat, black, heavy-looking, athletic shoes—not ideal outfits for swimming. Two of them had on life vests, but the third had removed his vest before he got into the canoe after announcing that it was uncomfortable and felt as if it would choke him.

The dogs and I stood on the shore calmly watching as this scene continued to develop. While the two boys wearing the vests splashed over to the upturned canoe and held on to it, the third boy began swimming for his vest which was quickly drifting toward the middle of the lake. Eventually he retrieved it, but he made no attempt to put it on again.

In addition to being inappropriately dressed for swimming, this third boy was just not good at it. After exerting himself to retrieve the life vest, he stopped flailing and simply began floating in the water with a sheepish look on his face.

I felt completely confident and almost casual as I handed Yogi the life preserver line and gave the command, "Go help." I called to the boy that help was on the way.

"Grab the life preserver. The dog will tow you in."

"Really? Wow!" he sputtered.

These were not test conditions. The boy was not splashing and yelling, "Here, Doggie, here!" Rather, he had become amazingly quiet, almost as if the stupidity of his situation had suddenly become apparent.

The look of surprise and relief on this teenager's face as my big Landseer swam toward him with the life preserver, circled him so he could grab it, and then began towing him to shore, was pure gold. Now, firmly gripping the life preserver and feeling more confident, he yelled to his friends, "Look! I'm being saved! The dog is saving me!"

With one boy safely on shore, Yogi was ready for a new test.

"Take the line. Get the boat."

Out went Yogi again, this time toward the other two boys who were still clinging to the half-sunken canoe. After watching the first rescue these two knew the procedure and one of them grabbed the line when Yogi approached.

The two boys were clearly astonished that Yogi could tow both of them and the boat as well. As the boy on shore watched this part of the rescue, he began dancing up and down the beach chanting, "A dog saved my life! A dog saved my life!"

As Yogi completed his second rescue and came out of the water, the chanting boy started over to pet him. But he stopped. This dog was just too big. The boy wanted to pet him, to thank him, but he could not muster the courage to approach him.

Finally, keeping their distance, the boys thanked me and Yogi for our help. Then, after dragging their canoe onto the beach, they sat down beside it and figured out that they had lost a paddle and a pair of shoes. They also discussed the fact that *somebody's* mom was not going to be happy. But after a few more minutes, they left to go call that mom.

It was time for me and my dogs to go, too. We had had a long day. The reason we had been late for water practice was because we were attending the Del Monte Dog Show in Carmel. The wonderful handler, Lori Littleford, had shown Yogi to Winners Reserve Dog that morning. My Newf had spent his whole day showing and working, working and showing—what an amazing breed.

As I packed up the equipment and put the dogs into my slime-encrusted SUV, the feeling of satisfaction in a job well done was almost overwhelming. Good dog! Good work! I wouldn't have it any other way. It is only in the working of these glorious dogs that everything comes to order, that a thousand years of human/Newfoundland companionship is revealed. I am *very* proud of my Yogi.

Summer Poris
Los Gatos, California, USA

Model Behavior

"Well, yes . . . Medvedka."

"Med . . . ved . . . ka. It means 'bear . . . female bear' in Slovenian."

"Oh, yes, she's a Newfoundland."

"Well, of course she's beautiful! Oh, yes! *Very* photogenic!"

"A dog food ad? In Santa Fe? Tuesday?"

A few minutes later I hung up the phone and looked down at the precious three-year-old lying at my feet.

"Wow, Med, how do you feel about becoming a *celebrity*?"

I took the "thump, thump" of her tail to mean she was willing to give stardom a try, so I grabbed her brushes and scissors and got busy. We don't get calls from advertising producers every day!

Since the Newfoundland was one of the breeds specified by the Pedigree people as being appropriate for their ad campaign, and since Newfs are few and far between in Northern New Mexico, Medvedka's name had immediately come up when the ad producer called Los Alamos Dog Club. Medvedka's a popular girl in our little town, and is well known for her therapy work. Although the invitation to pose for an ad was totally unexpected, being able to add "modeling" to her resumé would give it such a glamorous sparkle! Besides, it sounded like *fun.*

On the day of the shoot, Medvedka, my husband, Pete, and I arrived at the designated site to find many people milling around. Technicians were adjusting lights and reflective shields; staff members were setting up a misting machine, and another person was wetting down the flagstone path that was to appear in the photos. The photographer was arranging his tripods and cameras, and the wardrobe people were trying different hat and jacket combinations on a little girl.

After a few minutes, with everything in order, we all gathered around the production company's picnic tables and began eating, drinking, and visiting while we waited for the sun to reach exactly the right position. As we socialized, Medvedka amused herself by sniffing new scents and greeting new friends.

When it was finally time to go to work, Pete and I stood on the sidelines. The people-handler person, following the photographer's directions, began arranging the little four-year-old girl into various poses. A young and somewhat rambunctious Bernese Mountain Dog had also been invited to the shoot. The dog-handler person took the Berner in for the first shot. Somehow the Berner knocked the little girl down. This frightened her and she began to cry. While she was being consoled, the Berner was dismissed.

Next, Medvedka was taken in for her first shot. She was as calm and as cooperative as she always is. Soon the little girl was feeling braver and only slightly intimidated by her previous encounter with a big dog. In a short time, she and Med began enjoying this new game in which they were getting *all* the attention. Both were hams at heart, and they soon began having a good time.

In the course of the shoot, Medvedka was probably asked to change positions a hundred times. Every time she sat down, the dried leaves and grass on the ground stuck to her coat. So every time she stood up, two brush-toting staff members swooped in to clean her off. I just had to laugh, and to hope that these two young women were as amused by their special "derriere-dusting" assignment as I was.

The funniest part of the whole afternoon came when the photographer told the little girl to walk around and hug the dog from the other side. She stared at him for a second, then replied shyly,

"I can't . . . move. The big dog is sitting on my foot."

Throughout the three-hour, non-stop event, in which *hundreds* of photos were snapped, Medvedka maintained her poise and dignity. Indeed, among a group of remarkably laidback Southwesterners, she was easily the calmest and most patient of them all.

With her gentle, cooperative nature, Medvedka showed me, once again, that I had made the right decision three years ago when I chose to get a Newf. After our grown children's dear old Samoyed sled dogs died, I wanted another dog. I brought home piles of dog books from the library and read them all, but it quickly became apparent that the Newfoundland was the only dog for me.

When I finally located a litter of ten-week-old puppies in Colorado, I sat my husband down on the couch.

"Pete, I've found a Newfoundland puppy. It's an 840-mile drive and it will cost $1000. If this is unreasonable, tell me now and I'll reconsider."

"Don't you know I live to make you happy?"

His answer made me *very* happy! Only two days later, we visited the Colorado breeder.

Frankly, all the puppies looked identical to a non-Newf person like me. All of them were friendly and people-oriented and wanted to play. But finally Little Medvedka came up behind me, grabbed my long hair, and started to pull me back to the car.

It seemed as if she were picking us instead of the other way around. Of course I knew that was not exactly the right way to pick a puppy, but from that point on, I was hopelessly in love with this cheerful little soul. Within the hour, Pete and I were heading home with our frisky, black bundle. All three of us were happy.

And happy we've been with this beautiful girl ever since. Whether she's trotting into the house on shopping day with a grocery bag in her mouth, entertaining guests with an enthusiastic piano concert, or just quietly sitting with us at the end of the day, we treasure her presence. Medvedka brings us contentment and gives our life a special glow.

Louise & Pete Jandacek
Los Alamos, New Mexico, USA

Another Man's Treasure

Part 1

Brooke called. She said their Newf, Betty, needed to be placed. She explained that Betty had been limping. When her X-rays showed hip dysplasia, the vet had recommended surgery or euthanasia.

Brooke was not prepared to do either, nor was she willing to keep a disabled dog. She and her husband are runners and did not want a dog that could not keep up with them. When she tried to place Betty with the Humane Society, she was told they would put Betty down since no one would adopt a crippled pet.

I gave Brooke the usual options: 1) If she wanted to sell Betty, I would refer people to her and she could screen them. 2) If she wanted to give her away, I would pick Betty up, she would sign over her registration, and she would have to trust me to find her dog a good home.

Brooke was concerned about the $100 they had spent on the X-rays. She felt that the new owner should reimburse them for this expense. I told her several times that whoever was kindhearted enough to take Betty and keep her comfortable for the rest of her days, should not be expected to pay for the X-rays.

Option 2 is the one Brooke and her husband chose. Betty wasn't the right dog for their family, and they didn't want to be bothered with the mismatch any longer. Two days later I went to pick Betty up.

Brooke, her husband, and their two preschool-age children live in a very nice home on a hill. It is a three-story, split-entry with hardwood floors throughout and stairs everywhere.

I was told Betty sleeps in the garage. I realized she had to climb two flights of stairs to get outside. I noticed that the stairs were slippery. It didn't take a genius to figure out that this was not the right house for a dog with hip problems.

Then I met Betty. She is a large, well-mannered, five-year-old Landseer with a wonderful temperament and a constantly wagging tail. She is the perfect dog—almost. Her spirit is endless, but her body has limits.

I was relieved to see that her coat was brushed and clean. But she was overweight. Her family hadn't been exercising her because of her hips. I knew the extra weight was contributing to her limp.

I chatted with the owners for several minutes as I gathered the registration papers and some additional information on Betty's background. I learned that this was Betty's second home. Her original owners placed her with this family when they realized they didn't have time for two dogs and a new baby. They kept their older Newf and found a new home for Betty. Betty's breeder was no longer interested and was no longer in the area.

Brooke was still talking about the $100 for the X-rays. Once again, I explained that she would be getting no money from anybody.

Then the husband asked if I'd like to see their new, ten-week-old German Shepherd puppy. It had been bought from a backyard breeder just the week before.

I was stunned and saddened. This family had the perfect dog already, but they were tossing her aside for a puppy. Although they had taken care of Betty's physical needs, they had neglected her emotionally. She had never been physically abused, but they had never truly loved her.

When I took Betty outside to load her into my Toyota 4-Runner, she wouldn't get in. She was scared and confused. I didn't blame her. I was a total stranger and I was taking her away from the kids—her kids. I have no doubt that she would have protected those two young children with her life. She's that kind of dog.

But the children didn't seem to care that she was leaving. They couldn't stop playing long enough to say goodbye.

Finally the husband had to come out and help me lift Betty into the car. The poor girl was bewildered. As we drove away, she stared back at her second home until it disappeared from sight.

I never heard from the family again. They never called to find out if I had found a home for Betty. They just weren't that interested.

Part 2

Happily, Betty's adjustment to a new life went smoothly. She stayed with me for a couple of weeks. She slept in my bedroom on the floor, just as if she'd been sleeping there for years. She was perfect around the other dogs, constantly showing her friendliness by wagging her tail.

I could find absolutely no bad habits in Betty. She is a remarkable dog. Unfortunately, she just hadn't yet found any remarkable people to love her.

A gentleman was referred to me by a rescue group. He had been waiting for a female Newf to adopt for almost three years. I spoke with him by phone several times.

He and his wife have a single-level home with no stairs. They have grandchildren for Betty to protect and adore. He was willing to accept the extra responsibility of a dog with hip dysplasia—willing to give her the extra care she'll need for as long as she lives. He didn't even care what Betty looked like. He was prepared to offer her everything he could, knowing that she, in turn, would give him unconditional love. After all, Betty is a Newf.

Part 3

Betty, henceforth known as Freude, has been with us for almost three years. Ours is her third home, but it will be hers for the rest of her life.

Although I had long been familiar with Lord Byron's elegy to his Boatswain, I don't think I had an encounter with an actual Newf until a Seattle dog show in 1987 or 1988. But from that time on, I *liked* Newfs! I appreciated their calm, cheerful personalities and their exceptional loyalty. I had been rescuing Norwegian Elkhounds for years, but when the time came for me to have a new rescue, I wanted a Newf. I didn't realize it would take so long to find one, but it was clearly worth the wait. My big, loving girl is an absolute joy to me, thus my choice of the German word "joy" for her re-name.

I give Freude daily supplements to help with the joint pain and the arthritis, and through diet and gentle exercise, I have helped her lose all of her excess weight. She is down to about 118 pounds—the lighter she is, the longer she'll live. She has become more flexible and no longer limps. She enjoys her long walks, and although she's not as interested in swimming and wading as she was a year or so ago, she did go for a swim in Lake Washington in Seattle while at a dog picnic this July.

Freude is a very happy, very spoiled, very family-oriented dog. She spends at least twenty hours of each day indoors. During the day and evening she naps under the piano or wherever else she feels like flopping. At night, she always retires to our bedroom with us. This has been her chosen sleeping place since the very first night. She is definitely a house dog and prefers to be inside with her family both summer and winter. She goes to the door and barks or sighs when she needs to go outside, but it is never long before she barks to be let back in.

I cannot claim that Freude has no bad habits. If we're away from home for awhile she raids the indoor waste baskets and scatters the contents. However, she is respectful of loaded mousetraps, so if I remember the mousetraps, she remembers to stay out of the waste baskets.

She gave us another surprise not so long ago. After being with us for almost two years, she figured out how to get the lid off the dog food container we kept in the kitchen. By the time we got home, 1/4 of her five-gallon bucket of food was *gone*. After working so diligently to get her weight down, I'll make sure this doesn't happen again!

Freude has become a significant, well-loved member of my family. She recently turned eight years old and I have more difficulty dealing with the reality of her mortality than I do my own. As the saying goes, "One man's trash is another man's treasure." Freude is, and will remain, my treasure.

Wendy Pangle
Briggsbay Newfoundlands
Bend, Oregon, USA
(Part 1 & Part 2)

&

Larry Pratt
Puyallup, Washington, USA
(Part 3)

Spinner

My first Newf was a gift to the family from my dad when I was sixteen years old. He had neglected to mention the impending puppy purchase to my mother, who initially insisted that it be returned to the breeder the next weekend. However, by the end of the week Misty had worked her way into everyone's heart and was not returned.

This was fortunate because the previous year I had had a riding accident which resulted in a spinal cord injury. Misty became my steadfast companion as I learned to manipulate crutches and walk again. Except for her insistence on maintaining a large hole in the middle of the back yard, Misty was all sweetness and cooperation and love. Throughout her life she demonstrated exceptional obedience and willingness to please. She was dignified and gentle, the very model of Newfy decorum.

Then came my second Newf, Spinner. What a shock! He was five months old when my husband and I got him. He was obsessed with other dogs, almost unmanageable on walks, a determined escape artist, by far the most disorderly dog in his first two obedience classes, and *always* the naughtiest Newf at carting and water rescue events. To put it charitably, throughout his long puppyhood, Spinner was *completely nuts*!

But Dave and I persisted! Through rain and sleet and snow, we persisted. Through obedience and carting and water rescue, we persisted. Even through the births of our two daughters, we persisted. Socialization was ongoing. Training never stopped.

At last, when he was three years old, Spinner decided to behave. And when Spinner behaved, he was *spectacular*!

Amazingly strong and fast, with incredible stamina, Spinner became an outstanding draft dog. Dave held his lead and usually had to run to keep up with him when Spinner pulled the two girls and me in our Eskimo-style sled.

But his cooperation didn't stop there. Carrying all our gear in his backpack, he cheerfully accompanied the girls and me to the park, the day-care facility, the library, the skating arena, and the shopping mall. From an incorrigible, wild, rebellious puppy, Spinner grew into a responsible and totally trustworthy dog, lapsing into bouts of bad behaviour only when he felt he was off-duty.

I came to depend on Spinner for many things, but the help he gave me with our children was his most valuable, and his most appreciated, contribution. Because I am on crutches and could not pick up our toddlers or fend off unwanted approaches by people or other dogs, I relied on Spinner to protect them.

And protect them he did! Whether at home or on walks in the woods, Spinner always stayed near the children. He was *particularly* cautious around other dogs and unknown men, conspicuously placing himself between them and the children. With a stern growl, he would let other dogs know they were to keep their distance. With people he never growled, but he always eyed them warily and his message was crystal clear.

Interestingly, whenever Dave was with us, Spinner was not so vigilant. He followed his own agenda and often wandered out of sight. But any time my little daughters and I were alone, Spinner never left the children's side.

Spinner prevented many mishaps, both large and small, from occurring to our children. One of his most heroic interventions took place when Jennifer was three. She was riding her toddler bike with training wheels as we went for a walk. As she started down a slope, she began going too fast. She panicked and could not stop.

After quickly assessing the situation, Spinner plodded in front of her and halted, thus effectively stopping the bike with his body. Jennifer fell, but her fall was much less serious than it would have been had she crashed into the steep, rocky ditch toward which she had been heading.

In addition to handling crisis situations, Spinner also managed specific jobs. The year Anne began kindergarten, Spinner was given the job of walking her to the end of the driveway and waiting there with her for the school bus. For weeks Spinner did this job perfectly. Then one morning he stood up with Anne as the bus approached. Next, he followed her to the bus. Finally, he followed her *onto* the bus!

Imagine how thrilled the children were by this unexpected event! Gleefully they welcomed him and patted him and did everything they could think of to encourage him. He visited down the entire length of the bus and was let out the back door. He immediately trotted back to the front door and onto the bus again for another exciting round!

Spinner had such a jolly time with the children that he tried to get on the bus again the next day. But Dave was there to stop him. Afterward, we modified the bus routine so Spinner and Anne waited near the house. When the bus appeared, Anne walked down the driveway *alone* while Spinner supervised from the top of the driveway.

Although he never climbed on the bus again, Spinner continued to wait for it with Anne for the rest of his life. He was also always on hand when Anne came home, often bounding out of nowhere when he heard the bus coming and hurrying down the driveway to walk her to the house. Dave and I were forever grateful that he took his bus duty so seriously.

Throughout his adulthood, Spinner constantly demonstrated a great fondness for children and a penchant for keeping them safe. Not only did he stand watch over our own daughters, he also showed concern for other young children as well.

On one occasion while at the beach, our neighbor's little son wandered away from where his mother and I were sitting. Spinner, who was lying nearby, heaved himself to his feet with a big Newfy sigh, and went after the child. He walked around the little boy, licking his face and gently herding him back to his mother. This behaviour was repeated numerous times as the afternoon wore on.

The remarkable aspect about this incident is that the little boy has Down's syndrome. Spinner appeared to understand that he required special attention. While keeping a very close eye on this particular child, he seemed unconcerned about the wanderings of the other children.

Spinner won the Newfoundland Nanny of the Year Award two years running. This award is given by the Cerebral Palsy Association of Canada in cooperation with the Newfoundland Dog Club of Canada to a Newf that has displayed courage in protecting children or has contributed significantly to the well-being of a child or children.

Sadly, Spinner had to be euthanized just before his ninth birthday. Although he had cardiomyopathy, we had no idea he had a heart problem. Just six weeks before he died, he pulled me, and occasionally one of the girls, on a 5K hike. He was a dedicated draft dog and would have pulled until he dropped.

How I miss looking out and seeing Spinner lying under the climber as the girls play nearby. How I miss seeing him following behind them as they tramp about through the field.

I will always be grateful to this big, protective boy who was so much a part of my children's earliest years. It is a rare photo in the baby albums that does not include Spinner. He sits beside them in their strollers and playpens, and lounges near them in their baby seats. All of us miss him and his gentle devotion.

Joan Wormald
Campbellville, Ontario, Canada

A Gaggle of Girls

"Do you know all the kinds of dogs in the world, Mom? Can you name them all?"

"Too easy, Sarah! Big Newfs, Little Newfs, Black Newfs, Brown Newfs, White and Black Newfs, Baby Newfs, Girl Newfs, Boy Newfs . . ."

"Never mind, Mom. Never mind. I'll look it up in a book."

Showing unusual patience for a seven-year-old, Sarah accepted my joking with a smile. But the truth is, I was only half joking. In my world of dogs, I can see only Newfs. I've been this way ever since Natalie arrived two years ago.

I have my sister and brother-in-law to thank for this. When Natalie was seven months old, they sent her to me for my birthday. Our dear, old Chow had died, and although Natalie was their beloved baby, they knew she would be much more comfortable in Maine than she was in Key West, Florida. Having been a Cape Cod girl, Natalie had done little more than mope during the two months her family had lived in their new location. She just wasn't adjusting to the tropical heat and humidity.

On the day Natalie was to arrive, I was beside myself with excitement. Leaving my husband, Gary, and our three foster daughters waiting at home, a friend and I drove to Boston's Logan Airport to await her arrival.

Since her flight was over two hours late, I had already begun worrying when an airport employee approached with, "If you're the lady waiting for the dog, I need to see you in my office."

As pale as a ghost and with my heart pounding, I followed her. I expected the worst when she handed me a phone.

"Are you the owner of that big, black dog?" asked a cheerful, upbeat voice.

"Yes, yes . . ." I managed to stammer.

"Well, we *love* her! We *love* Natalie! Can you come over to the terminal and get her? We don't want to upset her by putting her crate on a train and sending her over to cargo."

My friend and I hurried to the terminal where we found two employees waiting for us on the tarmac in the unloading area. As soon as we arrived, six more baggage handlers suddenly appeared, one of them asking if we would take Natalie out of her crate so they could pet her.

It was love at first "re-sight." I hadn't seen Natalie since she was two months old, but she greeted me, and all of the others who gathered around, as though we were her long-lost family.

It was almost three o'clock in the morning by the time we got home, but Gary was up waiting for us. Within seconds our three little daughters came bounding down the stairs. The two younger girls bounced up and down with excitement as they patted Natalie and showed her around the house.

Their non-stop, bubbling laughter was interrupted only with gleeful questions about whose bed Natalie would sleep in and who would feed her breakfast the next morning. This homecoming had all the buzz and excitement of a Christmas morning, yet Natalie took it all in stride. The way she accepted the children, with tail wags and kisses, was so touching it took my breath away.

At the time, Star was nine years old, Sarah was five, and Nealy was four. Because of complications in their early lives, all three of our beautiful daughters have some special needs. It was immediately evident to me that one of their needs involved having a Newfoundland in their family. As I watched that early-morning lovefest, I knew we would never, *ever*, be Newfless again.

From that night forth, Natalie melted into our lives. It seemed as if she had been with us forever. She simply became another "daughter," clever, curious, and always generous with her love and kisses.

Star had not approached Natalie with the same enthusiasm of our younger daughters. Very early in life, she had developed a great fear of dogs, and even though she had been with us from the age of three, and had grown comfortable with our Chow, she was initially apprehensive around Natalie. However, watching the bond that slowly developed between my first daughter and my first Newf has made me a true believer in the Newfoundland as a perfect family dog.

Star accompanied Natalie and me to puppy classes and helped me train her. When Star's fourth-grade school project, "How To Train A Newf," was the class hit, I couldn't hold back my happy tears. Finally, on the day Star announced, "Well, Mom, I still don't like dogs, but I *love* Newfoundlands," I knew she had successfully cleared a giant hurdle.

When Natalie had been with us for about a year, Gary decided that if one Newf were good, two Newfs would be even better. About a month later, we adopted eleven-week-old Ceilidh.

I had worried about Natalie's reaction to a puppy. After all, she had been the only dog for over a year, and with three adoring little girls in our home, she was accustomed to getting almost constant attention.

I need not have been concerned. From the moment we brought Ceilidh home, Natalie was thrilled. Ceilidh was *her* baby. She took her under her wing and began showing her the ropes. She would even herd the children away and stand over Ceilidh when she needed a nap.

Ceilidh is fourteen months old now and Natalie still pampers her, letting her get away with anything. Sometimes Ceilidh is so rambunctious we call her "Rambo Puppy." Yet she often does things to let us know there is a calm, gentle Newfy inside waiting to get out.

For example, Ceilidh has always been fascinated by the dead moles our cats deposit on our driveway. To prevent her from licking or eating these creatures, we do a daily "mole patrol," disposing of them before she can get to them. Recently Gary let her out and walked in the yard with her. They came back inside and Ceilidh bee-lined to her jumbo beanbag bed, then lay down and gave Gary an unusually funny look. When he questioned her, she opened her mouth and out ran a mole! Giving her every benefit of the doubt, we think she was trying to save this little rodent from the cats. She was enormously disappointed when Gary let it outside.

While our puppy clowns and entertains our little girls, it is Natalie who helps me "mother" them. Four months ago, when five-year-old Kelli became our fourth foster child, Natalie was on hand. She stood without moving a muscle as Kelli gave her a few tentative strokes, then confidently put her arms around Natalie's neck for a long hug. I *felt* the message Natalie gave Kelli. It said, "We love you, Little One. Everything's going to be okay."

Natalie showed her mothering side again recently when Sarah got a four-inch splinter in her little foot. While I removed the splinter, cleaned the wound, and bandaged the foot, the other three girls sat with us, watching, and talking Sarah through her pain. Natalie joined us, crowding in to sit beside Sarah. Sarah put her arm around Natalie and grabbed a handful of black Newfy hair. Every time Sarah cried out in pain, Natalie braced herself and leaned against her. Natalie knew exactly what to do to calm Sarah.

After I got Sarah's foot bandaged, the two younger girls wanted me to check their feet for splinters, too. When I completed the inspections, Natalie put her big paw in my lap as if to say, "Me, too, Mom! Check my feet, too!" It was so cute and unexpected it made all of us laugh, and it seemed to have made Sarah's foot begin healing immediately.

Life with four human daughters and two Newfy ones never ceases to be amazing and wonderful. I am a different person since I became the mother of these six girls. I feel as if the world just opened up and said, "Take what you want that will make you happy." I took four children and two dogs. They have made me *very* happy.

I can't even remember what life was like before riding lessons and puppy classes, sticky fingers and sloppy kisses, girlie bows and Newfy hair, party dresses and Lupine collars, baby dolls and king-sized Kongs.

On a joyful day nine months ago, we adopted Star, Sarah, and Nealy. I feel blessed beyond bliss to be sharing my life with adorable children, a loving spouse, and two magnificent Newfs.

Beth Breton
Lebanon, Maine, USA

Star of Starr's

It was the waiting! That was the hardest part! Six months was a long time for one of our kids to be away—especially our two-year-old! But this was show business and our boy deserved his fifteen minutes of fame. Besides, Pappy was enjoying himself, and we knew he was the perfect Landseer for the part—even though we weren't sure exactly what the part was going to be.

It wasn't that we didn't know the story. As soon as we learned Pappy would appear in the film, we immediately bought and read the book. But the book version of *Hanging Up* didn't involve any pet at all, much less a Newfoundland. Apparently the big dog idea had emerged later, during the writing of the movie script.

In addition to knowing the original story, we knew a few other things. We knew Meg Ryan and Lisa Kudrow were to be in the movie. We knew Diane Keaton was to direct. And, most importantly, we knew we could trust Pappy's trainer.

Pappy's involvement in the movie began in the latter part of 1998 with a call from a member of the Newfoundland Club of Southern California. She told us a well-known movie-dog trainer was seeking a Landseer for a role in an upcoming film. She gave us the trainer's phone number, and my husband, Les, called to see what it was all about.

The trainer, Roger Schumacher, told us very little about the film, only that he thought the dog was to play Lisa Kudrow's pet but was not to be a major part of the story. He told us he needed a large Landseer who would be comfortable around people, camera equipment, and lights. We knew immediately which of our six adult Newfs met Roger's requirements. It would have to be Pappy!

Starr's Papillon (Pappy) was one of the three pups from a mating between Canadian/American Champion Topmast's Heir Apparent (Josh) and one of our girls, Brigantine's Summer Starr (Summer). Born with butterfly markings on his back, he was a beautiful puppy with a beautiful personality to match. He was the puppy we chose to keep. Now, two years later, he was a friendly, relaxed, outgoing guy with a love of novelty and adventure. However, he had had no training whatsoever.

Roger assured us that would not be a problem. So, a week later, with Pappy and his pal, Dancer, in tow, we met Roger at a park halfway between our home and his for an "audition."

Roger had other dogs all over the country he could have chosen, but he took a liking to Pappy and asked to use him. We were excited, but hesitant. Six months was a long time for our boy to be away from his family. We came home and did some research. Then, after many phone calls and much discussion, we finally agreed to let Pappy participate in the film.

During the six months of the filming, we were in touch with Roger often and he always assured us that Pappy was having no problems and was learning his stunts quickly. Our boy seemed perfectly happy living with Roger and his family and they certainly seemed perfectly happy with him. Roger mentioned several times how attached they had gotten to Pappy and how they would like to keep him. Of course that was never an option with us.

Every time we spoke with Roger, we pumped him for information about the movie. We wanted to know what Pappy was doing. We were curious about his specific scenes. We longed for *details*.

But Roger was noncommittal and vague with his answers. Given the nature of moviemaking, with many of the scenes that are shot not surviving the final cut, he wasn't making any predictions.

The six months passed, Pappy came home, and we began waiting for the movie. After the release date was changed three times, we started wondering if we would *ever* get to see our boy's performance! It wasn't until the advertising trailers started running on TV that we got our first glimmer of Pappy's role.

In February 2000, after Pappy had been back home for ten months, the movie was finally released. With excitement and curiosity, we prepared to go to the first showing in our neighborhood. We felt calm anxiety and anticipation. We were so proud, but at the same time, we were worried that Pappy might not look good, or that he would leave a bad impression of the breed.

Roger had been right. Pappy did not have a major role. Yet even though his scenes were few and far between, we were delighted with his work. We were pleased with his enthusiastic delivery and impressed with all his new tricks. Many of the tricks, such as "sit, down, and stay" had already become useful in his off-film life.

However, it wasn't until we saw the movie that we understood why one of the stunts he had learned had backfired on us. Shortly after Pappy came home, Les was working with him for the show ring. Every time he baited him, Pappy would take the bait in his mouth, then, strangely and for no apparent reason, spit it out. In the movie, Meg Ryan struggles repeatedly to give Pappy his "pills." He had been trained to make her job frustrating and difficult by spitting them out every time she put them into his mouth!

Only one stunt that Pappy did in the movie was a "trick" he already knew. No extra training was required. Before, during, and since the movie, when Pappy rides in a car, he really *does* like to sit in the front seat, and he really *does* try to climb over from the back seat to get there.

Although we think Pappy truly enjoyed himself during the experience, once his Hollywood days were over he immediately returned to his "regular guy" status in our family. Stardom had not changed him. Fame had not gone to his head. After all is said and done, we are glad we made the decision to let him appear in the movie. Not only did he have fun, but now he will live on forever on film. Pappy was a fine ambassador for his breed.

Les & Erlene Whitehead
Starr Newfs
Riverside, California, USA

Invisible Invaders

None of us *saw* the invaders. But all of us heard them. To me, their savage growls and vicious barks were simply unpleasant off-screen background noise coming from the TV movie I was watching, but to my two dogs, they were much more.

As soon as the fictitious dog fight began, Osa and Jammie awoke from the deep sleep they were enjoying in another part of the house and *hurled* themselves into the living room. Then, believing the TV dog fight was real, they reacted with unprecedented fury. Their pack was being threatened and they had arrived to defend it!

Osa, true to her Newfy instincts, rushed immediately to place herself between me and the *enemy*. As soon as she reached me, she whirled around, faced the TV, and with her hair standing on end, gave a deep, powerful growl. It was the scariest, most formidable sound I have ever heard her make.

Jammie, showing the more aggressive tendencies of her Akita-mix ancestry, charged right over to intercept the enemy. Facing the TV and standing directly in front of it, she lowered her head and began barking in a bloodcurdling, intimidating manner.

The speed with which my girls arrived for the battle, set up their perimeter defense, and began their counterattack, would do any military unit proud. Their plan appeared to have been prearranged and rehearsed!

When I caught my breath and realized what had triggered this combative display, I immediately tried to turn the TV off. But Osa, determined to keep me from harm's way, pushed me back on the sofa when I reached for the remote. After something of a struggle with her, I was finally able to grab the remote and end the terrible dog fight that had so alarmed my girls.

But the excitement didn't end there. Both girls were determined to make sure the enemy had definitely been ousted. For the next hour they did not leave the living room. They patrolled in tandem, sniffing, examining the windows one at a time, and checking the door that leads to the garage.

Each time they passed one another, they stopped and sniffed and licked each other. It looked as if they were reassuring each other that everything was safely back under their control. When my seven-year-old grandchild, Jessica, came in to join me, one or the other of the dogs insisted on staying right by her side the whole time she remained in the room.

At no time did our dogs show any aggression toward us. It was just very clear that they wanted to make sure their territory was secure and their pack was safe. I have observed and been fascinated with these two girls for over a year, but the way they communicated and worked together during this event was unlike anything I had ever seen. Their behavior was extraordinary.

Both of these girls are rescues. Jammie came first. She was the only female and the only white dog in a litter of six mixed-breed dogs who were born and have lived outside.

She was given to a young man who let her run loose. When the neighbors' complaints grew loud enough, he brought her back to the breeder and dumped her over the fence into the back yard with her littermates. These five-month-old male dogs immediately attacked her.

When Jessica happened to see her two weeks later, she fell in love with her. We had promised her a dog of her own, and despite Jammie's scrapes, scratches, and scars, this was the dog Jessica wanted.

Osa's background is quite different. She was turned over to Newf Rescue by people who loved her dearly but became unable to keep her. She is one wonderful, sweet, gentle girl. Her temperament is the best I have ever seen in any dog. In the year she has been with me she has gotten both her Canine Good Citizenship and her Therapy Dog International certificates.

Our two girls get along very well together even though their personalities are strikingly different. Osa is very calm, quiet, and relaxed, while Jammie is always watching, always listening, and always noisily reporting every "danger." When it comes to putting their heads in my lap and asking for hugs and kisses, however, both dogs are quite the same.

Although the incident with the TV dog fight has long since passed, Osa seems not to have forgotten it. She watches me closely now when I sit in front of the TV. The minute she notices I've slipped into "catnap mode," she barks at me loudly and startles me awake. The only thing I can make of this is that she thinks it unwise of me to fall asleep in front of a box in which a vicious dog fight has been known to erupt and might again erupt at any minute. So, as exasperating as it is not to be allowed napping privileges in one's own living room, I have to love her for her heroic efforts to keep me safe.

Donna Quinta
Woodbridge, Virginia, USA

Doggin' the Dogies

The third time's the charm, they say, and we *needed* some good luck. Our two previous attempts to round up these cows had been unsuccessful. During the last try we had managed to capture one heifer, but she had escaped over an eight-foot panel when we began loading her into the trailer. This herd had been in the desert too long. The cattle had become too wild. And these futile 150-mile round trips to gather them were becoming increasingly frustrating.

Cowhands for the afternoon were my husband, Bob, our eleven-year-old daughter, Christie, and me. Arriving at the designated pasture, we led our horses out of the trailer, saddled them up, and with new determination, set about planning our strategy.

While Bob and I rebuilt, reorganized, and reinforced the round pen into which we would drive the cows, Christie rode to the far end of the pasture searching for them. She was accompanied by her shadow, our one-year-old Newfoundland, Anika.

When Christie found the herd, one ill-natured cow immediately began charging Anika, so, *naturally*, Christie began charging the cow! Fortunately, before black hair, cowhide, and horse hooves started flying, the cow backed down. Realizing the danger to Anika and the difficulty we were going to have in moving the herd, Christie rode back to join us and report on her encounter.

Concerned about Anika's safety, we took her to the truck, put her in the back beneath the camper shell, and tied the hatch shut with hay string. This cattle-gathering expedition would be arduous enough without the involvement of a 130-pound, inexperienced pup!

Then the three of us got on our horses and headed out to pursue the wild bunch. When we were about halfway across the pasture, an exceptionally delighted Anika loped up to Christie's side. Had this big girl somehow liquefied and slithered out the back window of the camper shell?

"Oh, fine," I sighed. "A water rescue dog in the desert. The one thing this roundup was lacking."

We had come too far to turn around, we were losing daylight, and now the cows had spotted us and were beginning to move away. To further complicate matters, my horse lowered his ears, snorted, and charged toward Anika. From that point on, most of my attention was spent keeping my horse under control. Our chances of success were looking exceedingly slim.

Yet, we continued our quest. Attempting to keep the cattle together, Bob rode on one side of the herd, Christie on the other. My uncooperative horse and I struggled along in the rear. Anika, refusing to be separated from her young soulmate, trotted merrily along beside Christie's horse.

All went well for a few minutes, then Bob had to gallop his horse farther up his side of the herd to block an escape route. Shortly thereafter, Christie, our great little cowgirl, had to gallop her horse up the other side to prevent another escape.

With the other two cowhands flanking the herd, I was left in the rear with the responsibility of moving the cattle forward. Unfortunately, my "bronco," who had been lagging back in the sagebrush, now decided running through the herd to join Bob's horse would be more exciting than pushing the cows from the rear. So, once more, my efforts were focused on controlling my horse. All things considered, our venture seemed doomed.

Suddenly, Anika left Christie's side and bolted back toward me. What was she up to? Was she going back to the truck? Just before she reached me, she cut a sharp angle in front of me and, astonishingly, took up my place between Christie and Bob at the rear of the herd. Then this working dog went to work!

We have had Blue Heelers, Red Heelers, a Berner, and several other dogs with herding instincts, yet in all my years of chasing cows and knowing dogs, I have *never* seen an animal heel cattle like our young Newf did that day on that desert west of Salt Lake City.

Ears back, running fast, and keeping low, she portrayed the perfect livestock herding, heel-nipping, cow dog. She was all business. She was in charge. Tolerating no infractions and yielding no quarter, she heeled those ornery, unruly, wild cows straight into that round loading pen!

It was a beautiful sight, an *awesome* performance. From a gentle, black bear of a dog lumbering along beside my daughter, she transformed into an intense, precise, perfectly-synchronized, cattle-moving expert.

Bob was amazed. Christie was thrilled. I was shocked. And Anika? Even she looked a bit stunned at what she had accomplished. This was her first roundup. Never before had she seen a horse or a person attempt to move a herd of cattle. Heeling is difficult to teach even when it is bred into a dog. How did a Newfy come up with this skill out of the clear blue? Especially *this* Newfy?

Anika's first twelve months were spent in a pen with her sister. Life was not easy. Their breeder was having serious difficulties. Finally, the two dogs were all but abandoned and the breeder offered to give Anika's sister to another breeder. Visiting the dogs, the second breeder realized the situation had become desperate. The dogs had been neglected. The dogs were starving. Although she did not have room for the dog she had been offered, she knew she could not leave it in this situation. And she knew she could not leave its sister, Anika, either.

After rescuing both girls, the second breeder fed and groomed them, and began rehabilitating them. Anika was fearful and extremely shy, but the second breeder thought she might do well in our family.

We had had a heartbreaking, soul-wrenching experience with a sick Newfy puppy seven months prior to this. Eventually the puppy had to be euthanized.

The entire ordeal had left us sad and doubtful that we would ever have another Newf.

All of us were thrilled when we were contacted by the second breeder, but Christie immediately insisted that the Newfy would be *her* dog. She must have had ESP because that is exactly how things have turned out.

When we met Anika for the first time, she and Christie formed an immediate, and almost magical, bond. In the three months she has lived with us, the bond has grown even stronger. Anika worships Christie and follows her every step. When Christie is at school, Anika waits for her beside the twin bed where the two of them sleep. Being the youngest child, the "baby" in our family, finding herself so beloved by her Newfy has put a new sparkle in Christie's eyes. She realizes full well that she is a participant in an extraordinary match made in Heaven.

As for Anika's well-developed heeling talents, I'll be carrying our video camera to the next roundup and hoping for a repeat of her stellar performance. But whether what we witnessed was a one-time event or a life-long vocation, the memory of this beautiful young Newfy rushing in to help us will always remain among the fondest of our family memories.

Maurice, Bob, & Christie Erickson
Heber City, Utah, USA

Three Days In Paradise

"Holiday," they kept saying. "Holiday. Holiday."

Then one morning Mum and Dad started packing bags and boxes and putting them into my car. The Scratch and I were on to this immediately! We were going away!

To show our approval, we began prancing excitedly about the house. The more Dad yelled at us to "calm down," the more exuberantly we pranced. Scratchy and I *adore* car excursions.

Finally, the Scratch and I were boosted in among the bags and bundles, and off we headed, traveling north. Although we didn't know it at the time, we were on the road to Heaven. We were heading for Newf Paradise.

Yes, Scratchy and I are both canines. I, myself, am a dashingly handsome, two-year-old, black, seventy-eight kilogram Newf. I'm still not so sure about 7½-year-old Scratchy. She was already living here when I arrived ten months ago to re-house with my new mum and dad.

Oh, they *call* her a Newf, but no Newf I've ever met has been as hairy as she is. Still, she beats me to the bottom of the food bowl every night and she can hear the refrigerator door open from 200 yards away, so I suppose they could be right.

After riding for what seemed a small lifetime, we reached our destination. It was a little house on its very own beach. It was, as I already mentioned, Newf Paradise.

As the sun was still shining, Mum decided we had time for a swim. Across the beach we raced! Into the sea we plunged!

Since I seize every possible opportunity to scare Mum, I immediately took advantage of this occasion. I swam farther and ever farther from shore. Mum began yelling, "Norton! Norton! Come back! Please come back!" She sounded frantic and I knew she was probably pulling out her hair. However, I pretended I had water in my ears and couldn't hear. I didn't even give her a backward glance.

Meanwhile, never one for too much exercise, Scratchy splashed about in the shallows. When she wasn't scarfing down cockles, pipis, and other assorted gourmet gifts from the sea, she barked at me. In her usual bossy manner, she, too, was demanding my return.

Yahoo! I was creating a stir! I was getting attention! I relished having both Mum *and* Scratchy alarmed because of my behaviour!

Occasionally, solely to maintain their interest, I pretended I had had enough and swam back toward the shore. But just as Mum would attempt to clip on my lead, I'd grin, stick two fingers up at her, circle around, and splash back out to sea. It was a glorious game and I was winning!

A couple of hours later, declaring the contest over and myself the victor, I came ashore. By then I was really tired. I went into our little house for a sleep and didn't move another muscle until the following morning.

When I awoke at 6:45, I needed to go out *immediately*. So I licked Mum's face until she woke up and opened the door. After attending to my urgent business, I decided to explore the area a little more thoroughly.

There were two other little houses nearby, one of which had two Shelties in residence. The girl was very cute, but the boy was a bit mouthy. The grumpy boy yelled a few obscenities at me through the door. I ignored him. Then from the third little house came a high-pitched yapping. Totally unconcerned, I continued my explorations.

Suddenly, just as I was about to re-enter our house, the door of the third house opened and a little Jack Russell came flying out. He ran right up to me, called me a very nasty name, then rushed back to his house!

Well, I wasn't having that! I would follow him home and sort the situation out! Fortunately, I ran faster than Mum could manage on the gravel in bare feet, so instead of the lead dragging me back, suddenly I was free!

The Jack Russell's people had left their door open making it easy for me to dash in shortly behind their rude boy. The rotten little coward had hidden under the blankets with his mum and dad so I leaped onto their bed to find him.

Evidently, the mum and dad thought a monster had somehow gotten under their blankets. The mum began screaming and the dad started making noises I had never heard before. Arms, legs, and other body bits I cannot mention in a family publication, began flying through the air.

By the time my mum and dad arrived I had learnt several new words, and from the looks on their faces, I was in *serious* trouble. I was made to leave in a hurry while Mum and Dad were apologising profusely for my behaviour. (I never could make out why I was getting the blame 'cause the little one started it!)

Anyway, Mum and Dad took my pocket money off me and bought the people a bottle of grape juice to apologise, and I was in the dog house for the rest of the day.

But later that evening as we were watching TV, Scratchy made them forget all about my minor misdemeanour. The change in water, plus the numerous seafood items she had consumed on the beach, had upset her tummy. Midway through the rugby, her bottom exploded all over the carpet. The carpet was cream coloured. The explosion was not.

Scratchy and I were immediately dispatched to the deck for the night. (I never could make out why I was getting the blame 'cause the Scratch produced the problem!) Unfortunately, her discomfort continued through the night and dawn found me huddling pitifully in the only clean corner left on the deck.

The morning of day three of the holiday consisted of Mum and Dad pouring kettle after kettle of boiling water on the deck and scrubbing the carpet with various preparations bought on an early-morning shopping trip.

When they finally got everything clean, we went for a drive to give the carpets time to dry. Scratchy was still having problems and managed to make messes in the back of my car. I now know why Mum and Dad bought me a ute. They were isolated from Scratchy's messes! I, however, was not! Even though we stopped repeatedly so they could clean up the mini-explosions, I was very inconvenienced and forced to stick my nose against the small crack at the window.

We went back to our little house via the ferry. Thankfully, it was a warm day so Mum opened the back of my car. I stuck my head out, desperate for a breath of fresh air.

Suddenly a film crew appeared in front of me and started rubbing my head. Of course, Scratchy had to get in on the act as well. The crew was filming one of New Zealand's most famous personalities, an important Sir. Eventually, when the Sir realized Scratchy and I were getting all the attention, he came over and joined the crew in making a fuss over us.

Mum and Dad just stood back looking embarrassed about the smell permeating from the back of the wagon, and I made a point of advising everyone that the creator of the smell was NOT me! We were all quite lucky that there was a stiff breeze blowing that afternoon!

On the drive home the following day Mum and Dad kept muttering about kennels and dog sitters. I didn't understand why. They also had a lengthy discussion of something called "obedience training" before I would be allowed out in public again. (I never could make out why I was getting the blame 'cause it was the other dogs who created the disturbances!)

Oh, well. Whatever. In my opinion, our trip to Newf Paradise was a magnificent success. Scratchy and I were extremely pleased with this thing called "holiday." It was an exceptionally exciting event, and we are hoping it will happen again very soon.

Norton
&
Donna Crayston
Helensville, Auckland, New Zealand

Cantaloupe Fields Forever

Bosco never said a word. He never even smiled. But every time I petted him he would *lean* on me.

That's all it took. I was hooked. I was in love. I would run halfway across the UT Austin campus for that *lean*. I was pursuing a degree, but I was stalking a Newfoundland. I'd never even seen one before, and now I just *had* to have one!

My husband and I read all the Newf books we could find, then we contacted the Newfoundland Club of America for a list of breeders. Within weeks we were making the first of our three 12-hour, round trips to visit a Texas breeder.

"*Two*!" we told her. "When they come, we'll need *two*. And make ours black females, please."

The dad was an enormous Landseer, the mom, a large black. Their six babies were all Landseers—huge Landseers. We named our white and black girls Charlotte and Emily.

They were gorgeous! They stopped traffic! But the commotion they created in Austin paled in comparison to the stir they caused in the isolated Texas-Mexico border town where we moved when our girls were three months old. They were the only Newfies in town, the only Newfies our new vet had ever seen.

Three blocks from our home flowed a clear, spring-fed creek where Emily swam and Charlotte, submerged to her shoulder tips, head underwater and eyes wide open, *fished*. If there was anything more amazing to us than watching one of our Newfies swim, it was watching our other Newfy *fish*.

We *loved* these girls. Everyone *loved* these girls. Charlotte and Emily had more friends than we did. They knew people we didn't know they knew! One evening when we were walking them far from our neighborhood, a little boy came rushing toward us, waving and yelling. Hurriedly we put the girls into a "sit-stay."

He was a small child for a second grader, and he appeared so suddenly and swooped down so quickly we didn't have time to prevent him from giving our two girls tight, passionate hugs around their necks. I didn't know this child! I didn't know how our girls would react to his unbridled demonstrations of affection!

"These are my *friends*!" he cried from deep within a ruff. "I give them my sandwich every day."

No wonder our girls were so happy to see this little fellow. No wonder their tails were pounding and their mouths were watering! Of all the children who walked to school along our street, he was obviously their favorite. No surprise! He had already fed them a semester's worth of baloney sandwiches!

It was a sad Sunday when sweet Charlotte's heart stopped beating. She and Emily were playing chase games in the yard one minute, the next minute she was gone. She was only three.

My husband and I grieved, but Emily was devastated. She was heartbroken. She was beyond lonely. Emily needed a puppy. A few months later, we drove to Denver, Colorado, to get a little black Rose for Emily.

The breeder had several puppies. We were invited to go into their large mountainside yard and choose the one we wanted. Thankfully, we were rescued from that overwhelming responsibility when Rose chose us. With complete confidence she rushed over, crawled into our arms, and stayed. With complete confidence she took her place beside Emily in the back of our Bronco for the ride to the motel. With complete confidence she stopped in front of our door and waited while I caught up and opened it after a trip outside just before bed. We were her new family. There was no mistake about it.

Emily was delighted with her puppy and seemed awed by her confidence. Rose loved her big *tía* and rarely left her side. For the next nine years our girls filled our hearts and home with their joyful, loving spirits.

Then early one spring, we had to help our big Emily to the Rainbow Bridge. Our *wonderful* Emily. She adored people, adored swimming, adored her daily walks. Her size and physical beauty were striking. Her personality vibrant. Life was her party and she was thrilled that the rest of the world could attend. Yet the quality that guided and defined her was her gentleness. She had a gentleness so pure and so fine it could take one's breath away. She was in her thirteenth year and had been with us from the time she was eight weeks old. She was my soulmate, the heart of my heart.

We dug Emily's grave, large and deep, in a corner of our small suburban yard, and lined it with cedar shavings, armsful of mint stalks, and handsful of flowers. We lowered her beautiful body into the grave on a snowy white sheet and gently tucked the corners in around her.

I dropped in more mint and more flowers, covered the grave, and by adding extra soil, created a berm, a small, crescent-shaped hill. Emily's berm. Then with our darling Rose lying beside me, I spent days planting native shrubs and flowers on the berm, turning it into a butterfly garden. These were quiet, peaceful hours in which many tears and many memories helped me say goodbye.

Spring became summer and the native plants thrived. I was puzzled when I saw that a cantaloupe had sprouted in their midst. How could a cantaloupe seed have gotten there? I let the little plant stay. I didn't have the heart to destroy it. Cantaloupe was Emily's favorite treat.

As the summer progressed, the corner behind Emily's berm became a jungle. Passion vines and honeysuckle covered our side of the fence, purple hyacinth bean and trumpet vine tumbled over from the neighbor's. The cantaloupe vine wandered across the berm, down toward the fence, and finally got lost among the other vines crowding the corner.

One morning Rose took longer than usual in the yard. Finally I noticed her waiting at the back door.

"Oh, what did you find, Rose? What is it?"

Her tail was wagging. Her eyes were bright. Her whole body was announcing her excitement.

"What is it? Did you find a ball?"

I stepped back and our nine-year-old danced into the house, bouncing and high-stepping.

"Oh, let me see it, Sweetie!"

She opened her soft mouth and put her treasure into my hand. Gently.

It was wet. A bit slimy. But not marred, not a scratch. And it was ripe. Golden. A cantaloupe. Her favorite treat.

Then I was congratulating her. Slicing the cantaloupe. Feeding her portions. Enjoying her pleasure. Smiling through my tears. I hadn't been paying attention to the vine that had sprouted on Emily's berm. I hadn't noticed it blooming. I hadn't noticed it producing fruit.

Rose harvested eight more cantaloupes that season. A gift, a joy, a celebration, every single one.

The next year, and the next, I *tried* to grow cantaloupes for Rose. I cultivated special hills. I hoed and watered. I fertilized.

But we never got another cantaloupe. Cantaloupes, I was told, don't grow well in our area.

Our sweet Rose lies beneath her own berm now. Like Emily's, her berm is aflutter with hummingbirds and butterflies much of the year. The native flowers are nice but. . .I like to think about cantaloupe flowers. I like to imagine a big cantaloupe garden in the meadow in front of the Rainbow Bridge, over on the side, just to the right of the Bridge.

Emily and Rose play there with Charlotte. They form the welcoming committee at the Bridge. Smiling and wagging, they trot out to greet the newcomers. They show them around. They make them feel at home. And Rose. . .Rose always brings them a ripe cantaloupe.

Pat Seawell
San Antonio, Texas, USA

This story was published in the Spring, 2001, newsletter of the
Delta Society of San Antonio,
Delta Diary,
with permission.

The Nannys of My Childhoods

The winter my Nanny was fourteen months old, we were short of grass for the cows. To make up for this, I began supplementing their rations. Each day I would put two five-gallon buckets of molasses and a couple of bales of hay into the back of the van. Then, with Nanny on the front seat beside me, I would drive this extra food down to the cow paddock.

While I poured the molasses into the troughs, spread the hay on the ground, and greeted each cow with a much-coveted neck rub, Nanny would busy herself scenting rabbits. These were happy times. My animals and I all enjoyed our peaceful routine.

However, one morning when I returned to the van, I found Nanny with her head, neck, and shoulders in one of the empty five-gallon buckets I had left near the door. She was going at the molasses residue with enormous enthusiasm!

I called her name sharply. Although she attempted to look up at me, the sticky white plastic bucket completely encased her head. My girl had become a genuine buckethead!

Still, she shook herself free and looked at me. The sight of a molasses-covered Newf, even a black one, tends to leave one speechless! When I simply returned her stare and said no more, she resumed her "attack" on the molasses bucket.

Since the bucket was now on its side, she began pushing it blindly along the ground ahead of her, eager for more of that sticky treat at the bottom.

Somewhat amused, I collected the two buckets, put them in the van, and closed the door. Nanny gave me one of her looks. She had been enjoying that molasses and couldn't make out why I would want to deprive her of such sweet pleasure!

By then the cows were finishing their molasses and looking for more, so I thought it prudent to make tracks. In retrospect, I might have done well to leave Nanny there and allow the cows to lick her clean! Instead, leaving the van in the paddock, I began walking my sticky girl home.

Nanny didn't mind the walk, and with little encouragement from me, she took good, long swims in the water ponds behind the two dams we passed along the way.

I had hoped she would wash off some of the molasses, but the water was too cold. I ended up with a sticky dog who was also *wet*, and, once wet, eager to show how much she loved me in all the standard Newfy ways!

Much later, following gallons and gallons and gallons of warm, soapy water, an eternity with the hair dryer, and a thorough brushing, Nanny was as good as new. After riding in the van, scenting rabbits, slurping molasses, walking, swimming, romping around the paddock with her dad, being washed and massaged, being dried and groomed, Nanny retired to the family room and stretched out in front of the fire. Her long, contented sigh told me she had had a *perfect* day. And, despite all the additional work involved, I had enjoyed my day, as well. Watching my beautiful girl relax, I thought about my first Nanny and my introduction to this wonderful breed.

Some twenty-odd-years ago, I saw my first Newfoundland, a huge, magnificent Landseer. She was with a lady who stopped at our plant stall at Paddy's Markets. This Newf waited patiently while her mistress purchased some plants and talked with me about her incredibly docile, sweet-dispositioned dog.

Unfortunately, the owner was not certain what breed her dog was. She thought it was a Newfoundland crossed with a Samoyed to get the white markings.

That was it! I scanned the paper for months looking for a Newf-Samoyed-cross puppy. I saw no point in contacting a pure-bred breeder for a cross-bred pup.

One afternoon a friend of a friend of a friend contacted us. He knew some people with a two-year-old Newfoundland they had to "get rid of." Although this was only half of what I thought I wanted, I asked him to have the owners bring it by for us to see.

What a disappointment! Out of the car came a dirty, stinking, small, miserably undernourished Newf with a matted coat and fleas, to boot! Her name was Nanny.

The grandmother of these people had owned Nanny since she was a pup. Gran had now gone into a nursing home, and no one in the family could, or would, keep her dog.

From the moment Nanny and I saw each other, she never took her eyes off me. Those soft Newfy eyes blinded me to her outward appearance. I only saw her kind heart and beautiful disposition.

For her part, Nanny ignored her people's orders to "sit" and to "come." As far as she was concerned, these people no longer existed. She may have known why she was there, or just recognized a mutual need that was to be fulfilled.

To my parents' horror, I said, "Sold!"

Then I helped that smelly, black fleabag into the cabin of my truck. She lay across the passenger seat with her head on my lap. Her eyes were looking up at me the whole way home, and my eyes were looking down at her more than they should have been while I was driving.

My first Nanny had not known what play, or being brushed, or having proper, regular meals meant, but she quickly made up for lost time. In those days, I was working seven days a week, usually sixteen hours per day, getting our plant nursery started. Nanny accompanied me to the nursery every day. She could always find a muddy puddle to lie in where she could watch what I was doing. If

I moved away, she would come to me, shake, and get a cuddle for her effort. I am certain she thought I should enjoy being wet as much as she did.

During this period, I had little time for personal fun or socialisation, so my time with Nanny was particularly precious. Even hosing dirty water from her coat was a joy we could share. She provided an emotional outlet that was otherwise lacking, as I had not chosen to make time for personal relationships.

When my first Nanny's life ended tragically with a truck accident, I was almost inconsolable. She had only been with me for a bit over a year, but she left an indelible impression. I loved that wonderful, devoted girl. I miss her still.

That Nanny was my first Newf. Nanny, the molasses girl, was my third. In between I had Happy (a Landseer, not a Newf-Samoyed cross!). Both the second Nanny and Happy came to me as pups and enjoyed normal life spans. Now I look forward to my next Newf.

I am one of those people born "old," but with each Newf I have experienced the joys of youth. Although I did not have a Newf as a child, I become a child again with each Newf. My three gentle girls have left me with innumerable, happy memories.

Arthur Witten
Sydney, Australia

Blazing the Trail

She was a beautiful, eighteen-week-old puppy from a litter of two. Ever since her littermate had been adopted ten weeks earlier, she had become increasingly shy. She was timid about playing with other puppies and always had to be coaxed to leave her kennel run. She looked lonely. She seemed afraid.

The breeder had decided she would not breed this girl and had put her up for adoption. Unfortunately, no one wanted a shy puppy. The breeder's grandchildren had nicknamed her Annie—Little Orphan Annie.

She was not the puppy I had come to see. But she was the puppy I wanted. She was the puppy I would adopt. Immediately!

The breeder would not allow it. She knew I had deliberated for more than a month when choosing my first Newfoundland puppy. She was afraid my compassion for this shy little girl might change to disappointment. Anne had missed important early socialization experiences. Her shy nature might make her difficult to train for titles. The breeder insisted I go home and think about it.

I went home, but I never had a doubt. This was the puppy I wanted.

The next day my father (the cooperative, designated driver), Isabela (the well-behaved, one-year-old Newfoundland), and I (the eager, expectant mother) made the 1¼ hour return trip to get that special little girl. I had already changed her name. I would call her Sasha.

When Isabela met Sasha on the breeder's front lawn, she tried repeatedly to engage her in play. Sasha watched Isabela's antics, but she never joined in. Isabela finally gave up with a huff and sat down beside Sasha. I treated them both to dog biscuits.

That was the extent of their introduction and their interaction. With no further ado, we put them into the back seat of the truck for the trip home. With Isabela at 120 pounds and Sasha at forty-five, they were slightly crowded, but neither seemed to mind. Sasha appeared to love traveling even though this was her first ride.

Fear replaced poise when we reached home. Sasha followed Isabela into the house, but as soon as we crossed the front threshold, Sasha froze.

It had already been a day of many firsts for her: first grooming, first bath, first blow dry, first truck ride, and now, first time inside a human house. In addition to all these new activities, she had met Isabela and my father, and was now meeting my partner, Norma, and our grumpy, assertive, fifteen-year-old, alpha cat.

The day had been too much! Sasha scurried over to Norma and sat motionless at her feet. Norma patted her and spoke to her calmly. After almost an hour of Norma's quiet reassurances, we were able to coax Sasha to accompany us out into the back yard.

Always the gracious hostess, Isabela attempted to entertain her new little sister. She ran to her kennel, grabbed a squeaky toy, and hurried over to squeak it for Sasha. When Sasha made no effort to take the toy or play with it, Isabela dropped it at her feet and rushed back for another. One by one, she brought out all her toys. Isabela even tried prancing in front of Sasha with a toy dangling from her mouth.

Despite all the encouragement and the invitations to play, Sasha just sat close to Norma and stared at Isabela.

To round out her day of "firsts," Sasha was introduced to a crate. Her crate was in our bedroom, adjacent to Isabela's. After her long, stressful day, Sasha accepted this quiet refuge gratefully.

Everything went surprisingly well that first night, but early the next morning trouble began. When Sasha woke up in her new surroundings, she was frightened again and would not leave the safety of her crate.

I tried to coax her out. I hadn't forgotten that puppies need to relieve themselves as soon as they wake up. Little Sasha was anxious and overwhelmed. Nothing was familiar. She wanted to stay in the crate.

I doubled my coaxing efforts. I made all those short, repetitive, ridiculous sounds people make when they are calling a puppy. I needed to get Sasha out of the bedroom, through the kitchen, down the hallway, and out the back door.

Sasha wasn't house-trained. She wasn't leash-trained. She wasn't cooperating, and she was too heavy for me to carry.

At last Sasha exited the crate, but she was suspicious of her new environment. She lay down in front of the crate. I was getting concerned. My new puppy needed to get outside and I was doing a miserable job of getting her there.

With all my exuberant coaxing of Sasha, I woke Isabela. Sleepily, she stepped through the open door of her crate and sauntered into the kitchen.

Suddenly Isabela, who rarely barks in the house, let out an unexpected, "Woof." I left the coaxing detail and went into the kitchen. Isabela was standing at the cabinet door where we store the dog biscuits.

Isabela doesn't usually start her morning demanding dog biscuits, and I don't usually fulfill her every request. However, I wanted to return to the bedroom quickly, so I gave her a biscuit.

With the biscuit in her mouth, Isabela walked to the back door and stood there waiting. However, when I tried to open the door for her, she blocked the entrance and dropped the biscuit.

She returned to the biscuit cabinet and barked again. I had no idea what she was up to, but I really didn't have time to figure it out. Hurriedly, I gave her another biscuit.

This time she went into the hallway and dropped the biscuit. I couldn't understand this behavior. What was she doing? She *always* eats her biscuits!

Within seconds, Isabela was back at the cabinet asking for a third biscuit. She placed this one on the kitchen floor and returned to the cabinet for another. At this point, I realized there was a pattern to the placement of the dog biscuits. She was planning something, but evidently her plan did not include eating the biscuits! I thought, "This cannot be! She cannot be making a *biscuit trail* for the puppy!"

One by one, I gave her three more dog biscuits. One by one, she dropped them on the floor in a line that stretched between the back door and the bedroom.

With the sixth and final biscuit, Isabela reached the puppy. Gently, she placed the biscuit on the floor directly in front of Sasha.

Sasha, who had been watching Isabela place the last four dog biscuits, rose to her feet. Eagerly, she picked up her gift. Isabela stood beside her and watched her enjoy the treat.

When Isabela was satisfied that Sasha had finished eating the first biscuit, she proceeded to the second one. Then she stopped and looked back at Sasha, expectantly. Sasha accepted the invitation. She walked over and picked up the second biscuit.

I stared in awe as, biscuit by biscuit, and side by side, my two Newfoundlands slowly made their way through the house and into the yard. Isabela was communicating with Sasha at a level I had not imagined possible, and I was being given a rare glimpse into their world. I felt honored to witness this comforting and kind gesture one dog was bestowing upon another. My eyes filled with tears as I watched them. I realized that the only thing better than having one Newfoundland, is having *two*.

Although it took many months of training to gain her trust and build her confidence, today Sasha is a happy, well-mannered teenager. I can take some of the credit for her improvement, but Isabela deserves her share. She taught me how to train this puppy. Without her calm and gentle influence, my job would have been much more difficult. I am very proud of both my girls, the biscuit-loving puppy and the trailblazer.

Brenda Miele
Hudson, Massachusetts, USA

A Tempest In A Teabag

It was a lovely litter, a healthy litter, and in some exhaustion-induced moment of madness as the pups were being born, we began nicknaming them after brands of tea.

There was Tetley, an all-black male, and PG Tips, a black male with white toes. Then came Darjeeling. The list went on.

We had the male pick of this litter, and Tetley was it. At eight-weeks-old we brought him home, and he immediately began creating chaos and mayhem in our lives.

This little black puppy was the original bull in the china shop. If there was trouble to get into, he was in it. If there was a way to be naughty, he found it. He was stubborn. He was obstinate. He was a brat. We re-christened him "the thug."

The only problem was that he performed his every outrageous antic with a huge, bewitching grin. How on earth could I get annoyed with a hound wearing that innocent "who me?" expression all over his mush? It was obvious that his zest for life and for fun was at the root of all his mischief.

Now Tetley, being Tetley, was also selectively deaf. Quite often, if we called "Tetley," he would ignore us. But if we called him by his pet name, "Teabag," we would get his attention immediately. "Teabag" meant he wasn't in trouble and would probably be getting something nice. So, he basically went right off his Sunday title and responded only to his baby name.

Can't you tell what an idiot I felt going into the back garden and shouting, "Teabag!" The number of times the neighbors responded with, "No thanks, mine's a coffee with milk and two," only added to my embarrassment.

Not to be dissuaded by Tetley's immoderate behavior, we began preparing him for his first show. After much tearing of hair and quite a few profanities on our part, we had him all spruced up. His teeth were clean, and he was bathed, groomed, and trimmed. He was just at that lovely age where all the adult coat was not yet through. His tufts of puppy coat and fluffy ears gave him an endearing, baby appearance.

The first time in the ring with any of my dogs has always been a bit nerve-wracking for me. I can never be sure how they will behave. Not that it really matters too much with puppies, but in the back of my mind I always have that vague feeling they will make a fool of me. In Tetley's case, that vague feeling was replaced with certainty!

As we were walking into the ring, I noticed that Tetley put his head down to the ground, but I didn't give it a second thought. I was concentrating on getting my ring number and getting Tetley settled down.

Straight away the judge came over and began his examination. For the first few seconds, all went well. Remarkably well. Dared I hope I could make it through this without an awkward incident?

Then the judge opened Tetley's mouth. To the man's shock and to my horror, Tetley's mouth was. . *.full*. Tea leaves! His lips and teeth and tongue were covered with tea leaves! Tea leaves were swimming in the drool at the corners of his mouth!

Immediately the memory of Tetley putting his head down as we walked into the ring flashed through my mind. My immaculate boy with the dazzling white teeth had picked up a discarded teabag!

"Oh, Tetley!" I said, starting to chortle.

The judge took a step back and with a totally awed expression asked, "How on earth can you tell the brand just from that?"

That was it! I was finished! Giggling uncontrollably, tears running down my face, I had to tell this poor man that it was the dog's *name* that was "Tetley," not the stuff he was spitting at us!

The judge began howling with laughter and had to walk away to compose himself. He gave me a few minutes to sort out my little hound's mouth, and then he tried again. But every time he came near Tetley, he started laughing.

Eventually, the judge got himself together and my little Teabag went on like a dream. With a few stray tea leaves still in his mouth and a huge, mischievous grin on his face, Tetley took first place in his class that day.

I still see that judge from time to time, and he still asks about Tetley. He has told me that he's dined out on this teabag story on more than one occasion.

Tetley is now six and has mellowed a great deal, yet his very own, very distinctive personality continues to ring true. He has taught us a valuable lesson. For you see, we had wanted another Oscar, who, in our fifteen years of Newfy experience, remains our *perfect* dog. We had thought Tetley, being Oscar's younger brother, would fill that bill. What fools we were! We've had to think again!

Tetley has taught us to accept and appreciate the unique spirit that lies within each of these special dogs. He gave us no choice! He invaded this house with a vengeance. The day he walked in he made it obvious that he, with his own incomparable personality, was home to stay. May we never escape this wonderful madness that comes of being owned by Newfs.

Catherine Follows
Paddlebear Newfoundlands
Crossgates, Scotland, United Kingdom

A Boy In A Dress

The first shock came when I unlocked my front door and stepped into my living room. Toys! Toys! The floor was littered with puppy toys!

Just as I realized that four-month-old Brenin was not in his baby-gated area, but before I had time to panic, I got the second shock.

Something came tumbling and tripping out of the laundry room. It had Brenin's furry black head and furry front legs, but the rest of the body was. . .concealed. The rest of the body was wrapped in. . .something. *A dress*! My little boy was *wearing a dress*!

That's when I took note of Sophie. Lying right in the middle of this strange homecoming was my normally aloof and extremely dignified Akita. Her tail was wagging merrily. She had a huge grin on her face.

Strewn toys. Grinning Akita. A boy in a dress. What kind of revelry was this? Was my little cross-dresser orchestrating an orgy while I was out?

Evidently, after crashing through his baby gate and dragging dozens of his "puppy shower" gifts into the living room, Brenin sought additional ways to entertain himself and his seven-year-old Akita sister. He had gotten into the laundry basket and somehow managed to get his head through the neck and his front legs through the armholes of my short, blue denim jumper.

Actually, the fit was pretty good. The jumper accommodated Brenin's head and front legs perfectly. The back of the jumper stretched along his spine and draped down neatly over his tail. The only problem he was having was with his back legs. They kept getting tangled up in the skirt. The skirt kept causing him to trip.

My initial shock gave way to mirth. So *this* is a Newf! *This* is what all the fuss is about! You see, Brenin is my first Newf, but I had heard all about Newfoundlands long before I had ever seen one.

Several years ago, I had an exceptionally large, black chow/lab mix named Mick. People were always asking me if he were a Newf. My "What's a Newf?" usually brought rave reviews and many chuckles.

Finally I became so curious I began reading everything I could find about Newfoundlands. After I read Rhoda Lerman's *In the Company of Newfies: A Shared Life*, I was determined to live with a Newf someday.

Someday. When I had a house in the country. When I had plenty of room. When the circumstances were perfect.

Four years ago I was diagnosed with cancer. I had the initial operation and began radiation therapy. During the first week of my treatment, I lost my beloved Mick in a devastating way. It was a very bleak time for me.

I completed my treatment and received an excellent prognosis. I decided it was time to stop waiting for the perfect circumstances. A Newf would be my reward. A Newf would be the light at the end of my tunnel.

When I got Brenin, I discovered the house in the country was not necessary. The only room my boy wanted was that small space right next to me.

Now, 3½ years later, I do have my house in the country with the big fenced yard and the doggie door. I still have Sophie, and I've added another rescue, Rikki, the Husky. Happily, I'm now out of the tunnel, but in addition to his contributions as a Therapy Dog International, Brenin continues to be the light of my life.

He has been with me through many rough spots, and recently he even helped me during a small crisis. While I was working on the floor in front of my bookcase, a book fell and hit me in the head. Lying on the floor, dazed and in pain, I called for Brenin. He usually stays on the first floor, but I heard him clomping up the stairs right away.

With his Akita and Husky sisters watching shyly in the background, he hurried over and sniffed my prone body. Then he put his nose under my head so he could turn it and sniff it. Finally he lay down and stayed beside me until I was able to get up. It was not a big rescue, but having my boy watching over me was a comfort.

Just for the record, Brenin *still* looks good in a skirt. Members of our Colonial Newfoundland Club always enter the Christmas Parade in Colonial Williamsburg, Virginia. This year Brenin made an adorable Tinkerbelle in a fluffy white tutu with silver bells and giant fairy wings. It was wonderful to hear all the laughter and applause as we walked the parade route.

A few people mistook "Tinkerbelle" for a Christmas angel, but I just let it slide. Brenin's wings *were* incredibly large, besides, he's my angel every season of the year.

Judith Van Dyke
Knoxville, Maryland, USA

Crazy With Uncertainty

Lucy was awful! She was a terror! She broke through our fence and ran away every single day; she would not come when called; she climbed up on everything in sight; and that was just her *outside* behavior. Inside, she was a bucking bronco. She galloped through the house knocking lamps off tables, upturning chairs, and sending area rugs flying.

Once when we confined her to an X-pen in an upstairs bedroom she pushed the pen through the door and positioned it over the stairs so she could climb out the bottom. She took this opportunity to get onto a desk in our office and clear everything off the top. After shredding every piece of paper in the office, including my husband's plane tickets, she opened a closet door in our bedroom and polished off one of my new boots for dessert.

A week later she swept a big fishbowl off our coffee table. We came home to water stains on our hardwood floor and fishbowl accessories under our furniture. Two of our three fish were never found. We suspect *someone* enjoyed a sushi snack.

Every day seemed to bring a new peril and we were growing increasingly bewildered. All the books said Newfs were "gentle giants." All the books said they were "loving companions."

Within six months, our Newf had become a giant, but she was not gentle. And, worst of all, our Newf was not loving. She had no interest in us. She wouldn't *look* at us. Ever! Our Newf didn't even *like* us!

By the time Lucy was eight months old, we had completed three different obedience classes. Although she would sometimes act all right during the class, she would never mind her manners at home.

Finally we came up with a solution to our wild puppy problem. We would get a *second* puppy. If Lucy had a little brother, wouldn't she release some of her fire and energy in play? As incredible as it sounds now, this idea seemed logical at the time.

After we got little eight-week-old Winston, our hands were *really* full. He and Lucy got along beautifully—too beautifully. He idolized her and never left her side. She loved having a potential accomplice and worked overtime attempting to teach him her outrageous behaviors.

But despite Lucy's efforts, we could tell that Little Winston was a *normal* Newfy puppy. He was quiet and sweet and good and calm. He was *nothing* like the Tasmanian devil we had become accustomed to.

Having Winston made us realize just how crazy our Lucy really was. We had learned a few things about Newfs in the ten months we had had her. For one thing, we had learned the difference between a reputable breeder and a backyard breeder. Winston had come from a reputable breeder. Lucy had not.

Finally we decided Lucy was just not the right dog for us. She was a monster. We couldn't train her. We couldn't bond with her. She was too far out of our league.

And worst of all, we started thinking that Lucy was going to turn our angelic little Winston into one of her cronies. She needed a new home.

Our hearts were broken, but giving her up seemed the only thing to do. She was turning our lives upside down and inside out, and she had been doing this for almost a year.

Defeated and filled with sorrow, we put an ad in the paper. But when the phone began ringing, we changed our minds. We couldn't go through with it.

After another two weeks of horrors, we decided, once and for all, that we could not keep Lucy. By then I had heard of Newf Rescue so I decided to give the Penn-Ohio rescue group a call.

The person I spoke with listened to my story and told me she could take Lucy, but only after she sent someone out to see if she was aggressive. That weekend, a volunteer named Barb Collins came out to evaluate Lucy.

Barb took one look at Lucy's eyes and said, "This dog is *wonderful*! Are you sure you can't work with her?"

I told her about the obedience classes, about how hard we had tried, about how difficult our decision to give Lucy up had been. I also told her we were at our wits' end.

Barb told us she could take Lucy, foster her, and place her in a good home. But she couldn't take her until after Thanksgiving. Reluctantly we agreed to keep Lucy two more weeks until she could be picked up.

Barb also told us our girl's main problem was that she needed a *job*. She asked if, with her help, we would consider training Lucy. She said she would show us how to focus Lucy's energy into appropriate channels. We explained that we couldn't afford one-on-one training. She told us there would be no charge. The Penn-Ohio rescue volunteer was offering to help us rescue our own Newf! With new hope, we accepted her kind and generous offer.

Thus began our weekly training sessions, followed by homework throughout the week. The homework included socialization at pet food stores, long "down-stays," and umbilical cord lessons. All the training was done with positive reinforcement.

With Barb's help, we taught Lucy carting, water rescue, and agility. When we branched out to a Sacco cart, Lucy *loved* it. With this cart, the dogs pull the rider responding only to voice commands. Because the dogs are in the lead without a person in front, only dogs with great confidence excel at it. Lucy is a natural.

We have added job after job to Lucy's resumé in an effort to keep her brilliant mind challenged. Once I learned effective training techniques, Lucy responded beautifully. I still have to work hard to keep her interest, but the payoff is amazing. Last year she earned her therapy dog certification. This year she will try for her junior water title.

During the four years since we met, Barb has become a wonderful friend and mentor to me. We still train our Newfs together almost every weekend. She loves Lucy and is almost as proud of her as I am. Sometimes she teases me by saying she wishes she had taken Lucy when I was desperate enough to give her up.

To those of us who know what to do to make a Newf's life happy, giving one up sounds impossible at best, uncaring and irresponsible, at worst. But I have been on the uninformed side of Newf ownership. I have experienced the misery of having a wild, destructive, 125-pound puppy and the despair of not knowing what to do with her or how to do it. We loved Lucy and wanted to do what was right for her. But we were crazy with uncertainty.

Sometimes life is overwhelming. Sometimes life leaves you so confused you don't know what to do or where to turn. And sometimes life sends you an angel.

Karen Fuller
Lyndhurst, Ohio, USA

Magical Mr. Marsellus

Smoke and mirrors? Wire and string? How does Marsellus do these magical things?

Tonight he has conjured up a white spot on the top of his black head. Trust me, this white spot was not there yesterday. True, he has a white spot on his chest and a few white sprigs on the bottoms of his feet, but this spot on his head is new. He went out, romped in the snow, and came in with the white spot. I thought it was snow. I thought it would melt. It wasn't, and it didn't.

I should not have been surprised. Marsellus is quite good at producing spots. Even though his previous ones were black, they appeared every bit as suddenly as this white one did. It happened like this: one day Marsellus had a bright pink tongue; the next day Marsellus had a bright pink tongue with black spots! To make this even more startling, the black spot on the very front of his tongue is heart-shaped. Like a Valentine!

In addition to producing spots, our 2½-year-old Marsellus is a master of illusion. First, you see an entire chicken carcass on the kitchen counter. Then you don't! Next you see me panicking, wondering how to cushion all those sharp bones, putting in a call to our vet, e-mailing Newf-L for help while awaiting the vet's call. Next, you see a whole loaf of bread and two cups of cooked rice in Marsellus's bowl. Then you don't!

It seems our boy also wears an enchanted suit of protective armor. We became aware of this the afternoon our visiting nieces and nephews decided Marsellus was getting in the way of their *serious* soccer game and asked to have him brought in the house. One minute after they resumed their game, I heard what sounded like the china cabinet collapsing onto the floor.

The crash was caused by our 130-pound Marsellus hurling himself through the 1950's no-such-thing-as-safety-glass sliding door so he could continue participating in the backyard frolic. Although I have a few gray hairs I attribute to that day, Marsellus didn't have a scratch.

Of course Marsellus had been a master of escape long before the sliding-glass-door incident. First, there were the numerous crate escapes. Neither string, nor wire, nor padlock stopped him from bending his wire crate door and squeezing out.

Then there was the window caper in which he jumped outside through the screen. Fortunately, our neighbors saw him execute this amazing feat and called us at work. Unfortunately, they thought securing the door of his outside dog house with a wooden latch would contain him. Even though I hurried, the wooden latch was on the ground by the time I got home and Marsellus was visiting in a different neighbor's yard.

Marsellus also enjoys entertaining us with his working dog impersonations. Every time Jeff and his father do house renovations, Marsellus insists on hanging out with "the men." By covering himself with yellow sawdust and white drywall dust, he gives the impression that his day has been every bit as productive as theirs.

Although the aforementioned displays of sleight of hand and paw are impressive, the *most* magical of Marsellus's feats is the way he has transformed our lives. For example, our couch now requires two slipcovers to hide all the holes, and no longer has any springs. Our floors and wall are often decorated with black Newf hair and sparkling Newf drool. Our cars are crowded with poop bags, beach towels, and dog toys.

But the biggest changes are evident in our conversations. All our energy and interpretive skills are devoted to Marsellus's head tilts, his intriguing facial expressions, the way his eyes light up when we say "beach," and the low guttural sounds he makes when we are not giving him our full attention.

We wonder what he is thinking. We comment on the lovely tenor of his snore. We are charmed when he grabs a piece of firewood Jeff has just chopped and dashes around the yard with it. In short, Marsellus is the topic of all our discussions.

We just can't help it! We just can't stop! We are just two proud Newfy parents who waited for a long time to get our boy.

Jeff was set on having a Newf of his own one day. He had grown up with a friend who had a Newf, and he had always admired it. As soon as we began reading and learning about Newfs and meeting as many Newfs as we could, I knew I wanted a Newf in my life as well.

After three years of researching the breed and searching for a breeder, we finally welcomed ten-week-old Marsellus into our home. We have been mesmerized by his magic from the moment he became a part of our family. May the magic never end.

Lisa McInnis & Jeffrey Lonigro
Glen Cove, New York, USA

Desperately Seeking Assistance

Dear Newf-Listers,

Help! Our nutritional needs are being compromised by our two-year-old Newf, Bruin. Always a chow hound, his latest exploit has exceeded our coping strategies. Our situation has become desperate!

First it was the kitchen counters. As soon as Bruin noticed that's where we left our bread and cookies, he learned how to stand on his hind legs and identify their exact location. He would then swipe them onto the floor, tear open the packages, and proceed to have a little picnic.

Oftentimes he would pilfer his prize and escape with it to his crate domain. Hours later I would discover what little remained. Occasionally there would even be an unopened package stored there! Perhaps he was hoarding treats for the long winter.

We tried several avoidance techniques including the noisy can pyramid on the counter, the snappy mousetraps on the counter, scolding, and yelling, but nothing discouraged Bruin for long. Food kept disappearing.

We finally resorted to clearing our kitchen counters. True, having perfectly empty counters is not decorative or colorful, but it works. The problem was solved.

Next, it was the lazy-susan corner cupboard. As soon as Bruin recognized this as a food source, he figured out how to open the door and whirl the shelf around until the peanut butter (his personal favorite!) spun into view. He would then remove the jar, *unscrew* the lid, and proceed to have a little snack.

We wedged a chair in front of the cupboard. Needless to say, having a chair extending into the main thoroughfare of our kitchen is not attractive or convenient, but it works. The problem was solved.

Bruin then focused his thieving behavior on the little dorm-sized refrigerator in the garage. As soon as he realized that's where we kept our beer and soft drinks, he learned to open it and select the beverage of his choice. He would then remove the can, puncture its aluminum sides, and proceed to quench his thirst.

We exercised the All-American option and wrapped the refrigerator with duct tape. This presented absolutely no challenge for Bruin. He simply used the tape as a convenient handle and continued stealing our beverages.

Finally we moved the small refrigerator to the basement. Of course tripping up and down a flight of stairs every time we want a beverage is not easy or practical, but it works. Bruin doesn't *do* basements. The problem was solved.

Unfortunately, as perplexing as these pilfering episodes seemed, Bruin was merely enjoying a few appetizers. He has now moved on to the main course! In this venue of over 1,000 "Newfie people" we dare to hope that at least one of you has encountered (and solved!) our most recent Newf-induced problem. Please share your solution. Please come to our aid. For you see, Bruin, the food filcher, has now graduated to the kitchen refrigerator!

Evidently, the refrigerator raids began about two weeks ago. I had noticed that leftovers seemed to be disappearing more rapidly than usual, but I didn't think much about it. We have three teenage boys in the house, and growing boys will be growing boys. Then one afternoon I found half a cantaloupe, still ice cold, lying on the deck in the back yard. Hmmm, how curious.

I decided one of the kids must have left it out on the counter within Bruin's reach. But, when I accused them of this, they all pleaded innocent.

It wasn't until the following afternoon that the cantaloupe mystery was solved. I walked into the kitchen and caught Bruin, the real culprit, standing with his head in the refrigerator!

Then to my chagrin, he gave me a nonchalant, "Can I get you something while I'm in here?" glance, and returned to his browsing! I gasped and clutched the counter. I could hardly believe my eyes!

That was three days ago. Since then, Bruin has helped himself to food from the refrigerator every chance he gets. Yesterday it was a bag of grapes, a leftover chicken breast, and a quarter pound of bleu cheese.

Although I found and followed his grape trail, by the time I reached the deck where he had carried his booty, it was too late. I found nothing except stems and empty containers.

We have tried putting a chair in front of the refrigerator but he has been able to push it away. We can't block off access to the kitchen because that's where we have our doggie door to the outside.

Do you Newf-Listers have any suggestions? You are our only hope! Please help us before we starve!

Mary Ann Bowers (who is now standing guard over the family food supply)

Kody (four-year-old Newf who is enjoying the spoils of his brother's thievery)

Bruin (who is just another teenage boy standing with his head in the refrigerator)

Mary Ann Bowers
Mansfield, Ohio, USA

Neighborhood Watch

When I answered the knock on my door this morning, I was surprised to see my 83-year-old neighbor from two doors down standing on my front stoop. I was even more surprised when she told me that two of my dogs were at her house and asked if I would come get them.

Certain that all six of my dogs were exactly where they belonged in their own back yard, I thought she must be confused. But I decided to humor her and walk back up the street with her. Besides, I thought it might be easier for me to handle a neighborhood dog crisis than it would be for her.

Glancing toward my back yard as I followed her down the steps, I was simultaneously shocked and horrified. The side gate was standing wide open! Jack, Cree, Maria, and Charlevoix were all sitting innocently in the back yard peering though the gate with great interest. But Sam and Tuggy were missing!

Near panic, I looked quickly toward my neighbor's house. She had been right! There they went! Sam, my big, black Newfy, and Tuggy, my little, brown American dog, were happily jaunting off down the street.

My elderly neighbor stood beside me as I squatted down and called my two escapees. With obvious disappointment, they hesitated, looked back, turned around, and then reluctantly sauntered back home.

Feeling embarrassed about the whole situation, I quickly placed them in the back yard and made sure the gate was well secured. I couldn't imagine how they had gotten out.

At this point my neighbor began telling me how much the dogs had frightened her four-year-old grandson who, with his mother, was visiting her. Wanting to reassure the child and to retain his grandmother's good will, I walked her home and apologized to her grandson and his mother. I explained that the dogs did not want to hurt anyone, they just wanted to be friendly.

To my astonishment, the mother stated, "Don't be sorry. They were the best baby sitters I could have ever had!"

Slowly, and with the help of another neighbor who had witnessed the entire event from across the street, the story unfolded. From her window, this neighbor had watched as the little boy began riding his tricycle up and down the busy street in front of his grandmother's house. After about twenty minutes, she saw Sam and Tuggy trot up to him and "shepherd" him back to his grandmother's house.

As soon as the dogs got the child onto his grandmother's driveway, they assumed a guarding position. Tuggy sat facing the street. Sam sat facing the little boy. Sitting side by side at the end of the driveway, they effectively prevented the little boy from returning to the street.

They maintained their watch for about ten minutes. It was only when the grandmother and the mother came out the front door looking for the little boy that the dogs ended their vigil. When the adults appeared, the dogs went up to greet them and were given pats on the head. With this exchange, the dogs turned the care of the child over to the two women and proceeded on down the street to visit some of their dog friends.

As incredible as it sounds, Sam had evidently become uncomfortable about having an unaccompanied four-year-old riding a tricycle up and down our busy street. It was a particularly hazardous situation because there are no sidewalks along this street. The little boy was simply riding along beside the passing traffic. After watching him for awhile from behind the fence, Sam had decided to put an end to this dangerous behavior. Somehow my notorious escape artist managed to open the gate, and with Tuggy as his accomplice, he had "escorted" the little boy to safety.

Wanting the child's experience with dogs to end on a positive note, I asked the mother if she and her son would like to come with me and meet the rest of the pack. She accepted my invitation enthusiastically and, knowing his mother would be with him, the little boy was delighted with the idea as well.

I was so proud of my little dog family as each one sat patiently waiting his or her turn to be petted by the child and his mother. The mother, already awed by Sam and Tuggy's guarding initiative, was very impressed with how well-behaved all the dogs were. We talked about teaching dog obedience and the importance of being consistent. She concluded that raising a well-behaved dog is very much like raising a well-behaved child.

By the time the visit was over, the mother was considering adding a Newfy to their family. She spoke of contacting the Newfoundland headquarters when she returned to her home state.

"I know my son will be safe and doing what he is supposed to be doing if a Newfoundland is around," she said.

"And that is what?" I asked.

"Staying in the yard where he is supposed to stay!" she replied, looking her child right in the eyes.

As my visitors returned to my neighbor's house, I blessed the day some ten years ago when God, my husband, and the breeders agreed that I should become the human parent of our first Newfoundland puppy. Since then we have added four more Newfs to our family and adopted one American dog. (Actually, Tuggy adopted us. But that is another story!)

All of our dogs work, or have retired from working, as Best Friends 4-H Club volunteers. Best Friends is the only 4-H Club in the U.S. that teaches dog obedience, agility, and anatomy to disabled children and young people. The children and young people of our club range in age from eight to twenty-five years old.

Best Friends teams each child and his or her dog with an instructor. By working one-on-one, the instructor adapts the commands for both the child and the dog, and prepares the youngster/dog team for competition at the Berrien County Youth Fair. If a family cannot afford the expense of owning a dog, Best Friends provides a volunteer dog with which their child can participate. I am happy to serve as the Volunteer Training Instructor/Coordinator of this program, and I could not be prouder of my little group of 4-H youngsters and dogs.

I won't lie. Having five Newfoundlands and one American dog in our family pack does come with a few negative notes. Keeping the dogs clean and well groomed takes time. Keeping the house and the yard presentable takes time. And my dogs do not become good citizens automatically. They have to be taught good manners and the rules and regulations of our home. Our teaching assignment is on-going and never-ending. It takes time, effort, patience, common sense, trust, and love. It also takes an understanding of each dog's personality and quirks, and *many* doggy treats to accomplish our goals.

Yet I have been rewarded tenfold. Not only do people admire and sometimes even seem a little jealous of my wonderfully well-behaved dogs, but I have also gained the love, trust, and respect of six members of my family—five big Newfoundlands and one little American dog.

Linda Shannon-Chaillet
Shannollet Kennel
Benton Harbor, Michigan, USA

Windi the Weather Woman

When Windi was returned to her breeder, I offered to show her. She already had her Draft Dog title and four single points. I had finished her dam and her brother who both eventually earned their Versatile Newfoundland awards. Her sister and her sire had also earned VN's. I felt she deserved the same Versatile Newf recognition as her relatives.

When she picked up a four-point major the first time we entered the ring together, I knew we were on our way. Within the year, we had completed her Championship, both water titles, and her Companion Dog, making her VN a reality.

But even before our successful showing, Windi had thoroughly won my heart. Her joy of life and love of car rides were infectious. Although I knew it was a long shot, I decided to try breeding Windi one more time. She had been bred four times before she was returned to her breeder, but none of the breedings had been successful. I never knew whether it was the nutritional supplements I had been giving her or just that she liked living in California, but the fifth breeding produced five beautiful puppies.

I had lined up help to watch the puppies around the clock during their first week. Windi and her new family were monitored every minute of every night and day. I was taking no chances.

Although Windi enjoyed the company, she couldn't figure out what all the fuss was about. She was a *great* mom. Competent. Confident. She kept the puppies and the whelping box immaculate. She acted as if she had been raising puppies for years.

Our only hurdle proved to be the weather. It was one of the wettest, most unpleasant Februarys we had ever had in Northern California. But at four weeks old, it was past time for the puppies to be introduced to the great outdoors. Despite the uncooperative weather, they needed to stretch their little muscles. They needed new sights and new smells. So, on a relatively pleasant afternoon, with Windi's careful supervision, I carried the five excited youngsters out to the pen on my grassy lawn in our fenced back yard.

After watching the puppies for awhile and becoming convinced that they were safely enjoying themselves, I left them in their mother's care and went back into the house. A few minutes later, Windi came in. By trotting back and forth between me and the door, she showed me she wanted me to come outside.

I went out and checked on the puppies. Everything was fine. They were playing chase and tumble games. They were having a wonderful time. I reassured Windi that things were as they should be and returned to my cleaning project in the puppy room.

In less than two minutes, Windi was back at my side *insisting* that I come out again. As soon as I stepped into the yard, she hurried me to the puppies. I stood and watched more chase and tumble games. I saw no problems. I saw no cause for concern. Once again, I reassured Windi and went back inside.

Almost immediately Windi joined me. This time, instead of leading me to the back door, she led me to the whelping box. She climbed into the box and lay down. Then she gave me the *saddest* of looks and heaved a deep, mournful sigh. She could not have been more explicit in her request.

This time when I went outside to check on the puppies, I finally understood Windi's concern. It had begun raining. Raining *hard*! Although the puppies seemed delighted with this new development, I didn't want them to get wet and chilled. It was clear that Windi didn't like that idea, either.

As quickly as I could, I gathered up the gleeful, wriggling puppies, dried them off, and returned them to the warmth of their whelping box. Of course I got drenched in the process.

Although it rained twenty-one of the twenty-nine days that February, I continued taking the puppies outside to play. However, from that first day on, I paid close attention to Windi. When she came for me, I would hurry out and hustle the puppies into the house immediately. Usually, I would have only a minute or two before the downpour began. I might have been a slow learner, but I was lucky. Windi had been a patient and persistent teacher, and she was much more reliable than any of the local weathermen!

Lori Littleford
San Jose, California, USA

We Also Serve

It was a lovely thing to happen to us. An honour. And, in our more than thirty years of breeding Newfoundlands, it was the most unusual and unexpected request we had ever received.

We were told there was to be a ceremony at Earnscliff, the official residence of the British High Commissioner in Ottawa. It would be hosted by His Excellency, Sir Andrew Burns, High Commissioner to Canada. The guests would include a group of veterans who had fought in the 1941 Battle of Hong Kong. Representatives from Quebec City's Royal Rifles, the Winnipeg Grenadiers, and additional units from all over Canada were to be present.

General Sir Roland Guy, past chairman of the People's Dispensary for Sick Animals, the leading animal veterinary charity in the United Kingdom, would be arriving from Britain to present the Dickin Medal for Bravery, posthumously, to Gander, the dog who had been the Royal Rifles' mascot. Gander was a Newfoundland.

The organizers of the event wanted a stand-in for Gander. Would we be willing for our 3½-year-old boy, Marcarpents Rimshot, to participate in the ceremony? Would we be willing for him to represent the Newfoundland who had sacrificed his life to save seven wounded Canadian soldiers?

We accepted the invitation without hesitation. Rimshot is calm and comfortable among large groups of people. He is confident and friendly. We knew he would conduct himself with dignity befitting the occasion. He could be trusted to take the ceremony in stride.

One of a litter of ten, Rimshot has been with us since birth. As I was drying him off seconds after he arrived, I took a liking to the stocky little boy and offered him to my husband. We have both been happy with our decision to keep this puppy. He has grown into a truly handsome Newf of about 185 pounds.

The day of the ceremony arrived and we presented ourselves and an exceptionally well-groomed Rimshot at the appointed hour. We were led to the far end of Earnscliff's formal entry hall, then asked to turn around and face the front door. As we waited in the middle of the hallway, the veterans lined up along both sides of the hall between us and the door.

Within minutes, the front door opened and the veterans came to attention as Mr. Fred Kelly, Gander's handler and former Rifleman of the Royal Rifles, was shown in. Prior to this event Mr. Kelly was ill and had been hospitalized, but when he heard that the medal would be presented, he had insisted on being present.

Mr. Kelly's face came alive as he spotted Rimshot. Filled with emotion, he walked toward us. Rimshot licked Mr. Kelly's hand in greeting and we handed the leash over to him. Then the veterans, led by Mr. Kelly and Rimshot, walked into the drawing room and the ceremony began.

During the presentation, General Sir Guy recounted the three documented instances in which Gander played a part in helping his human comrades.

In the first instance, Gander attacked invading Japanese troops on the beach. In the second, he saved several wounded soldiers from capture or immediate death by forcing a unit of the invaders to change the direction of their march. In the third instance, the one for which the award was presented, Gander grabbed a live hand grenade that was tossed into a group of wounded soldiers and ran away with it in his jaws. He was killed instantly when the grenade exploded, thus saving the lives of several soldiers by giving up his own.

General Sir Guy reminded us that the Dickin Medal was instituted in 1943 by Maria Dickin, who founded the People's Dispensary for Sick Animals in 1917. The medal, which bears the words "We Also Serve," honours animals for acts of extreme bravery in wartime. It has come to be called "the animal Victoria Cross," and has previously been awarded to fifty-four other animals. Gander's medal is the first to be given since 1949, and the first given to a Canadian animal military hero.

With Rimshot at his side Mr. Kelly accepted the medal on Gander's behalf. "This is the greatest day of my life," Mr. Kelly said. "Seeing this beautiful Newfoundland dog, exactly the same colour as Gander, brought back memories from sixty years ago."

We were immensely proud of Rimshot as he stood regally in the drawing room throughout the presentation. It was a particularly moving ceremony, and watching the veterans' faces, especially that of Mr. Kelly, was a very emotional experience for us.

After the formal awarding of the medal, it was presented to the director of the Canadian War Museum. The medal will become a permanent part of the Hong Kong exhibition. It, together with Gander's story and the stories of his courageous friends, will help keep alive the memory of this chapter of Canadian history.

To say that Rimshot was a big hit with the veterans would be an understatement. At the conclusion of the formalities he was repeatedly taken for pictures or given cuddles by the veterans, the media, and anyone else who was present. Despite the heat in the overcrowded room, Rimshot didn't even drool. Evidently he understood that the occasion called for proper manners.

To us, Gander's courage and bravery brought to light the courage and bravery of this particular group of Canadian veterans. Undertrained, inadequately armed, and numerically overwhelmed, they were dispatched halfway around the world to garrison the island of Hong Kong. When they were finally forced to surrender, these men endured the cruelest of hardships for over 3½ years. Many of their comrades did not survive.

We were honoured to have had our Rimshot participate in this inspiring ceremony. We think it is important for Gander's story to be told and celebrated as widely as possible. This heroic Newfoundland was the epitome of what our breed is supposed to be about. In 1808, the English poet, George Gordon, Lord Byron, in his famous elegy for his Newfoundland, Boatswain, described him as having had ". . . all the virtues of man without his vices." Such was the Newfoundland called Gander.

Nina McNamara Coté & Marc Coté
Marcarpents Kennels
Bainsville, Ontario, Canada

www.cnwl.igs.net/~marcarpents

Tattletales and Training Tips

Early last spring, Lucy, my three-year-old Newfy, experienced a frightening health problem. Seemingly overnight she lost her muscle strength, her appetite, and her desire for water. She was lethargic and so weak she could hardly move.

We rushed her to our vet, then on to a specialty clinic. Her body temperature dropped from a normal 101 degrees Fahrenheit to 89 degrees in three hours, and she was suffering renal failure.

With amazing insight and luck, the vet at the specialty clinic recognized the signs of Addison's Disease, which in addition to renal failure, causes the potassium/sodium ratio to become totally unbalanced. Without waiting the twenty-four hours for the results of the definitive ACTH Response (Adrenocorticotropin Hormone) test to be returned, the vet immediately began treating Lucy as if she had the disease. We were fortunate that she did this because her initial diagnosis was correct. Lucy was, indeed, experiencing an Addisonian crisis.

I learned that Addison's is a non-curable disease caused by non-functioning adrenal glands which no longer secrete cortisol. It is however, a very treatable disease and dogs can live their normal life span if given the appropriate medications. I now give Lucy a monthly injection of a synthetic hormone that replaces the cortisol, and I supplement her with Prednisone which replaces the glucocorticoids her body no longer produces.

Initially Lucy was given fifteen milligrams of Prednisone daily, and although this is an acceptable dose for a dog her size, it is not without side effects. One of the most obvious signs of high doses of Prednisone is extreme hunger and food-driven aggression.

Never shy about hinting for snacks *before* her diagnosis, Lucy became bizarrely obsessive about food after the Prednisone treatment began. She would glue herself to the floor in front of the biscuit jar and *implore* me with soulful eyes and soft, entreating "woofs" to give in to her desire.

Hugo, a year younger than Lucy and still very much a baby, would follow Lucy's lead and park himself just behind her. Then he would look from her to me and back to her, wondering if something were supposed to happen.

Soon Lucy would begin drooling, and Hugo would immediately begin drooling in sympathy. Nothing works as well at producing guilty feelings and a melting heart as the intent stares of two impossibly adorable, 130-pound, black Newfoundlands engaged in synchronized drooling.

Finding foods to satisfy my two hungry dogs without adding unhealthy weight to their frames became my constant challenge. One of the alternative treats I offered them was Romaine lettuce leaves. This crisp, crunchy snack immediately became popular.

One evening I gave both Lucy and Hugo an appetizer of Romaine lettuce leaves before dinner. As always, they inhaled these leaves and begged for more. I assured them that their dinner would be served soon, and I went upstairs for a second.

Suddenly, I heard Hugo barking loudly; he sounded excited and quite agitated. Since barking of any kind is unusual for him, this particular outburst brought me running.

As I hurried down the stairs, I could see Hugo standing in the kitchen doorway. Between intense bursts of barking into the kitchen, he would anxiously look back over his shoulder to see if help were on the way. As soon as he saw me coming, he directed his attention solely toward the kitchen and doubled the volume and forcefulness of his barking. By then I was almost afraid of what I might find!

A thief! Hugo was telling me there was a thief in my kitchen! By the time I arrived, Lucy had not only stolen the head of Romaine lettuce from the kitchen table, she had devoured the last of its leaves. And, recognizing a crime in progress and not wanting to suffer the blame, the Beastie Boy had been tattle-telling.

But the real blame lay with the medication. The pre-Addisonian Lucy would never have taken anything off the table, and the "leave-it" command had never before failed. I looked at my big, hungry girl and sighed.

Today, a year after her Addison's diagnosis, Lucy is on a very low dose of Prednisone. She takes only 1.25 milligrams every other day, so she is less compulsive about food.

However, as those of us who have been on diets well know, old habits die hard. Lucy will always gravitate to the biscuit jar, and Hugo, not wanting to be left out, will always be close behind her. But now she has added a new twist to her requests for treats. She has worked out a bartering system that is quite effective, and she has successfully trained me to respond to it. She searches out a high-value item such as a towel, some underwear, a hat, or a glove. Then with the item in her mouth, she parades through the house until I notice her. (If I don't notice her, she will literally come up to me with the goods in her mouth and toss her head up and down, making her ears flop in a very charming way.)

Once Lucy has attracted my attention, the fun begins. With me following her and, of course, Hugo following me, we make several joyous circuits through the house. Finally, Lucy, the Pied Piper, ends the parade at the biscuit jar. She sits down and Hugo moves around to sit behind her. When we are all in position, Lucy spits out the item she has been carrying, gives me "the eye," and *waits*. I would have to be as blind as a bat and dumber than a box of rocks not to realize what I am supposed to do.

Lucy also plans ahead for future trades. I have watched her bury a few trade items in the bottom of her toy basket. If I am missing a sock or hairbrush, I know exactly where to begin my search.

According to a friend who stayed with Lucy while I was out of town, Lucy snatched her tube of toothpaste out of the guest bathroom and buried it in Hugo's basket. Unfortunately Hugo was not around, thus missing a golden opportunity to tattle on his big sister.

Life with these two is never dull. Busy, dirty, hilarious, poignant, but never, *never* dull. Newfoundlands are kind and loving dogs, and Lucy and Hugo are no exceptions. When I lie in bed at night, with Lucy's big, warm back against mine and Hugo curled up next to her, all is right with my world. Thank goodness I have a king-sized bed and a husband who loves these two as much as I do.

Marie Acosta
West Bloomfield, Michigan, USA

Sweet Dreams (Interrupted!)

Shuffle, shuffle, shuffle. Flooooof! Shuffle, shuffle, shuffle.

Somewhere amid my layers of sleep I heard it, but I was tired. Exhausted.

Shuffle, shuffle, shuffle. Flooooof! Shuffle, shuffle, shuffle.

It was my husband, Mike, who had been sick all week, but because of his coughing and nose blowing throughout the nights, neither one of us had been getting much sleep. I dozed off again.

Shuffle, shuffle, shuffle. Flooooof! Shuffle, shuffle, shuffle.

Why did I keep waking up? The room was quiet. Mike was peacefully slumbering beside me. Wearily, I went back to sleep.

Shuffle, shuffle, shuffle. Flooooof! Shuffle, shuffle, shuffle.

What was going on? I opened my eyes and in the dim light of the bedroom I saw our one-year-old Newfy, Elliot, come through the doorway.

Shuffle, shuffle, shuffle. Flooooof! Shuffle, shuffle, shuffle.

That boy! That funny, mischievous boy! Elliot is our first Newf and I thought he was too old to be getting into this kind of trouble. Quietly, and one by one, Elliot was stealing tissues. He would pull one from the box, take it into the next room, eat it, then return for another prize. He must have been pleased with the convenience of the pop-up box.

Shuffle, shuffle, shuffle. Flooooof! Shuffle, shuffle, shuffle.

A big, black 100-pound Newfy *tiptoeing* in the night. What a concept! What a sight! I couldn't stop giggling. Soon I was laughing so hard I woke Mike up.

Busted! Although Elliot was understandably disappointed that the party was over, he seemed quite pleased with himself. He knew he was clever. He knew he was cute. And he knew we would agree with his self-assessment.

We did. We still do. Elliot, who is over three years old now, continues to be everything we had wanted. And we had wanted him for a long time.

Even before we were married, we had wanted a dog. Then somewhere along the line we saw a picture of a Newf and our hearts melted on the spot. Immediately our focus changed from wanting a *dog* to wanting a *Newf*.

During our three years of apartment living, we thoroughly researched the breed. When we learned there was a Newf-owning family in our town, we contacted them. Could we please meet their Newf? Could we please have just a peek?

The photographs we had studied had been wonderful, but they had not prepared us for the magic of a flesh and blood Newfy. Oh, those eyes! Those beautiful, brown eyes! They looked straight into our souls!

Countless kisses, endless belly rubs, numerous comical accounts of life with a gentle giant, and many, many Newfy hugs later, we knew we had found our breed. We went home and doubled our research efforts.

The dozens of nanny-type stories we read only increased our determination to have one of these amazing bear-dogs. When we had a Newfy, it would be devoted to our babies. When we had babies. *Perfect*!

During our years of researching Newfies, we were also saving to buy our first home. The minute (quite literally!) that our offer on a house was accepted, we called the president of our local Newf club. She was able to recommend a breeder who was expecting puppies just before we were to move into our new home.

We had a phone interview with the breeder, then made two visits to her home, some four hours away. A new house *and* a new puppy. These were exciting and happy times.

Elliot was born in September and came home with us just before Thanksgiving. He was the gift we were most thankful for that year, and we have been thankful for him every day since.

We truly adore our big boy. Every single night before we all go to sleep, we shower him with kisses, hugs, and whispered sweet nothings. Once Mike and I laughed to ourselves that maybe Elliot had come to dread our happy shout of "Bedtime!" every night. Maybe we were too demonstrative. Maybe we were too doting.

But when we tested Elliot by going to bed without a flurry of affection, he was upset. He was worried. His bedside pacing and his questioning looks told us we had forgotten something. Something *important*.

After a few minutes we hopped out of bed and lavished our boy with the usual loving routine. Afterward, his smile still spreading from ear to ear, he relaxed and fell asleep. We have never bothered testing him again.

Elliot has changed our lives in many ways. Interspersed among the nanny stories we read before we got him, there were many drool and shedding stories. We thought those were amusing, but exaggerated. However, now that we live with Elliot we have come to know that drool and shedding may, indeed, be amusing, but those stories were *not* exaggerated. Newfies *do* necessitate extra house cleaning. Newfies *are* high maintenance creatures.

But the rewards are great. For example, Elliot has taught us to savor the simple things. When he stops for his sniffs on our morning walks, we stop, too—and notice the sparkle of the frosty dew on the lawns, and hear the hammering of an industrious woodpecker in the distance. Then with a cheerful wave of his silky black "flag," he walks on. But we'll be stopping again soon. To smell the roses. Who could ask for anything more?

Mike & Angie Read
Augusta, Georgia, USA

In Love With the Jazzman

November 5th. A Friday. It remains a blur.

Could I do right by this guy? Would I make mistakes training him? Was I up to the challenge of raising a giant breed? Would my family accept him? Why couldn't I think of a name for him? Should I have taken this plunge?

Akc (All kinds combined) is the "breed" I had always loved, the "breed" I had always chosen. I had two, dear, old geriatrics, and two, four-year-old, 32-pound, long-haired, golden girls, Thunder and Lightning. The girls were littermates whom I was training in obedience, as well as water work and carting.

Yes, water work and carting. With the Newfy people and their Newfies. That's why I had fallen in love with Newfies. That's why I had decided I would adopt a Rescue Newf when my old guys went to the Rainbow Bridge.

That fall, when two of my Newfy friends' girls had puppies, I stayed away. Purposefully. I did not want to be tempted. It would be a few years before I would be ready to adopt a Newf.

Then I was approached about a special Newf puppy. He had been born with the front part of his left eye undeveloped. Although the difference between his two eyes was only noticeable upon close observation, he had no vision in his left eye. Of course the puppy had never been told about this. The puppy was seeing everything he wanted to see. Merrily, and with great enthusiasm.

I had had to do some soul-searching. I already had four dogs. Rescues. I was an Akc woman. A Newf had not been in my immediate plan. A puppy had not been in my plan at all. And, knowing myself well, I realized I had to make my decision *before* I saw the cute, cuddly, three-month-old, black furball I'd been told about.

Finally I made up my mind to adopt the puppy. But now that I was on my way to pick him up, I began feeling anxious. Nervous. Tense. I was almost overwhelmed with "new mom" worries.

Happily, these insecurities did not last long. Within days the puppy had found his place in our pack and I had found the perfect name for him. When his saxophone stuffie became his favorite toy, he became The Jazzman. I would call him Jazz.

Then began the bonding. How can I describe the depth and the intensity of the connection that has developed between Jazz and me? I have loved all of my dogs and don't want to take away from my relationship with any of them, but my attachment to Jazz is unique. Newf people tell me it's a *Newf* thing. Non-Newf people tell me it's a *guy* thing. All I know is that Jazz and I are fused together with a bond that grows ever stronger.

Jazz's first year went by with two surgeries and some medical issues that were really "issues" only to a nervous, first-Newfy mom. We survived.

Jazz won the hearts of my family members, even those who are not particularly dog fans. Slime became conditioner, black hair on light carpets became an acceptable decorating accessory, and my big puppy learned to play gently with his little golden sisters and my parents' miniature Schnauzer.

Jazz's second year began his life of fun. We resumed the obedience and water training we had started before the surgeries. And we added a third activity—camping.

After wearing out a little Ford Probe, I decided an extended cab pickup with a camper shell would be a sensible car for this family. So, what do you do with a camper shell, but go camping? Jazz needed to experience the beach and salt water! Jazz needed to experience snow!

Our first "trip" occurred on our driveway and included Jazz, Thunder, Lightning, and me. How many legs fit on a sleeping pad? How long can a Newfy go without a drink? How hard is a metal floor? How hot can a camper shell get on a "cool" November night in Texas?

That first trip lasted ninety minutes. The next morning I was off to get an air mattress, a battery-operated fan, and *lots* of containers for Jazz's water.

Except for driving through Houston during rush hour the Wednesday before Thanksgiving, despite having planned *not* to, the beach trip was wonderful. But we did draw attention. People seemed to think a single woman camping alone was unusual. A single woman camping alone with three dogs was unique. A single woman camping alone with three dogs in the back of a pickup was downright *bizarre.*

Jazz loved the attention he got from his fellow beach bums. He loved running on the sand and wading in the water. Although he had learned to swim in the lake at home, he did not have the confidence to swim in the waves. I did get into the water once to encourage him, but I didn't stay long. We will have to go back when the water is warmer.

With the beach experience successfully completed, it was time for Jazz's first snow. From Central Texas, New Mexico is the nearest source of the cold, white stuff. So, a couple of weeks later it was back into the pickup for another long drive.

Late that evening we arrived at Sumner Lake State Park in New Mexico. It was almost closing time. The ranger gave us a weird look and told me we could have our pick of the sites. We were the only campers. It was 30 degrees outside and getting colder. Do New Mexican campers have more sense than Texan campers?

Getting too hot was not a problem that night. I was prepared with two sleeping bags and four blankets. I had a hat, some gloves, and several sweaters. How many legs fit on an air mattress? How close can Thunder and Lightning snuggle to Mom? Jazz was the only member of the family who did not spend the night shivering.

The next day we forged on to Taos and *snow*. We found a lovely campground. With *people*! It took Jazz, being the true Newf that he is, a few steps to figure out how to walk in the snow. Then he was off! Chasing snow! Catching snow! Having a magnificent time. A National Forest and a remote ski resort parking lot in low season are perfect places for a Newf to get his fill of the fluffy magic.

Our second night in Taos was cold, really cold, 0 degrees. The golden girls and I huddled tightly together, but our shivering never stopped. Jazz's water froze in his bowl, but he was in seventh heaven. Happy. Frisky. Rarin' to go.

I'm pretty tough, and I pride myself on sticking things out but—the *girls'* health was at stake. Right? The next day we drove to Santa Fe and "camped" in a warm, cozy, motel room. Jazz just had to accept it. Majority rules.

Jazz was so busy with activities, I hadn't been planning to add carting for a few more months. But then, a *sale* was announced. On the very cart I wanted! How could I turn down a *bargain*?

After working so patiently and so long to teach Thunder and Lightning to pull their little cart (often with my Chihuahua-mix, geriatric guy sitting proudly on the cart seat), I was amazed at how quickly and easily Jazz took to carting. (Yes. I know. *Born* to cart!)

Although he still has a way to go, Jazz is gaining on the golden girls, and last week he dazzled me with his ability. As usual, he was tagging along, leashed to their cart, while the girls were out carting.

Despite their training, all three of the dogs get excited when they see a loose dog or cat. I can control the situation when I'm paying attention, but when a yappy, little dog approached us, my mind was elsewhere. My three started barking.

In the ensuing cacophony, I somehow tripped over my own feet and ended up on the shafts of the cart. I survived, but two of the shafts did not.

As I assessed the situation, traffic backed up (all one car of it!). On this narrow, back street, the man driving the car had no option but to wait while I determined that the girls could not pull the cart with two shafts detached. The man seemed sympathetic and understanding. He didn't honk. At least I didn't *hear* him honk.

I leashed the girls, detached them from their cart and its pieces, and, while holding onto three leashes, finally got the "wreck" off the street. The driver of the car moved on, but the people working in their back yards continued enjoying the carting entertainment.

I walked the dogs home, planning to return in the pickup for the cart. But then I remembered that Jazz is a *carting* dog! I would give him a *mission*!

Leaving Thunder and Lightning in the house, I hooked Jazz to his cart and the two of us returned to the scene of the accident. I loaded the girls' little cart into Jazz's big cart and off we went.

Jazz was so proud of himself! He was strutting! He was holding his head high! Once or twice he looked back at the load piled in his cart. This was his first real job and he knew it was important.

As for me, I couldn't stop smiling. My heart was full of love for the Jazzman. But then, my heart is *always* full of love for the Jazzman. My purple boy—purple collar, purple backpacks, purple carting harness, purple crate. Because purple is a royal color. And the Jazzman is undeniably my king.

Cathy Comstock
Belton, Texas, USA

Harvest On Cattail Pond

Typha angustifolia. Cattail. "Never let it loose in your pond," the garden book cautioned. "It's aggressive; it grows anywhere there's standing water; and, it will crowd out everything else."

It *was* aggressive! It was encircling my parents' 3/4-acre pond with its dense, seven-foot stalks. It was closing in fast. The Newfs were not going to like being crowded out. This pond had always been *their* territory.

Enter Winnie, our alert, energetic, fifteen-month-old bitch. Sizing up the aggressive cattail situation, she began an aggressive campaign of her own. Standing shoulder deep in the pond, she would stick her head completely under water for a few seconds. Then, like some big, black, lagoon-dwelling creature, up she would splatter from the deep. With her mouth full of cattail plants! She was pulling them up by the roots!

But she didn't stop there. With the white, tuber-type roots sticking out one side of her mouth and the long green shoots sticking out the other and trailing behind her, she would slosh through the water and wade onto the shore.

At first I thought that was the end of it. I thought once she had retrieved the cattail plants and dropped them on the ground, the game was over. But when I watched more closely, I realized Winnie was *eating* the cattail tubers. With gusto! As though they were some rare, exotic treat!

Within days, five other members of our Newfy herd were following Winnie's lead. They, too, were devouring cattail tubers with enormous enthusiasm. But Ollie, Macky, Sarah, Daisy, and Rosie weren't doing their own harvesting! No! These water-loving Newfs were staying high and dry on the shore. These water-loving Newfs were waiting for Winnie to procure the succulent, corncob-sized morsels and deliver them!

Each time Winnie waded ashore with a clump of cattails, the other five eager Newfs would crowd around to share her snack. Then, as soon as every tender tuber had been eaten, Winnie would wade back into the water and return with more. Although it was obvious that *six* Newfs were enjoying the new delicacy, only *one* was doing all the work! Poor Winnie!

Into the summer and through the fall Winnie continued dragging cattails out of the pond. She and the other Newfs continued devouring the tubers. First, I wondered about possible ill effects from ingesting cattails. Later, I wondered what I might be missing. Had Winnie discovered some rare gourmet fare? Should I be lining up on the shore with the other hungry diners?

An inquiry to Newf-L brought a few literary references to humans eating cattails, but evidently no one had ever heard of cattail-eating Newfs. Browsing through a desert survival handbook, I learned that I would be *lucky* if I found cattail tubers. But, because of the stagnant nature of most desert water, I was advised to *broil* them. Fresh cattail tubers, I read, taste a lot like asparagus.

Leave it to Winnie to make this discovery. *Nothing* gets past this bright, happy Newf. She is the puppy we kept from our 1999 litter, and she has given us no dull moments since. Although she is a total clown, she is also one of the most keen-minded Newfs we have met in our eleven years of breeding. She is an inquisitive, curious, vivacious girl.

By the time the pond froze in November, the aggressive cattail plants were history, six of our Newfs had developed a passion for tender white tubers, and Winnie had become an expert in underwater plant extraction.

Since our Newfs so excel at pond reclamation, we're considering offering them for hire in our community next spring. We can guarantee their diligence, they work for roots—or asparagus, and they demonstrate remarkably efficient teamwork. What employer could hope for anything more?

Dee Adrian
Breakwater Newfs
North Salem, Indiana, USA

This story was published in the July, 2001, newsletter of
Wisconsin's Native Plant Society,
Botanical Club of Wisconsin,
with permission.

Omaha

It was a wish come true for my husband, George. On June 6, 1944, D-Day, as a young Combat Medic with the 29th Division, he had landed on Omaha Beach. Now, fifty-five years later, he was boarding a plane for his first return to Normandy. He would participate in the celebration of D-Day and visit the beautiful Saint Laurent Sur Mer Cemetery where many of his comrades are buried. He had been looking forward to this trip for the greater part of a lifetime.

Our friend, Sue, and I took him to the airport for his ten-day visit, and with many last-minute reminders and much excited anticipation, we waved him onto his plane. But as soon as he departed, Sue and I hurried back to the car and raced off to a different airport. We had another important mission that evening, a *secret* mission. Returning to Normandy hadn't been the only thing my husband had wished for!

Several months earlier, we had lost Charlie, our dear, eleven-year-old Newf/Lab mix, and my husband had been heartbroken. He had mentioned that since Charlie had been such a great dog, he would love to have a Newf someday.

When I heard him say that, sparks went off in my brain. He *would* have a Newf! I would see to it that he had a Newf! A sweet, little, Newfy puppy. The *perfect* gift. Then I had to get practical. I wondered how I would pay for a Newf. Hubby would use the tax refund money for his trip, but how could I afford a puppy? I discussed the situation with our vet and told him I would just have to get lucky because it *was* going to happen. I *was* going to get my husband a Newf.

Unbeknownst to George, I found a Newf breeder who was delighted with my idea and agreed to help me with the puppy conspiracy. I sent a deposit and told her I would like to have the largest male of the upcoming litter. I also told her I had already chosen the name "Omaha" in recognition of the part my husband and all the other members of "The Greatest Generation" had played in the invasion of Normandy.

For the next three months, I exchanged information and snapshots with Sandi, Omaha's lovely and patient breeder. Among many other things, she learned that we live in the country, and that my husband is retired and home alone for twelve hours a day. Among many other things, I learned that Omaha's dad was a Landseer and his mom a black Canadian Newf.

Just before George left, I played the lottery. I got lucky. I won $5,000. This more than covered both the trip and the puppy. When I told our vet my good news, he gave me an astonished look. Then he raised his eyes heavenward and cried, "There *is* a God!"

On the day George was to leave for France, things did not go exactly as planned. I received a worried call from Sandi. The airline had advised her she would have to send the puppy right away because the weather was heating up so quickly.

As it turned out, George was boarding a plane for Paris at approximately the same time Omaha was being boarded for Washington, D.C. I like to think they were both in flight at the same time and perhaps their stars crossed! Then, as George was sipping his first glass of champagne aboard a French airliner, Sue and I were taking a ten-week-old, twenty-eight-pound Newfy out of his crate for a first look-see.

Omaha did not go with us when we picked up my husband ten days later. George walks with two canes and has had three heart attacks, so I decided he didn't need a Newfy surprise at the airport. But when we got home, George stopped to take a few things from the car. I hurried into the house and let Omaha out. George spotted him almost immediately.

"There's a black puppy on our carport. Where did he come from? He looks like a Newfoundland."

George gave me a quick glance, "You didn't!"

"I DID! MEET OMAHA!"

Shortly thereafter, Sandi called to see if our puppy were answering to his name. When I told her he had known his name since the very first day, she laughed.

"No wonder," she said. "My husband and I called him by name since the day he was born. And guess what? The whole *litter* answers to Omaha!"

Now, at two years old, Omaha has grown into a handsome young man of almost 150 pounds. Yet he is just as energetic and full of tricks as he was as a young puppy. We love the way he solves problems, and we are constantly entertained by his sense of humor.

George still laughs at an incident that happened one morning not so long ago. As I was leaving for work, I went to say goodbye to Omaha and found him sitting on the porch by his food bowl.

Noticing that he had not finished his breakfast, I said, "Omaha, you didn't finish your kibble. Shame on you!"

Omaha looked up at me and down at the bowl. I had to return to the house for something and when I came back out, I saw him still sitting and looking at his bowl.

When I went over to him, I saw he had put his favorite stuffed animal—a brown, long-tailed monkey—into the bowl. He had placed the monkey face down as if it were eating. I laughed and ran to tell my husband.

He said, "It looks as if Omaha has made a monkey out of you!"

Omaha is fond of all his stuffies, and many of his ideas and plans center around these toys. One spring night after a rain, I heard big paws running back and forth over the porch. Then I heard something being dragged, clinking as it went.

When I investigated, I found Omaha had inadvertently left his cloth ducky out in the rain in the mulch of the garden. When he remembered it, he had raced across the porch, into the garden, and retrieved it.

Then, noticing Ducky was covered with mulch and evidently finding that unacceptable, Omaha had promptly "bathed" him in his big water bowl and laid him on his blanket to dry. Next, since the water in his bowl had become filled with dirt and floating mulch, he had dragged it across the porch and tossed it, bowl and all, onto the lawn.

Some people thought I was crazy to get such a big dog at this stage in our lives. My husband has problems walking and cannot take Omaha for long jaunts. Yet, instead of sitting inside all the time, George now gets out nine or ten times a day to play toss with Omaha and give him his treats and his water and his hugs. When I come home in the evening, George always has entertaining stories to tell me about their day.

In a deeper vein, I did not give our puppy the name "Omaha" lightly. When my husband suffered his first, almost fatal, heart attack, a poem started to flow as he began to recover. He titled the poem "Return to Saint Laurent Sur Mer." It ends with these lines:

> Here in this marble orchard where seeds of valor were sown
> You may find the noblest saints of all though some remain unknown.
> And when the harvest is gathered in heaven's final edition,
> The Book of Life will know the names of all who made this mission.
> As I turned to leave, a voice seemed to call after me.
> Please don't forget the price they paid to keep our country free.
> Greater love has no man than to give his life for others.
> Then just before I reached the gate I turned to my sleeping brothers.
> Humbly with my head bowed I said this little prayer:
> Dear God, bring multitudes to visit Saint Laurent Sur Mer.

My husband participated in a battle on a beach in Normandy. It was a pivotal experience in his life. In my heart of hearts, more than fifty-five years later, the soldier and his dog are both celebrated with the word "Omaha."

Phyllis Roberts
Mt. Airy, Maryland, USA

Floral Design 101

My curious black puppy watches intently as bright yellow lemons drop from the table and roll across the flower shop floor. I wait to see what will happen next. After living with this wonderful breed for almost twenty-five years, watching the workings of intelligent puppy brains is still a favorite pastime.

"Hmmm, toys!" she thinks. "Must be for me. . .it's all for meeeee!"

After a quick chase and some batting about with her paws, Cosi picks up one of the lemons with her mouth. A fine mist of citrus oil tickles her nose as her puppy teeth graze the skin.

"Whaaaat the. . .?" she wonders as she shakes her head.

She drops the lemon and it begins rolling again. What's a four-month-old Newfy to do? If it rolls, chase it! If you catch it, pick it up! More citrus mist is released into her mouth as she gives the lemon another shake.

"Aaaghh! This thing must be tamed!" she decides, and she sinks her teeth into the lemon's soft skin.

This time I see *juice* squirting. Cosi drops the lemon and shakes her head. She begins licking the inside of her mouth and the air around her mouth.

My puppy is surprised, but undaunted. After a moment of collecting her thoughts, she pounces on the slightly flattened lemon with both front feet. Again! Again! Over and over she pounces until the lemon is only a pulp of its former self.

Satisfied that she has hunted this lemon down and subdued it, she focuses on another one. With a renewed surge of enthusiasm, she begins batting it around.

Then, gingerly this time, Cosi picks up the second lemon and trots it over to her big, dignified, Landseer brother. She wants to share her bounty. She wants Sirius to examine her prize.

Three-year-old Sirius has been coming to the shop since he was twelve weeks old. He has been a therapist, a rug, a cheerleader, a diplomat, and a nanny for crying children. He has also assisted in plenty of fruit-enhanced floral creations. Having once pilfered grapes and strawberries from a completed arrangement, and having often chased kumquats and oranges across the floor, he eyes his little sister stoically. Cosi's lemon holds no surprises for him.

Sirius's patience and tolerance are exceptional. He is already surrounded by sticks, leaves, and other discarded floral foliage that Cosi has dragged to his sleeping space. He is half covered with the spoils of her active morning.

However, he gazes thoughtfully at the lemon. It seems to bring back a memory. Then, as if to say, "Okay, Kid, have I got a game for you!" he stands up and shakes off the debris.

He walks over to one of the lemons still lying on the shop floor. Gently he picks it up, carries it to the Newfy water bucket, and drops it in. Cosi is fascinated. She watches wide-eyed as he repeats the process several times.

When the last lemon splashes into the bucket, Sirius turns and looks at Cosi with an air of expectancy. Five lemons are floating in the water. Floating. . .floating. Cosi approaches the water bucket. What's a four-month-old puppy to do?

Cosi begins bobbing for lemons. She starts with only her nose in the water, then she includes her face, next she submerges her head, blowing bubbles all the way. Finally she plunges into the bucket with both front feet and digs and shakes and dips. Water is flying and Cosi is "grrrring" through the bubbles. Bobbing for lemons isn't as easy as it looks! My entire staff and all the customers who happen by spend the next half hour doubled over with laughter as Cosi, the Newfoundland baby, shows us how to mix work with fun.

Sirius watches Cosi's antics from his space. He likes teaching her, and he seems happy to have been of service. My big boy *always* seems happy to have been of service. Sirius is my "savior" puppy. I had lost my previous dear Newfy to age, and I thought I could not bear to have another. Then I realized I couldn't bear *not* to have another.

My life at the time was nothing but work, work, work, and I rationalized that if I got a puppy and brought him to the shop, we'd both get the best of both worlds. He would get to spend the day socializing with his "pack," and I would have a legitimate reason to get outside and see the blue sky several times a day.

The plan worked perfectly. But. . .if one Newfy is good, wouldn't two Newfies be better? Didn't Sirius need a little sister?

The two-Newfy plan is working beautifully. But I'm not crazy. Since Sirius and Cosi are such good companions, I wouldn't upset their harmony. I wouldn't jeopardize their relationship by bringing another puppy into this compatible situation. It looks as if next time I will simply have to get *two* puppies.

I wonder. . .how many Newfies can I fit into a flower shop? And. . .how many Newfies can I teach floral design?

Gigi Rhodes
Pleasant Hill, California, USA

My Well-Organized Angel

Schedules. Priority lists. Calendar notations. I organize my time. I stay on top of things.

Our eighteen-month-old Newf, Einstein, knows and appreciates my routines. However, yesterday his Thursday schedule was altered when my husband, Jay, came home at noon to wait for the cable man. Of course Einstein was thrilled to have his dad's company and stayed right by his side all afternoon.

When I got home just after five o'clock, Jay told me Einstein had not eaten his breakfast until 3:30 in the afternoon. I wasn't too surprised. Einstein has never been a big chow hound. Sometimes he doesn't eat his breakfast at all. But knowing he had eaten at 3:30, I decided I would get a few things done before fixing his dinner.

I wasn't five minutes into my first chore when Einstein came over and began dancing all around me.

"Okay, Einstein, I'll take you out to potty."

I got my jacket on, got his leash on, and we went outside. But Einstein didn't need to potty.

"Oh, I get it! You just wanted to play!"

I tossed his Kong a few times, but he just stood there giving me a "why in the world did we come outside" look. Soon he led me back to the door.

I hung up my jacket, put away his leash, and tried to continue my chores. But in no time Einstein was dancing beside me again. This time he added some insistent barks which he directed right into my face.

"I just took you outside. You didn't need to potty. You didn't want to play."

Einstein replied with more dancing and more barks.

"Oh, you want to play *inside*. Okay, let's find some toys."

Once more, I tried to engage our boy in play. But he was simply not interested. All I got for my effort was a worried stare and more barks.

"What do you want, Einstein? Really, I'm trying to listen, but I'm not getting it. You don't want to potty. You don't want to play inside or out, and you can't possibly be hungry for dinner yet."

At the mention of dinner, he immediately thumped his front legs down into a play bow.

"Dinner? Einstein, you want *dinner*?"

Einstein popped up and danced around with his tail wagging ecstatically. His frantic, demanding barks were replaced by soft little woofs. His smile spread from ear to ear and saliva began glistening at the corners of his mouth. Dinner. I had said the magic word.

I was positive he would not be hungry for at least two more hours. Yet, there was no question about what he wanted. He had communicated his wish very clearly.

All right. Okay. Since food was obviously what he wanted, I would fix his dinner. Then maybe he would stop disturbing me. Then maybe I could get a few things done.

As soon as I began the Newfy dinner preparations, Einstein lay down next to me and dropped his head onto his paws with a contented sigh.

"Okay, here you go, Einstein. Are you ready for your dinner?"

When I put his dish down on his mat he raised his head and gazed at me.

His expression said, "No, thanks. I had a late breakfast. I just wanted you to *make* my dinner. I just wanted you to stay on *schedule*."

Then his head dropped back onto his paws, his eyes closed, and his nap began. Apparently getting his human to follow her normal routine had been very tiring.

Two hours later, Einstein slowly ate his dinner. He had gotten hungry about the time I had expected him to. But I had learned my lesson. Einstein knows what should be done and the order in which it should be done. He both supports and *endorses* my regard for schedules. From now on, his dinner will be served at the proper hour.

Since Jay thinks I'm somewhat obsessive about my routines and schedules, he found this incident hilarious. But it's only one of Einstein's many amusing incidents. He has kept us smiling from the beginning. Within minutes of entering our home for the first time, our new, 18½-pound puppy made a brilliant attempt to escape the sticky Alabama heat by climbing into our refrigerator. Sliding the orange juice jug and other assorted items aside, he settled comfortably onto the bottom shelf and flashed us a big, satisfied grin.

As with most Newfies, keeping cool continues to be one of Einstein's priorities, and since we moved to Rhode Island he has reveled in the winter snows. This morning I watched him play in the fresh powder that fell during the night. First he flopped onto his back and began wriggling around. I thought he was trying to grind the snow as close to his skin as possible.

While still on his back, he smashed the left side of his face into the snow and ground deeply. Next, he smashed the right side of his face into the snow and repeated the process.

It was only after he stood up that I realized what Einstein had *really* been doing. Our artistic boy had been making a snow angel! It was a *plump* angel with three heads and four short, stubby *wings*. Precariously, it perched at the apex of a huge, fan-shaped pedestal.

Inspired by his accomplishment, my black angel made two more snow angels before dashing off to search for sticks and other treasures buried under the snow. As usual, his life was *bubbling* with excitement!

Einstein adds an extra bubble of excitement to our lives as well. I had to wait for over four years between deciding that I wanted a Newf and getting my first puppy. But this funny boy was well worth the wait. He keeps us smiling. He keeps us entertained. And, most importantly in his opinion, he keeps us on schedule!

Sue Elkins
Rumford, Rhode Island, USA

Surrounded By Sweetness

Ephraim doesn't mind if they can't speak. He doesn't mind if they don't know what day it is, or what year. It doesn't matter to him if they have food on their shirts, or even if they smell bad. He just walks over to them and sits by their sides. He lays his head on their laps, or on an arm of their wheelchairs, or on a side of their beds.

Even if they can't reach out to pat him, his quiet presence seems to touch the hearts of these elderly people who used to run and laugh and play and sing and love and be responsible for others in their lives. Always warm and gentle, Ephraim sits and gives them his affection and a bit of his strength for a few moments. Week after week he gives, he gives, he gives, and he asks for nothing in return.

Not long ago we were asked to visit a lady who had been sick for a few days. She was unusually weak and depressed, and had not come out of her room or spoken with anyone since she had become ill.

Ephraim sat by her bedside and she slowly reached her hand out to him. He was very still as she rubbed the fur on the back of his neck.

When it was time to move on to the next person, the lady asked, "Will you come back again?"

I knew that Ephraim had once more gone into the silent, mysterious world of Alzheimer's disease and given his love to someone who lives there. She had returned with him briefly to his world, so she could invite him back to hers.

Even though his breed is famous for its gentle, loving temperament, Ephraim's temperament is *exceptionally* gentle and loving. We realized this when we visited his breeder and were invited to choose our puppy. We had read several books about choosing puppies so we felt confident we knew all the things to look for.

When my husband, Ted, got down on the floor and called to the eight-week-old puppies, Ephraim ran to him and kissed him and kissed him and kissed him. This little guy was *gentle*. This little guy was *loving*. We didn't have to look for anything else. We knew Ephraim was the right puppy for us.

As he has grown to adulthood, Ephraim has become even more gentle and loving. Now, at the age of five, our big boy is sweetness itself. It was because of Ephraim's wonderful temperament that we decided we could bring our second Newf, Tiny, into our family. We knew we could rely on him to help us with her transition and adjustment.

Tiny came to us as a five-month-old, pet-store puppy. The people of her first family had loved her, but they had not trained her. She had already become a very forceful, overly confident, headstrong little girl when a sad change in their circumstances made it impossible for them to keep her.

The first thing Tiny did when her family brought her to our home was race to the pond in our fenced back yard and plunge in for a swim. This was before she had even said "hello"! Although Ephraim, who had been in the yard awaiting her arrival, was initially startled by her audacity, he seemed to become amused by her enthusiasm. Shortly after she finished her swim, they became friends. Even Meeshack, our mixed-breed boy who doesn't always like other dogs, decided Tiny was all right.

Her first family looked at our big back yard, looked at the camper we had gotten so our dogs could travel with us, and looked at how well Ephraim and Meeshack got along with a strange, new, rambunctious puppy. They knew Ted and I would love her and care for her. So from that day on, Tiny was ours.

But Tiny was a challenge! We started her right off in obedience school and she, like Ephraim before her, became the class clown. She went on to Level 2 Obedience, and this class was followed by a beginning-level agility course.

We worked hard at training her and redirecting her energy, and Ephraim, with his patient, gentle influence, made our job easier. He helped teach her manners; he helped calm her down.

Although Ted was in love with Tiny from the start, I thought I could never love her like I loved Ephraim. But I was wrong. During the 2½ years she has lived with us she has made a place for herself in my heart. She can sit gazing into my face, giving gentle little kisses to my chin for as long as I can sit gazing into her face, giving gentle little scratches to her ears. How could I not have a place in my heart for a dainty, little, 100-pound girl whose eyes say, "Oh, Mom, I love you so much! You can never even imagine!"

When Ted had the flu during the winter, Tiny would go to our bedroom every evening and crawl up on the bed beside him for a few minutes prior to going to her crate for the night. I'm not certain whether she was trying to reassure herself that he was okay or just trying to tell him that he is loved. In either case, she accomplished both objectives. She seems to have become as sweet as Ephraim, after all!

We have had Newfs for only five years, but now I cannot imagine life without them. Shortly before we got Ephraim, my dear, loving, eighteen-year-old kitty died and I was so filled with grief, I wasn't ready for another cat. Yet, within a week, I knew we needed another pet in our house.

When we decided on a dog, Ted got the book *The Right Dog For You* by Daniel F. Tortora, Ph.D., and we read it from cover to cover. All the tests and questionnaires "herded" us in the direction of working dogs, and of the working dogs, Newfs seemed like a good match. We read about and studied Newfs for several weeks, but when we met our first Newf puppies we realized this wasn't a *good* match. No! This was a match made in heaven. May we be blessed with Newfs forever.

Ted & Melanie Peck
Lebanon, New Hampshire, USA

http://www.newfemporium.com

The Music Critic

About four years ago my singing voice developed the wobble that older women get. Since I didn't have time for the practice and coaching necessary to eliminate it, I decided I would *stop singing*. Graciously. Didn't Beverly Sills retire at the age of fifty?

Last week I got an invitation to join a reunion of my 1961 high school choir. This had been an extraordinary choir. It had been directed by a couple of gifted musicians who had gone on to much bigger and better things.

I was thrilled. I was excited! I *needed* to go! I signed up, bought plane tickets, and began rearranging my schedule. Ooops! Suddenly I realized I would need to *sing*!

I got out some vocal practice tapes and popped one into the stereo tape player. The first exercise was on focus and volume. It involved saying "hello" in loud and soft voices.

My Newf, Saralinda, is five. She has lived with me since she was ten weeks old. Except for listening to me follow along with very loud songs on the radio or croon a few funny, little, silly songs to her, she has never heard me sing. But I hadn't started singing yet. I was just saying "hello."

Saralinda *knows* "hello"! It means someone is coming to visit. It means excitement. It means pats, hugs, and kisses all around. So, when at 10:00 P.M. in the middle of my kitchen I began saying "hello" in all kinds of voices, she flew into action. People were arriving! She needed to greet them!

She ran to the front door. She ran to the side door. She ran to the back door. She ran out the dog door and all around the yard.

It was hard for me to concentrate on focus and volume while giggling.

When I stopped saying "hello," Saralinda finally stopped running. She sat down and did her head tilt thing with the eyebrow effect.

By then the tape had moved on to actual vocalizing and I was attempting to sing scales. My girl was not sure she liked this. Why was I making coyote calls? Why was I acting weird?

Saralinda came to a tight sit right in front of me. In case I had not noticed her, she switched her bottom and sat even straighter. She uses this sit when she *really* wants something. She uses it to say, "See how straight I am sitting? You clearly must reward this perfect sit with a bit of that really great-smelling stuff you have there."

"BARK! BARK! BARK!"

Had my Newfy become a music critic? Maybe she wanted me to be quiet. Maybe she was trying to sing along. Or, maybe she was just imploring me to produce the phantom visitors so they could pat her.

Although I still don't know what she was trying to tell me, I do know that she is a very special girl. I grew up with various dog breeds and mixes, and acquired the privilege of living with a Newf when I married. But Saralinda is my first personal Newf. Now it will be Newfs for me, forever.

Saralinda has her Canine Good Citizen certification and has passed her Delta Society test. She has a little blue cape and some patches that I might actually sew on it when the rest of my life slows down a bit and we can begin visiting at the local pediatric hospital.

Saralinda will enjoy cheering and comforting children, and as a family physician, I can recognize good medicine when I see it. Newfs are *exceptionally* good medicine.

Chris Robb
Rehoboth, Massachusetts, USA

A Dog For All Reasons

Baby gates. Wire crates. X-pens. Portable, soft-sided Cool Crates. Each of these has entertainment value, and our Newf, Lakhota, welcomes variety. Indeed, breaking out of confinement is the pastime he enjoys most.

We assume Lakhota was born with this fascination for escaping. When he came to live with us at ten weeks old he was already honing his Houdini skills. By the time he reached five months, he had mastered his baby gate. Some of the time he would just sail right over it from a standing position, but his lazy approach was to knock it down with one well-aimed head push and casually step over it.

When we began putting him in a wire crate, Lakhota found the door latches intriguing. Soon he began opening the latches whenever we left home, and, to our horror and dismay, marking his accomplishment by peeing on our bed. My side, of course!

Realizing he needed an additional challenge, we added six leash clips to the door. Apparently Lakhota found leash clips boring because after they were added, he stayed in his crate for a few days. Little did we know that he was planning his greatest escape to date.

The afternoon my husband, Lenny, informed me that Lakhota had escaped from the crate, I *knew* that was impossible. I was *positive* I had latched the crate door with the six clips before I left for work. Lenny started laughing and suggested I go take a look.

I couldn't believe my eyes! Instead of exiting through the door, Lakhota had bent the rod that holds the crate together, pushed out a side panel, and set himself free.

X-pens? They were all right, but not very challenging. "Up, over, and out" is the name of Lakhota's favorite X-pen game. This boy excels at jumping.

Although Lakhota found his baby gate, his wire crate, and his X-pen somewhat interesting, his greatest thrill came when we zipped him into a Cool Crate. This immediately became his favorite, most exciting toy.

If we failed to zip the Cool Crate completely closed at the bottom, a quick unzip with his nose led to freedom. Boring. No challenge. It was only when we zipped him in properly that he discovered the real joy of the Cool Crate. His mesh-sided, fabric crate was *mobile*!

The first time we left Lakhota in the Cool Crate, I came home to find it on its end, door side down. Lakhota was sitting on the door. But the alarming thing was what I found hanging on the crate frame! While tumbling around in our bedroom, our boy had gotten the crate rods caught in the slats of my closet door. This resulted in him pulling the closet door completely out of the frame. Apparently

Lakhota had spent the afternoon dragging my closet door around the room with him.

After that episode we lashed the crate in place using a series of leashes which we wrapped around the legs of the bed and stuffed under a heavy dresser, then clipped to the stake rings of the crate.

This leash method worked, so we had good luck for awhile. Then we used the Cool Crate at a United Kennel Club show in Davie, Florida. After I showed Lakhota, I zipped him into his Cool Crate and returned to the ring to watch the next group of dogs. Since I was going to be within sight of Lakhota, I didn't think about securing his crate.

Suddenly, I was startled to hear the chairman of the host club laughing hysterically from the top of the announcer's platform. Simultaneously, about twenty people began yelling, "Catch the crate! Catch the crate!"

I turned to see Lakhota coming to join me. He was still in his crate, but he was rolling it end over end like a hamster in a Freedom Ball! He had already managed to turn one corner and come down a long corridor. Now he was poised to roll through the entrance gate to the showing area.

The next day people kept asking me if I owned the "rolling crate," then laughing uproariously when I sheepishly admitted that Lakhota was, indeed, my boy.

At home or at dog shows our boy seems to find trouble at every turn. But when he is working, he becomes an exceptionally well-behaved, careful dog. I have multiple sclerosis, and while I am still quite able to do so, I am training Lakhota to be my Service Dog. Consistently, he becomes serious and cooperative the minute we go to work. Lenny and I joke that living with Lakhota is like living with Dr. Jekyll and Mr. Hyde.

Lakhota is almost two now, and he has been going everywhere with me since he was ten weeks old. When we are working, he will go anywhere and do anything I ask of him. He'll even go down a slide in a playground. If we go into stores where the shelves and display tables are crowded together, Lakhota walks as close to me as is physically possible. If an area is so tight he cannot turn around, he backs up to get out of that spot. He began doing this on his own initiative.

I have taken him into all manner of stores including shops in which expensive china and such are displayed, and he has never knocked anything over. I wish I could say the same, but I am a little more clumsy than Lakhota.

Ultimately, Lakhota is going to be doing balance and bracing work for me. He will be getting a harness with a fixed handle so he can learn to stand and brace for me when my balance is off. Also, using his carting and wagon-pulling skills, he will help me with grocery shopping and other tasks that require carrying heavy loads.

Training Lakhota myself has been an incredibly rewarding experience because it has helped us discover absolutely everything there is to know about each other. Lakhota has learned to trust me implicitly, and I have learned I can rely on him.

We thought Lakhota was making a substantial contribution to our family by entertaining us with his escape artistry and working for me as a Service Dog. However, recently, he made yet another contribution, a *monetary* contribution. Lakhota appeared in a TV commercial and received his very own paycheck. Now he has his own banking account and is able to pay his own handler's fees.

Lakhota's TV opportunity came when an animal wrangler needed a Landseer for a Huggies Diaper commercial. Finding a Newf in Florida, much less a Landseer, is not easy. Lucky Lakhota just happened to be in the right place at the right time.

In the pre-casting interview I was asked if Lakhota likes children. I laughed and explained that the younger they are, the more captivated he is by them. Then I was asked if Lakhota *licks*. This question *really* made me laugh! I explained that there were few times when Lakhota does *not* lick.

Lakhota spent three days doing the casting of the babies. His task was to lie on the floor and lick every baby who came up to him. Whenever a baby didn't come quite close enough, Lakhota took it upon himself to creep along the floor until he could sniff its feet and give its toes kisses. He *loved* his job! He must have kissed the toes, and often the faces, of 300 different babies before the four babies were selected for the commercial.

The commercial was shot on the balcony of a house with Lakhota lying in the open doorway playing with, licking, and receiving treats from a baby. He did great work and everyone on the set fell in love with him. He was quite the charmer!

I have had other dogs, but Lakhota is my first Newf. Since I am a certified lifeguard and Water Safety Instructor, a large water dog was very appealing to me. Yet even though I studied the Newfoundland breed for five years before I was able to have one, nothing I read prepared me for Lakhota. He is my amazing, wonder boy.

Bonnie Giacovelli
Jupiter, Florida, USA

www.pb.quik.com/bonniet

The Rug That Came To Dinner

Sunday, April 8, 2001, is a day that will be forever etched in my memory and in the memories of some of the residents of Lake Waukomis, Missouri.

The day began normally enough. Calvin, our Search and Rescue Newf, Doug, my husband, and I were going out to practice with the local dive rescue team.

As usual, Calvin began barking and whining with excitement the minute I started packing the Suburban and continued carrying on until we got to the lake. Upon arrival, he did his usual exuberant "meet and greet" of all the dive team members.

This practice was to be a bit different from most in that prospective dive team members had been invited to attend. While we got to know these new people, they would learn what we do by working with us. When Calvin saw that we had guests he was delighted. New people! Yippee! Victims! What a joy!

People familiar with Calvin know that he is nice and cooperative for one reason and one reason only: to get stuff! But unsuspecting strangers are often lured in by his admiring looks, his cute tricks, and his endearing kisses. Once he has the new people under his spell, he takes advantage of them and becomes his usual outrageous, demanding self.

At this invitational practice, one of the visiting couples, in particular, was drawn to Calvin. They had Saint Bernards and, being partial to large dogs, spent a great deal of time admiring Calvin. Throughout the day, they were loving on him; slipping him hot dogs; playing fetch with him; rubbing his ears, and in general, treating him like a king. They even took pictures of themselves with him: in the water, on the dock, on the boat.

As the day went on, things proceeded quite well training-wise. I was making progress coaching Calvin in scent detection, and Calvin was making progress in bamboozling his new admirers.

When the training was over and it came time for Calvin to be put back in the Suburban, the nice couple asked if they could put him away for me while I helped clean and store the dive gear and training equipment.

I was grateful for their assistance, but not long after they took Calvin up the hill to the truck, the man came running back with a leash in his hand. His first words to me were, "Calvin's gone!"

I just looked at him, then started running up the hill. I was disgusted with myself. I should have known better than to have put 8½-year-old Calvin into the hands of people he was so easily manipulating. To a lesser degree, I was also disgusted with Calvin for being such a cunning handful.

As I ran toward the Suburban, the man kept pace with me while telling me that they had taken Calvin's leash off before they put him in the truck and—whammo! Calvin had taken off!

When I got to the top of the hill the man's wife was crying. She told me she had called Calvin but he had just ignored her and taken off. She said she was worried that I would be mad, and added that she was afraid Calvin might not love her.

By then I was *really* upset with myself for not taking care of my own dog and *really* annoyed with Calvin for taking advantage of his new admirers. Of course I didn't have the heart to tell this lady that Calvin actually *didn't* love her, that he *hadn't* loved her all day, and that he considered her just another in his long line of *victims*!

So, I simply asked the obvious question, "Which way did he go?"

But neither the husband nor the wife knew. They hadn't noticed!

I asked the couple to stay put and watch for Calvin while I took off with my eyes peeled and my ears straining to hear the usual sounds of an escaped Newfoundland: dogs barking and people screaming.

I started down the street and had walked past five houses when a man who was outside gardening asked if I were looking for the "big, black dog that just ran by."

Before I could answer, I heard a scream. I wasn't sure which house it had come from, but two minutes later a lady walked out her front door with Calvin in tow. As soon as she spotted me she called, "Is this dog yours?"

Numerous things were running through my head, but the only thing that came out of my mouth was, "What did he do?"

The lady started laughing as her husband and her two or three pre-teens crowded behind her in the doorway.

It seems Calvin had used the door-opening skills I had taught him to get into their house. Then he had shocked the family by trotting into their kitchen where they were in the middle of dinner. They watched in utter disbelief as he did a quick scan of the counters, then plopped himself into a "sit-stay" beside their table as if expecting to be served a plate.

It was only when Calvin sat at their table smiling that the woman had regained enough composure to scream. Her outburst startled their new "dinner guest" and he had taken off through the back door. Quickly realizing that he was trapped in the back yard, he had trotted back into the kitchen.

I started apologizing profusely for Calvin's behavior, but the husband began laughing uproariously. He said that two good things had come from Calvin's arrival: 1) His wife had recently brought home a flea market find—an old, black, bearskin rug. He hated that rug and had told his wife that God would get even with her for bringing home such a gruesome thing. When Calvin joined them at their table, the wife screamed because she thought the rug had come to life and she was being punished for bringing it home! 2) As a family, they would always have an interesting story to tell about the evening the bear rug came to dinner.

I was overjoyed that the evening had ended safely, in spite of some unusually stressful minutes. But then Calvin is an expert at creating stressful minutes. He has *always* been pushy, demanding, energetic, and vocal. He lets me know if his dinners, his walks, or his training sessions are not on time. If we get off schedule, I have to listen to him complain. Yet, despite the drawbacks, I wouldn't trade him for anything in the world. He has lived with us since he was eight weeks old. He is our second Newf SAR dog and we have been training together since he was ten weeks old. Calvin is my baby boy, and I love every inch of his black bearskin.

Nicki Gundersen
Lenexa, Kansas, USA

http://www.droolingdogs.com/dogs.html

A similar version of this story was published in
The Heart of America Newfoundland Club Newsletter, April/May 2001.

Mother of A Different Feather

Even though there is nothing subtle about a Newfy nudge on the leg followed by a 164-pound, 30-inch-tall girl wheeling around and rushing away, my three-year-old Jacqué had to repeat her request several times before she got my attention.

I was busy. I was inspecting the large 70'x70' area inside the kennel yard. I was concentrating on my job—cleaning the grass, examining the toys, and checking the wading pool. Additionally, I was carrying on a brilliant conversation with my other two Newfs, a handsome, five-year-old, 197-pound fella named Tux and a sweet, ol', ten-year-old, nanny girl called Hazel, who were "helping" me. I was also making the occasional comment to the resident crows who hang out on the kennel fence hoping for a handout.

Jacqué wasn't helping me. This was, in retrospect, rather odd, as she is an "in your face" kind of girl who rarely misses an opportunity to be a part of the action. But other than the time she spent rushing out to nudge me and hurrying away, she was staying inside the little converted cabin that serves as the dog house.

When I finally stopped my work for a second and focused on Jacqué, I realized she was not allowing the other dogs to go into the cabin. I half registered the fact that she had been giving a small woof, a growl, or just blocking the door when either of the other dogs came near.

Then, for the third or fourth time, she rushed out, gave me a nudge that nearly knocked me into the wading pool, and hurried back inside the cabin. As I mentioned, Jacqué is not a petite girl, nor is she subtle.

"What is it Jacqué? What's up, girlfriend?" I asked.

Finally understanding her request and her urgency, I followed her into the cabin, squeezing through the narrow doggie door.

Once inside, I found Jacqué in a "down-stay" position. The big smile on her face and the thump, thump, thump of her wagging tail let me know she was glad I had *finally* gotten her message. Another second passed before I noticed the tiny creature on the floor in front of her.

"Oh, Jacqué. . .a baby swallow," I whispered. "You found a baby swallow."

I bent to inspect the small bird and discovered an uninjured but soggy little bunch of fluff. Hearing bird noises, I looked up and saw a good-sized mud nest built high up in the rafters right above where Jacqué lay with the baby bird. This little fella had fallen out of its nest and Jacqué had been protecting it from harm and keeping it warm by nestling it in her chest ruff.

The baby swallow seemed quite calm. It was just looking around and peeping every time its mama swooped through the cabin.

"Oh, good girl, Jacqué! Good girl! Stay! I'll get a ladder."

I set up the ladder and, with Jacqué watching intently, I carefully picked up the tiny swallow and returned it to the nest. I saw two more swallow babes peering at me as I did so.

As soon as I got down from the ladder and moved away, the mama returned to check on her family. Then I heard what sounded like happy little bird noises.

Once Jacqué was satisfied that the baby bird had been safely returned to its proper place, she visibly relaxed. With her job finished, she was ready for a rousing game of wrestle with Tux.

Despite her abundant energy, Jacqué is a wonderfully sweet girl. When she came to live with us at eight weeks old, she wasn't terribly interested in us humans for quite a while. She preferred being with the other dogs. However, after she finally warmed up to us, she became an avid people lover. Before long she was not-so-gently shoving her way through the dog crowd in her attempts to get all the pets, kisses, and hugs. She is always the first to bound onto the couch or the bed with us and her favorite thing is exchanging "jowl kisses" with my husband.

Being an extra large girl, and very demanding now, Jacqué is often rather boisterous and clumsy in her attention seeking. She sometimes squashes us in our bed or crushes us on a chair or couch in her enthusiasm. And she is always barking at any intrusion of other animals or people into the yard.

Given this exuberant nature, I thought Jacqué would have been the first of our three dogs to harm the little bird, accidentally or otherwise. Other than being gentle with toy "stuffies" which all the dogs treat with care, she had never before exhibited any mothering or protective instincts. Yet she was certainly careful and protective of that tiny baby swallow. I was so touched and so proud of my big girl. What a sweetheart!

Lin Holt
Whiskey Creek Newfoundlands
Joyce, Washington, USA

The Devoted Music Fan

Busy! That's what we called him. That's what he was. We had never had a more curious, inquisitive puppy. Rocky was just plain *nosy*. He monitored me, my housemate, and our three cats constantly. He had to know everything that was going on at all times.

He also found remote controls, books, and toilet paper very entertaining, and devoured more than his share of each.

But the most memorable of Rocky's puppyhood traits was his absolute refusal to sleep in his crate at night. Even though it was in the same room where I slept, and even though he could see and hear me, my eight-week-old puppy would begin howling and crying and whimpering and whining the moment the lights were turned off.

In hopes of calming him, I tried putting all sorts of items in his crate with him—an alarm clock wrapped in a towel, his toys, his stuffed animals, an old shirt with my scent on it, a hot water bottle. But nothing worked. Except for the occasional exhaustion-induced nap, he howled throughout the night until the lights were turned on again the next morning.

After a few days of this I became a walking zombie at work, but I knew I couldn't give in or the crate training would be ruined. His breeder kept assuring me that he would settle down. A month passed. Six weeks. Rocky was still howling all night. *Something* had to be done. I called his breeder for more ideas.

This time she suggested I try playing "soothing music" for my puppy at night. Thus began a period of "trial and error" in which Rocky rejected several bands and many vocalists. First I tried all the tapes I had that might be "soothing." Next I tried all the tapes my friends and co-workers loaned me that might be "soothing."

I had almost given up on the music idea when the breakthrough I had been longing for came. Anne Murray. "Anne Murray's Greatest Hits." As soon as I put this tape in the player, Rocky got quiet. Then he stared at the speaker and cocked his little head to one side. Next he relaxed and began listening. I had found a voice and a singing style that appealed to my pup. Finally! Within a few minutes, Rocky was peacefully slumbering. Within a few minutes more, so was I.

From that night on, for many weeks, Anne Murray sang both of us to sleep. Rocky simply *loved* listening to her. He seemed to like the range of her voice, the highs and the lows, the way she goes back and forth. Whatever it was that he liked, the sound of her voice became his cue to settle down and go to sleep.

Our wild, sleepless, little busybody has grown into a calm four-year-old boy. But he still loves listening to Anne Murray. Recently while I was scanning radio stations in the car, Anne Murray came on, but the radio scanned on. I glanced at

Rocky in the rear view mirror. He was cocking his head and listening intently. But then she was gone.

He looked at me and I scanned back to her song for him. When it came on again, I could tell he was very pleased to hear a favorite voice from his childhood. As he listened contentedly, I reminisced about sleepless nights and thanked God for Anne Murray.

Since Rocky has always had an enormous love for people, I wanted to give him the opportunity to visit the residents of a local nursing home. Although he did very well in his class for therapy dogs, I was a nervous wreck on the night he was to be tested for his Therapy Dog International certification. I knew the floors in the hospital where the test was conducted were buffed and polished every night, and even though Rocky is great with people, my 160-pound boy is afraid of shiny, slippery floors.

When we entered the hospital corridor Rocky hugged the wall for dear life. But as soon as people began making a fuss over him, he forgot about the shiny floors. There were other dogs being tested that evening, but Rocky was the magnet everyone seemed drawn to. Patients, nurses, and orderlies all wanted to pat him and ask questions about him. With all these people around to allay his fear of the floors, Rocky passed his exam with flying colors.

It isn't unusual for Rocky to attract a crowd, and as with most Newfoundlands, he often steals the show. Recently he participated in a blood drive at Angell Memorial Animal Hospital in Boston. Although there were approximately sixty other dogs participating, Rocky was the one who caught the reporter's eye. That's why it was my "big, black-haired, shaggy, drooling, brave and mostly oblivious" boy who was featured in the story about the blood drive that appeared in the April 1, 2001, *Boston Sunday Globe.*

Deciding to take Rocky to participate in the blood drive was not difficult. I felt this was one way I could repay the vets and staff at Angell Memorial. When Rocky was seven months old and again when he was nine months old, we went there for his hip surgeries. He had triple pelvic osteotomy (TPO) on one side and darthroplasty on the other. Because of the skill of the surgeons and the excellent post-surgical care of the staff, he now runs like a Greyhound rather than being crippled and in pain.

As each dog left the hospital it was awarded a bright blue "Pet me, I gave blood" bandanna, but when it came Rocky's turn, the technician had to tie two bandannas together to fit his big, shaggy neck. Rocky seemed happy enough to have the bandannas, but he was even more interested in the second gift, a twenty-pound bag of dog food.

Because of Rocky's hip dysplasia he is neutered and cannot be bred nor shown. But he is priceless to me and to all the folks he visits at Devlin Medical Center in Lynn, Massachusetts. One of the ladies who lives there actually asked if she could buy him from me so he would never have to leave.

People who have been afraid of dogs their entire lives have been drawn to my big boy. They want to touch him or just stand close to him. They can see his gentle and kind nature in his eyes. I call this Rocky's gift. From the time I was a little girl, I have always loved Newfies and wanted one of my own. My grandparents were from Newfoundland so I joke that I have no choice. It is in my *blood* to appreciate Newfoundland dogs. Whatever the reason, there is something special about the breed and something extra special about Rocky.

Cathie Logan
Lynn, Massachusetts, USA

Mocha's Moments

Much of my joy in living with a big Newfoundland comes from the *small* moments. These times with my dog have a magical quality that make me slow down, focus on the present, and appreciate my good fortune.

Right now, I can see our three-year-old Mocha lying on her side in our tile entryway. She is a 120-pound brown beauty who is spending the afternoon sleeping, sleeping, sleeping. She is preparing herself. Boosting her stamina. Building her energy. Our girl works the 7 - 11 evening shift.

After dinner, my husband, Bill, sits down at his computer, and I go to bed with a book. As soon as Mocha sees that the two of us are settled, she gets busy. She begins by climbing onto the bed beside me and leaning her head against my shoulder. I feel her warmth and her heart beat. I hear her contented sigh. I lower my book, bury my hand in her ruff, and look back on my day. . .and on my life. Stress melts. Tension vanishes. Problems disappear. For several moments the two of us are quiet and still, and completely at peace.

As soon as Mocha is satisfied that she has helped me put everything in perspective, she leaves our bedroom and goes downstairs. It's time to give her other human his share of attention.

The first thing she does is duck out the dog door to find a toy in our back yard. Back inside, she approaches Bill with the toy in her mouth. She sits beside him, chomping on it as she waits. She chomps. She waits. She shakes her head. She wiggles.

With one eye still on the computer screen, Bill takes her toy and tosses it across the room. Enthusiastically, she fetches it, sits down beside him, and chomps. And waits. And shakes her head. And wiggles.

Finally, Bill reaches out for the toy, and round two of the game begins. She pulls. He pulls. She pulls. Ultimately the man wrestles the now saliva-soaked toy away from the dog. He pretends to toss it and she races across the room. She turns around to face him and he "drills" it to her. She catches it! The game proceeds. Fetching. Wrestling. Faking. Throwing. Catching.

They play until Mocha catches the toy at least twenty times and Bill starts to lose interest. As soon as Mocha notices his enthusiasm lagging, she comes over and *gives* him the toy. No more hard-to-get. No more keep-away. They play catch a few more times until Bill finally hides the toy in exasperation and attempts to get back to work.

This is Mocha's signal to up the ante. Now the nudging starts. She pokes her nose under Bill's arm and pushes upward. Again. She drools a little swath of slime on his chair, then a little dribble on his keyboard. Next, she pokes her nose under his arm again. Time for a full chin and chest rub.

Before too long, Bill and Mocha come upstairs and into the bedroom. Mocha, proud of her good work, is smiling. Bill, unable to finish his work, is complaining.

"It's okay, Darling," I say. "It's time for bed, anyway. Let's hit the hay."

Once all the lights are out, I hear Mocha preparing her huge dog bed on the floor near my side of the bed. It's made of either excelsior or pine shavings packed inside a protective case and covered with a fluffy plush fabric.

PAWPAWPAWPAWPAWPAWPAW. . .turn, turn.

PAWPAWPAWPAWPAWPAWPAW. . .turn, turn.

PAWPAWPAWPAWPAWPAWPAW. . .turn, turn, turn.

I cannot see her, but she seems to be doing some sort of loud, scuffling, doggy dance in the dark there beside me. It goes on. And on. Although she will sleep in various locations during the next eight hours, this bed and dance is where her night begins.

Finally, she gets it right and lies down with a long, huge, serene sigh. It sounds as if all the air has been let out of a giant inner tube. When Mocha sighs, tranquillity reigns and all is right with the world. Whenever I feel stressed, recalling this nightly "Mocha moment" helps put things right.

About four years ago, we decided our Lab-mix, Sam, needed a friend. When Bill told me that the beloved dog of his young adulthood had been a Newfoundland, I knew that was the dog for me. I had met his dog once, long before we were married, and it had been everything I dreamed a dog should be.

After researching the breed for several months, we found just the right breeder and were put on a waiting list. We understood it would be six to twelve months before we would get our puppy.

But only three weeks later another buyer changed his mind about a ten-week-old puppy, and the breeder offered her to us. We decided to "sleep on it."

The next morning an e-mail arrived with her photo. That's all it took! I gulped and said "yes." "Yes" to huge quantities of fur collecting in corners. "Yes" to copious amounts of dog saliva on furniture, floors, walls, and ceilings. "Yes. *Yes*!" There is *nothing* more fetching than a Newfoundland puppy!

When the breeder brought Mocha from the nursery and placed her thirteen pounds of adorable fluff in my arms, she most resembled a small, chocolate-colored sheep with miniature jowls. I had already fallen in love with her from her picture, but now my heart went BOOM! We had our Newfoundland and Sam had his friend.

Sam was the one who really raised Mocha, and he did it with amazing patience and grace. Typically she would latch onto his neck with her little jaws, running along beside him—back and forth, over and over—all day long. Sam was the main focus of Mocha's incredible puppy energy. Bless that dear, old dog. Nowadays, Mocha is several times larger than he is, and as she revels in her prime, he grows ever whiter around his chops.

Mocha is an alert, sensitive girl who understands much of what we say. We noticed that when guests react in a negative way to her drool, her feelings are hurt. I now intervene by insisting that while it's okay to withdraw from swinging tendrils of slime, it must be done with tact and love. To help the situation, we always fold a daintily embroidered linen tea towel neatly over her collar when guests are coming. We use this "Jowl Towel" for deftly dabbing the moisture from her lips and chin.

In addition to being sensitive to human speech, Mocha is also wonderfully affectionate. In times of great love spilling over, such as when she greets us, her lower jaw vibrates in an open and shut motion. This is her delightful way of saying, "I love you." It always brightens my day and is one of my favorite "Mocha moments."

Mocha is our well-loved, chocolate-colored treasure. We know how lucky we are to be able to live with this marvelous girl.

Bill & Anne Anderson
Dublin, California, USA

Sheba Wants A Cracker

Sheba is five years old, and Sheba is plump! We knew when we rescued her two months ago through the Great Lakes Newfoundland Club that there was a diet in her future. We just weren't certain how long battling the bulge would take.

After our vet examined her, he helped us work out a reducing plan wherein Sheba will take her weight off slowly and sensibly. With time and patience, she will be as lean and fit as our other three weight-appropriate dogs.

Although Sheba loves her food and is now convinced that she's been put on a crash diet, the rest of us know she hasn't. Aside from the five bagels she stole off the counter and ate a week ago, she is doing quite well. I *think* I see a loss already. I *think* I felt a rib this morning.

Sheba's adjustment to her new home, her new humans, and her new dog siblings has gone smoothly. However, her adjustment to our Eclectus parrot has created something of a problem. It's not that she's having trouble learning to live with Mambo; rather, she's having trouble accepting the idea that he gets yogurt-covered cranberries, dried apples, dried banana chips, dried cherries, and peanuts with his pellets, but she does *not.*

From the first day Sheba joined our family, she has been fascinated with Mambo's food. She makes it her job to "vacuum" under his cage several times a day. I think he actually throws treats out to her in response to her begging. In any case, she has sampled all his food and evidently finds it a most desirable supplement to her reducing diet.

For two weeks she had been watching me *closely* each time I put the fruit bags away in a drawer of the computer armoire. Today she decided she had had enough "watching." Today she decided it was time for a fruit fest! While we were away from home for about thirty minutes, she opened the armoire drawer, pulled out all six (yes, SIX!) bags of parrot food, ripped them open, and ate every last ounce.

By the time we got home, all that was left of the approximately nine cups of Mambo treats were cellophane bags and empty peanut shells!

When I found the evidence of the heist, Sheba wagged her tail happily and looked at me with those "I love you, Mommy" eyes. I just had to laugh and give her a big hug and a kiss. She is so adorable and so cute I couldn't bear to scold her. Anyway, aren't all dieters entitled to an occasional binge?

Amy Lane
RiverRock Newfoundlands
Washington, Michigan, USA
www.NewfCentral.com

Watching Baron Bloom

It's official! Our six-year-old Newf, Baron, can curl his huge, floppy lips up enough to bare his teeth! He can snarl and growl and bark *ferociously*! Even more importantly, Baron has proved that he knows *when* to display these protective behaviors and when they are unnecessary.

Baron's opportunity to protect his family came last week when he was riding with my husband, John, in my truck. They had stopped at a traffic signal behind several other cars. The light turned green and the Mercedes behind them rammed into the back of the truck.

When a small, sporty car, even an expensive one, hits the bumper of a truck, the passengers of the truck feel very little impact and there is no damage done to the truck. Baron, in typical laidback Newfy fashion, noticed the impact and looked interested, but not at all concerned.

My truck is a full-sized Ford F150 work truck, not one of those cute little trucklettes. It is hardly a vehicle that can go unnoticed! Additionally, the responsibility for avoiding what lies in front of one's vehicle always falls directly on the driver. Nevertheless, the driver of the Mercedes jumped out of his now slightly wrinkled car and proceeded to wave his arms and yell angrily as he walked toward my husband.

But Baron would have none of that! His response was immediate and loud. The man heard his fearsome barking, took one look at his snapping teeth, and hastily retreated. Baron, however, continued glaring at him and growling softly.

John was surprised by our big boy's behavior. In the 2½ years he has been with us, Baron had never before delivered such an impressive warning. When he joined our family, we already had Blizzard, our Great Pyrenees. Blizz excels at protective mode, but Baron seldom initiates defensive barking and has never approached it with the same seriousness as the Pyr. I really don't expect him to, as I feel one 100+ pound dog is enough to keep the UPS driver and the fallen tree branches at bay.

But now Baron had accepted the full responsibility for protecting John. Even as a police car roared into view with emergency lights flashing and siren screaming, Baron continued focusing his attention on the Mercedes driver who was by then standing quietly beside his crumpled car.

Baron understood that the police officer was not a threat. While he stood near John writing the accident report, Baron was his calm self again, wagging his tail and begging to be petted. However, when the officer went back to speak with the Mercedes driver, Baron returned to his defensive guard mode.

Although I had always known Baron would come to our aid if necessary, this was the first time that such an occasion had arisen. He showed excellent judgment in this situation, and I was very proud of him.

Baron's confidence in protecting my husband is particularly appreciated in view of his background. He came to us as a very timid dog with many insecurities. He had spent much of the first four years of his life confined to the dim basement of his original home.

At first the world was a scary place for Baron and he just wanted to spend his days hiding in a corner. But gradually we exposed him to new sights, sounds, and surroundings. Starting with small groups of family and friends, we moved on to softball games and community events with lots of people. He was especially cautious when any man would make a sudden move in his direction, and he was often seriously and inexplicably fearful of certain areas of certain floors.

But even though he was sometimes frightened during this socialization period, he never made the slightest aggressive or defensive move toward anyone. Since his fear reactions are very subtle, we were the only ones who could tell when he was afraid.

A city bus driver unknowingly helped Baron get over his uncertainty about buses. I was alone with him at a shopping mall when a bus pulled up toward us. I stood calmly to signal to him that it was okay to be near a noisy vehicle. He stood with me but kept a watchful eye on the bus. Astonishingly, the driver stopped the bus, got out, and asked if she could pet my dog! Baron was delighted with her cuddles and caresses, and now looks hopefully for his friend every time he sees a bus.

Eventually Baron was comfortable in any situation, including watching freight trains and a drum and bugle corps complete with waving flags. During his first year with us he learned that pats and hugs are good, that toys are fun, and that back yards are designed for playing. People just seemed to gravitate toward him and he learned to enjoy their attention. As he became happier and more secure, he even developed a sense of humor and a real talent for amusing people.

Baron makes us laugh every time he uses psychology on Blizz and our other dog, Jesse. Of all the dog toys we have, Baron is interested in only one—a gray bear named Theodore. If another dog has Theo, Baron will pick up a different toy and prance across the room with his head held high, making little happy noises that say, "This is the best toy in the world!" As soon as the other dog drops Theo to check out the world's best toy, Baron grabs him and takes him off to a quiet corner. This is the only time Baron ever touches another toy.

Baron is with us because I happened to see an ad in the paper for an adult Newfoundland. His first family had purchased him as a puppy in a pet store, but he had grown too big and become too hairy and too slobbery. They told me they had kept him in the basement most of the time because he was too large to live in the house. These were not bad people, but they had been uninformed about the characteristics and needs of a Newfoundland. After attempting to cope with him for four years, they were happy to sell him to anyone who would pay their price. To those people Baron was a piece of property that had not turned out as they had expected. To us he is a member of our family. We've watched him blossom and grow into a patient, wonderful, *protective* boy. It never ceases to amaze us that this warmhearted Newfy was unwanted.

Angela Mertens
Pleasant Prairie, Wisconsin, USA

The Band Played On

It was *time*. Leash training. Social manners. Small-child-present behavior. We had been practicing these skills ever since I had subscribed to Newf-List 2½ months earlier. I was pleased with Dawson's progress. He had been doing exceptionally well. So I decided he was ready for a *test*, an official *outing*.

The Kenai River Festival was going full swing in a park only four blocks from our home. This would be perfect! I had read the Newf-L discussion about taking a Newf to a public event. I used that information to plan my strategy.

Dawson and I would walk to the park so he wouldn't be overly energetic at the festival. Later my husband and children would drive over in the van with Dawson's water dish and water. I had a good plan. I felt confident.

The walk to the park went well. Then Dawson and I walked across the grounds and entered the fairway where booths were set up along both sides. As we came into sight, all conversation, chattering, and giggling ceased. Suddenly I realized all eyes had turned to *Dawson.* In the silence I could almost hear the jaws as they dropped.

I had learned many things about taking a Newf to a public event, but no one had prepared me for *this!* At least the *band* kept playing!

"Oh, Dawson, please don't do anything embarrassing right now," I secretly hoped.

Then we started down the fairway and the murmurs began. The questions commenced. The people began approaching.

"Man! That's a *big* dog!"

"What *kind* is it?"

"How much does he *eat?"*

"He's beautiful! May I pet him?"

As we slowly made our way to the end of the fairway, my 2½-year-old Newfy was a super-well-behaved gentleman. He welcomed the hugs and pats and squeals from the humans, both big and small. He accepted the new smells, new sights, and new sounds. He posed when a man took out his camera and asked to take his picture. He even greeted a German Shepherd and her owner with friendly curiosity.

I was overwhelmed with the attention Dawson attracted. Walking down the fairway with him was an experience I could never have imagined. When we finally reached the end, I took Dawson around behind the booths for a quiet moment.

My boy had won many friends and influenced many people, and I was thrilled with his behavior. But I was also exhausted. Public appearances take *lots* of energy. I needed a break!

Today I can look back on Dawson's first public event with a smile. Now that he has been with us for over a year, I'm well accustomed to the attention he attracts when we're out. I'm well accustomed to answering the questions about him that are inevitably asked. But I am still awed by his gentleness and by the sweet surprises he reserves for our family.

Often these sweet surprises involve our children. Last spring, when our six-year-old daughter held a dandelion up to his nose for a smell, he very gently accepted it. And ate it. Maybe he thinks dandelions are special doggie treats and was pleased with his little mistress's thoughtful gift. Or maybe he just thought she had mistaken a dandelion for a doggie treat and didn't want to hurt her feelings.

Later in the year during a bedtime tucking-in session, I got to my seven-year-old son last. He lay on his stomach, eyes closed. Knowing that the kids sometimes pretend to be asleep to point out that I took too long tucking in their siblings, I lay down next to him for an extra cuddle. As it turns out, he really had fallen asleep, but I thought he was "acting."

Dawson walked into the room so I said, "Dawson, give Pete his good-night kiss!"

Jumping onto the bed, Dawson stood directly over Pete, putting a front paw on either side of him. With his rump still in the air, he lowered himself onto his elbows until his chest was resting on Pete's back. Then he lay his muzzle right next to Pete's face—a perfect "good-night kiss" posture.

I wasn't expecting anything close to this! "Give a kiss" is not a formal doggie command in our house. When did he learn this? Who taught him this? Dawson does lean in close when I say "give a *hug*," but this kissing behavior was entirely new.

I couldn't help laughing while trying to persuade Dawson it was time to end the "kiss." Pete was groaning weakly. He could only squeeze a tiny bit of air into his lungs with a 120-pound dog on his back. Surprisingly, my son didn't remember any of this in the morning and doesn't even believe it happened!

Of course not all of Dawson's family activities meet with our approval. A few days ago I made a batch of cookies, and each of the children enjoyed two while they were warm. Then I left the rest of the cookies cooling on the dining table. Minutes later I returned to find all of the cookies gone, Dawson licking his chops, six disappointed children, and one disgusted husband. Dawson seemed rather proud of his clever trick, but not one member of his human family applauded.

We still have much to learn about our boy, but we're making progress. When we adopted Dawson from a family that was moving, we knew nothing about Newfs, but we had heard of their sweetness. All we knew for certain was that Dawson needed some *serious* brushing.

After we had had Dawson for about six months, an acquaintance suggested we subscribe to Newf-L. What a wonderful surprise! What a wealth of information! Reading about other Newfs transformed our relationship with Dawson.

We had thought he would be more comfortable living outside where it is cool rather than inside our warm house. But we learned from Newf-L that Newfs can live indoors with their families, indeed, they *need* to live indoors with their families. Dawson has been inside with us ever since and we're all much happier with this arrangement.

Although we knew little about Dawson's background when we got him, we've learned quite a bit since then. Initially, I met a woman who had been Dawson's neighbor at his first home. She was stunned to see him in such good condition and with such good manners. She told me he had been quite a runabout, helping himself into other people's houses and generally making a nuisance of himself. I would never have dreamed he could have been like that. Not my gentleman! Not my shadow!

A few weeks after meeting his former neighbor, we met the owners of Dawson's parents. From them we've learned that he has his mother's gentleness and sweetness. He also has her strong determination to keep moose out of the yard! Somehow having learned more about him gives new meaning to his life with us and makes us more aware of what makes him "tick."

We all love our big boy and are thrilled to have him in our family. And, we are forever grateful to all the subscribers of Newf-L who take the time to share important information with people like us who are new to this remarkable breed.

Nenette Rogers
Kenai, Alaska, USA

www.rogersark.com

Goldilocks In Galilee

It was a lovely summer morning and my three Newfs and I were enjoying our walk. We were just outside the village in the open countryside behind our house. This is a quiet, peaceful area where we see only farmers here and there working in their fields.

All the farmers are accustomed to our early-morning excursions and usually wave as we pass. One morning one of them called from his tractor, "Hi, Miri. You look like Goldilocks with the three bears." My hair is blonde. My dogs are big. Perhaps there *is* a resemblance.

On this particular morning, we seemed to have the area all to ourselves. But suddenly the tranquillity was shattered. Rounding the corner of an olive orchard, a complete *patrouille* of soldiers riding in open Jeeps roared into view. This is not an unusual sight, as our army often uses the countryside for training and maneuvers.

As the Jeeps bounced along the sandy road toward us, huge clouds of dust billowed all around them. Since my dogs were off-leash, I called them to me and we stood—a middle-aged woman, two black Newfs, and a big Landseer puppy—waiting by the side of the road for the *patrouille* to pass.

The first two Jeeps flew past us, but the third Jeep in the long convoy came to an abrupt stop right in front of us. Of course this caused some confusion as, one by one, all the Jeeps behind the third one halted.

Clouds of dust were still swirling as the young soldier who had stopped in front of us began speaking to me. Under his big helmet, I could see his face was black with dust.

"Good morning, Ma'am. Those are beautiful dogs you have," he called down to me. "Aren't they Newfoundlands? Yes, I read all about them. They are most wonderful dogs who rescue people from drowning and have swimming webs between their toes, right?"

I was so astonished and so pleased to have this young man recognize and admire my dogs! He was only about eighteen years old, and he seemed very serious in his quest for information. When I nodded and told him he was correct, he got such a big smile on his dusty face!

By then, some of the soldiers in the Jeeps behind him had begun honking their horns.

"Hey, what do you think you're doing holding us up?" another soldier shouted.

"Well, sure pleased to have met your dogs, Ma'am!" he said.

Then the young man put his foot on the gas pedal, gave us another big grin, and in a cloud of dust, followed by the rest of the convoy, he was gone.

I smiled down at my three dogs: Dee, the big, high-spirited girl I had gotten from a Russian immigrant breeder, through an interpreter, seven years ago when I just *had* to have a Newf—*immediately*; Jubilee, the beautiful two-year-old I had imported from Italy after I did my homework and knew I wanted to build the Newf breed in Israel, and Kissy, the six-month-old male puppy I had imported from Portugal after I decided it might be easier for the white dogs to bear our summers.

Yes, the young soldier was right! My dogs *are* beautiful! Newfs are rare in Israel, and Kissy is the only Landseer in the whole country. So, they often draw attention. They often make people gasp and stare. But this morning had been different. This morning my Newfs had stopped a *convoy*!

By then the sun was getting higher so it was time to get the dogs home. Summer heat is something we know about and respect here in Israel. During our warmest months I have to be careful with my Newfs. Yet by taking a few extra precautions, I am able to keep them comfortable despite the high temperatures.

Since a regular exercise routine is essential to maintaining their health and *mine*, I walk the dogs daily. However, we take our main walk early in the morning and I *always*, even on short walks, take along a bottle of half-frozen water and a drinking bowl in case of emergencies. Other things I do to maintain the dogs' comfort on walks, as well as put smiles on their faces, include patting their bellies now and then with a wet cloth and squirting their heads with water from a spray bottle. Once we return home, they cool off with an ice cube or two. They lick, crunch, and play with these treats on the lawn before I take them inside.

During summer days, I keep the dogs in the house with the windows and curtains closed to keep the house cool. Sometimes I leave the ceiling fan in the living room spinning, and when it is exceptionally hot, I leave the air conditioner on. They relax and sleep all day until we come home from work in the evening.

Early morning is the best time for a walk, but I try to give the two younger dogs another walk in the cool evening hours, even if it's after dark. Instead of taking them out to the fields in the evening, I take them on a leash into the village. Dee doesn't need as much exercise as Jubilee and Kissy do, and the truth is, the sidewalks in our village are not broad enough for the four of us!

Although keeping Newfs comfortable through an Israeli summer requires some thought and planning, it is not a difficult task. I make the same kinds of adjustments anyone living with Newfs in a hot climate needs to make. During the hot part of the day, my dogs are never given any strenuous exercise. Rather, they always have a cool place to rest and they are always given an adequate amount of water. Unlike most bruins who sleep through the cold days of winter, my three bears sleep through the hot days of summer. I am happy with this arrangement, and so are they.

Miri Abramson
Yama Valley Newfoundlands
Yavneel, Israel

April the Hun

When I returned home after running some errands, April greeted me at the door with welcome wags, as usual.

"Leaves? Where did you manage to find leaves in the house? April, how did you get dried leaves all over you?"

My four-year-old Newf gave me a cheerful smile, then trotted down the front stairs to the yard. That's when I noticed she had a hitchhiker thoroughly entangled in her pantaloons.

"My hairbrush! April, how did you manage to get—wait a minute! Those aren't *leaves*!"

I had done it again! I had forgotten to jam the upstairs bathroom door open before I left the house. And she had done it again. She had gone into the bathroom to enjoy the cool linoleum floor and gotten trapped when the door had accidentally swung closed.

Had she just relaxed and taken a nap? Nooooo. Had she just waited for Daddy to come home and let her out? Nooooo. Those brown bits in her coat were *wood chips*. Those white specks were *drywall*. My little trooper had made her *own* way out of the bathroom.

She could have escaped the easy way through the nice, soft drywall. Instead, she had chosen to depart through the door. Subsequently, she had dug a huge, Newfy-sized hole in order to do so.

All that was left of the bathroom door was a shell and a floor full of sawdust and wood chips. One look told me I would need to replace the door, the trim, and the jamb.

April's jobs would be easier. First, she would have to find a new place to nap, and second, she would need to let one toenail grow back to its normal length.

I must admit, this door demolition event took me by surprise. It's not that I didn't know she was capable of such a feat—I hadn't nicknamed her "The Hun" without reason. Her puppy days and young adulthood remain a blur of astonishing activities which include, but were not limited to, stealing the Christmas turkey one year and indulging in a private holiday feast, and pilfering a full 1-kilogram (2.2-pound) jar of peanut butter from the pantry one morning and devouring it in my bed before I woke up.

But we hadn't had any "incidents" for almost a year and I had been lulled into a false sense of security. Now I realize April is like a volcano that slumbers peacefully between dramatic eruptions. Now I know life with my first Newf will continue to be a joy ride of unexpected events.

Before April came to live with me at the age of 7½ weeks, I had loved Newfoundlands for many years. I had done exhaustive research on their temperament and personality. But my research fell short in describing April. Yes, she has a gentle temperament. Yes, she has a lovable personality. But she is also an extremely clever girl with a wildly creative imagination. It's that *spark* in her eye when she is thinking up something outrageous that makes me smile. And since she is almost always thinking up something outrageous, I am almost always smiling. But now I have been forewarned. Now I know April's spark is volcanic!

Sean Manson
Mount Uniacke, Nova Scotia, Canada

The Corncob Kid

Something was wrong—*seriously* wrong. In addition to always being a clown and always being mischievous, Dillon had always been a voracious eater. But for two days he had refused his food. On the morning of the third day, he was vomiting water.

Although he was acting normal in all other ways, his refusal to eat and his vomiting were not normal. Within minutes I had him in the van heading to the vet's office.

A series of X-rays confirmed that Dillon had a blockage in his small intestine. Soon we were back in the van making the two-hour drive to a surgical clinic in Los Angeles, and by late afternoon Dillon was waking up from his first major surgery.

The surgeon assured me that the surgery had been successful. He had found the problem and removed it. He explained that the blockage had been caused by a piece of corncob. He told me it was an inch long with the circumference of a silver dollar.

Of course I was extremely concerned about my boy, but after the surgery Dillon's blood panel was perfect. He was a bit dehydrated, but that would be easy to correct since I had caught the problem early. Because he was an otherwise healthy 2½-year-old, the surgeon told me I could expect his recovery to go well.

I knew exactly when that corncob had been eaten! Two weeks earlier, my husband, Tom, had come home from running some errands to find that Dillon had opened the door to the kitchen cabinet where we keep the trash, dragged our large trash can into the back bathroom, and scattered its contents all over the floor. Tom was leaving on a trip later that day, and had prepared a delicious meal the night before—steak, salad, and corn-on-the-cob.

By the time I broke the news about Dillon in a phone call to my husband, I could laugh a bit.

"Tom, remember that *wonderful* dinner you cooked just before you left? The steak and the corn? Well, that was the most expensive dinner we have ever eaten!"

Tom never asked, "How expensive is expensive?" Instead, he wanted the details of our ordeal and reassurances that Dillon would be all right.

When our credit card bill arrives, he will learn that the trip to our local vet's office was $133.00, and the trip to the surgery center was $1650.00. The grand total for our steak and corn-on-the-cob dinner was $1783.00. And we didn't even have wine, coffee, or dessert!

We've always known Dillon will go out of his way for food. Ever since he came to live with us at the age of eight weeks, he has been interested in all things edible. We came home one day to find him standing on top of our dining room table with a cube of butter in his mouth. Another day he surprised us by opening the cabinet where the canned foods are kept, rolling canned foods all over the house, and greeting us with a can of tomato soup in his mouth.

Actually, the boy puts all sorts of things in his mouth! Glass Christmas tree ornaments come immediately to mind, and at his Water Rescue Dog test, he somehow managed to hold an oar in his mouth so he could swim with it sticking straight up from the water like a flag.

Dillon is our fourth Newf, but he is the first to teach us the importance of using child-guard locks on cabinets, the necessity of double-checking closed doors, and the value of disposing of corncobs in Newf-proof receptacles. Although keeping him out of mischief sometimes seems to be our full-time occupation, his enthusiasm for life and his sense of humor are infectious. We love our energetic boy and are very grateful that his corncob-eating venture had a happy ending.

Peggy Lange
Rossmoor, California, USA

So, Where's Your Purse?

It all happened too quickly. It all seemed unreal. Ours is a family that approaches any new project carefully. We read books. We consult authorities. We investigate possibilities. In truth, we tend to examine things until everyone loses interest.

Oh, we had *started* our research. My husband had *seen* one Newf. We had *read* one book. But at that stage an ad appeared in the paper. When we spoke with the breeder, she told us she was bringing her thirteen puppies down to the vet for heart checks. If we met her there, we could take our pick after the sire's owner chose his two.

If we met her there! Then my husband did something totally out of character, something absolutely unheard of in our family. He rushed across town and took our three kids—two teenagers and an eight-year-old—out of school! Then off they sped to the vet's office!

Within minutes of their arrival, the four of them had chosen a puppy from the back of the breeder's truck. They brought him to the center for the treatment of physically handicapped children where I worked, and he spent the rest of the day peeking out at me from under a wheelchair.

Newf puppies should carry warning labels! Newf puppies make rational people act irrationally! As I said, it all happened too quickly. It all seemed unreal. And we were not prepared. Not for our first Newfy! Not for Bear!

When he had been with us for three weeks, Bear decided he was the leader, the alpha, the ruler of our roost. No questions asked. No votes taken. No second opinions sought. Bear was eleven weeks old. We were in trouble!

Acting quickly, we enrolled Bear in an obedience class for puppies. As soon as it become obvious that he wasn't taking me very seriously, my husband took over his training.

One of the main problems I was having with Bear was his unrelenting determination to grab and shake my arm or my sleeve every time I left the house. Occasionally, he would sink his sharp little puppy teeth into my purse as I attempted to get out the door.

When I discussed my dilemma with a local breeder, she suggested I put something suitable in Bear's mouth prior to leaving the house. If his mouth were already engaged, perhaps he wouldn't grab *me*.

I tried to think of something appropriate. A purse? He loved my purse. Would he like a purse of his own?

I searched through my closet until I found a purse I no longer needed. When I presented it to Bear, he was absolutely *thrilled*. He grabbed the purse and ran through the house to the front door. He was ready to go! He was ready for a ride in the van!

From that day forward, the phrase, “Bear, get your purse!” was our boy’s signal that we were ready to leave the house and he was included. As soon as he heard the phrase, he would begin racing around looking for his purse. As soon as he found it, he would skid to the door. Once outside, he always dropped his purse and hurried to make a quick piddle. Then he would grab up his purse again and rush to the van.

If Bear happened to be outside when we invited him to get into the van, he would give us a quick look, then bound to the door of the house. As soon as someone let him inside, he would begin a frantic search for his purse! We had to wait until he found it because he resisted all attempts to get him on board until he had his purse. He let us understand, in no uncertain terms, that he could not *possibly* get into the van without it!

For the rest of his wonderfully-long, twelve-year life, Bear never left home without his purse. As each one of his purses got a bit ragged (from carrying—never from deliberate destruction), I would get him a new one at a garage sale.

He loved his purses and often carried them with him when we reached our various destinations. He was particularly fond of showing off his purse at our vet’s office and would literally drag me to the door in his eagerness to bask in the excitement his visits always produced.

In his later years, I sometimes replaced his purse with garage sale stuffed animals, but the signal remained the same. “Bear, get your purse” never failed to send him into a frenzied search through the house.

Bear was always an integral member of our family. Because he was so lively, we focused his energy on training, and he introduced us to the whole Newf world. He learned to cart and went on to get his Companion Dog, Draft Dog, and Team Draft Dog titles. He loved carting and drafting. At the age of ten he walked in the Syracuse St. Patrick’s Day Parade. He was so full of love and life that he *never* wanted to quit.

When it was time for the kids to go off to college, we were too busy with Newf activities to suffer empty nestitis. Because of Bear, our children were able to get on with their own lives without *too* much parental involvement. By the time Bear was a year old, we had added Halcy. Then came Kriket. He was followed by Patti and her brother, Zeus. Zeus recently died at the age of 12½, and now we have three-year-old Zena.

We learned two valuable lessons from Bear: 1) training is necessary if a dog and a human family are to live together in harmony; and, 2) training should begin on Day 1.

Bear was always a character and a clown, but he never forgot to test us occasionally for alpha status. He knew that pack survival depends on a strong leader, and he wanted to ensure the survival of his pack.

Bear also taught us not to take ourselves too seriously. He was our first Newf, and we probably made a few mistakes with him. But Newfs are the most giving and forgiving of God's creations. And our dear Bear was the most giving and forgiving of all.

Beth Sell
Cazenovia, New York, USA

Sweet Seduction

Being new to the world of Newfoundlands when our first pup came to live with us, we had no idea how attached they got to their people. Our little Holly shadowed us, rarely letting us out of her sight.

As the months went by, we sometimes had to venture out without her. She couldn't adjust to being alone, and developed separation anxiety. Try as we might, nothing we did to reassure her worked. So, we resigned ourselves to the fact that another Newf would have to adopt us to keep Holly company.

We are fortunate to live just around the corner from Sam and Joyce, wonderful breeders of Newfoundlands and great friends. When we explained our plight to Sam he said, "Why don't you take Emma Lou home for a visit and see how it works out?" (Three Newfs later, we would learn that "take home for a visit" actually means "stay at your house forever"!)

Emma was ten years old at the time. She is a retired Search and Rescue dog with a remarkable record. She has the gratitude of many, many families in the Pennsylvania/Ohio/West Virginia tri-state area.

Stories were also told about Emma having a sweet tooth when she was younger. I vaguely remember something about her devouring a five-pound bag of sugar.

But Emma acted her age now. She had to be lifted into the van. She had to be helped out of the van. All her moves were made with care and seemed to take such an effort.

Just as we had hoped, Holly was delighted to have a friend and housemate, and Emma seemed happy with her new situation.

About two weeks after becoming gleefully aware that Emma was here to stay, my son, Matthew, and I went out shopping. My husband, Tom, stayed home with the pooches, but he was quietly working on the computer and not a Newfy soul realized he was home.

Not more than five minutes after our departure, Tom heard a peculiar noise coming from the kitchen. It sounded like nails scraping on glass. It would start, last for a second or two, then stop. This pattern repeated for about two minutes before he decided to investigate.

Tom quietly walked toward the kitchen. As he rounded the corner, a wondrous sight caught his eye. Have you ever heard of selective memory? What about selective arthritis?

For there, up on the island in the middle of the kitchen, back legs dangling two feet above the floor, was ten-year-old, arthritic, "carefully help me into the van, please" Emma Lou. She was poised to grab a bag containing doughnuts.

Tom could hardly contain his laughter while gently lifting Emma back to earth. He was also amused to see that Holly, realizing Emma was behaving badly and not wanting to be implicated, was hiding around the corner.

Emma is fourteen now, and that sort of climbing antic is out of the question. She is spry for her age, but nonetheless, not as active as she was at ten. Still, we always hide the doughnuts—just in case.

Julie McKenzie
Aliquippa, Pennsylvania, USA

Drooly Thoughts

One part spit and one part drool,
I wear it on most days at school.
My students all exclaim, "What's *that*?"
It's an ever-lovin' slobbery *splat*.

It's on the wall and on the rug,
We look at it, and smile, and shrug.
It's medium-sized, or big, or tiny,
Sometimes drippy, always shiny.

We look for them with anticipation,
Clinging, dangling Newf decorations.
It's on my car and in my shoe,
How far it'll fly, I've not a clue.

Holly launches them moist and fast,
Solly ejects them with a sonic blast.
Then there's Emma all neat and nice,
She's *never* dripped, even once or twice.

It's everywhere and every way,
It gives us joy each night and day.
I've never spotted it atop our roof,
'Cause we don't have a flying Newf.

It's just a part of Newfy lore,
Like furballs on the bathroom floor.
A wonder, another proof,
That we love being owned by Newfs!

Tom McKenzie
Aliquippa, Pennsylvania, USA

Bathtime for Atticus

It was *that* time of the month for the dogs again! The Mobile Dog Wash was coming! Atticus had so far been more than a bit reluctant about this event each month. So, what would he be like this time?

As soon as Atticus saw the trailer with the hydrobath in it, he knew what was coming. It had stopped at his house twice before. He watched as Simon, the dog-wash man, came forward to greet him.

Simon had gained the cooperation of our other Newf, and he was determined to make good with Atticus. Atticus gave him a tail wag and even a slobbery lick on the chin.

I took this as a positive sign. Atticus knows Simon is the dog-wash man, but evidently he holds no grudges.

We managed to get Atticus up the ramp this time without *too* much effort. Clearly, we were making progress. The battle that was Atticus's first wash began when he went into "drop mode" on the road in front of the ramp. That day, his protesting continued throughout the whole bathing adventure.

I did not attend the next wash; I decided instead, that David, my husband, would organise Atticus's second arrival to the bath. (I did not get much of a report on Atticus's behaviour. However, while shaking his head later in the day, David uttered, "Atticus isn't too keen on getting a bath.")

But now, after successfully getting Atticus up the ramp, getting him into the tub for Bath #3 was another matter altogether. Once we had him turned around to face the bath entrance, Atticus decided a "drop-stay" was the best weapon against the next step toward cleanliness.

I took the front end while Simon lifted the back end. HEEEAVE! Atticus decided dignity was the most important thing and gave only a little resistance. He did, however, still have a few more ideas up his furry sleeve. Once in the tub, he quickly plonked himself into a "sit-stay."

I decided at that time that Atticus's lust for nibbles might help with the rest of the bathing, so I ran back to the house and retrieved some tasty morsels.

Simon reported that as soon as I was out of sight, my almost-one-year-old puppy stood up to try and see where I had gone. This made the start of the "wetting down" stage a bit easier. However, as soon as I returned, Atticus sat down once more.

But not for long! I produced a morsel which instantly brought results. Atticus stood up again, rested his head on the side of the tub, and waited for his treat.

Naturally, as the bath continued, there were times when Atticus wasn't getting little treats (or bribes?). During these moments he really did his best to show his displeasure. But, he did this in a dignified manner. Being a

Newfoundland, he didn't bark, bite, growl, or try to exit the bath. No. Atticus *sulked.*

He did this by bowing his head as far as he could while standing, and pressing it into one of the corners of the tub. Of course when I said his name, he would lift up immediately to see if I were offering another morsel. Now, that is "sulk mode" with *attitude*. Atticus is *not* dumb!

I know it wasn't funny to Atticus, but, gee, it made me laugh when Atticus did his best to make Simon and me feel as if we were the nastiest people around. I was amused, but also a little embarrassed about Atticus's sulking in front of Simon. He showed himself to be quite the "performer."

At last the soap and rinse cycles were finished and the drying began. Atticus does NOT like the dryer! I don't know whether it's the noise or the warm air blowing on him, but *something* about the drying process truly urks him. He gave me the "I've had enough, please let me out of here" look.

Even though Simon started the dryer on low to help him become accustomed to the noise, and we both talked gently to him during the process, Atticus was clearly not amused. But after two previous visits from this noisy thing, he decided to *tolerate* it.

Then there was only one more hurdle to cross. But this was where Atticus finally drew the line! For no amount of sweet talk, for no number of tasty bribes would he change his mind. He wouldn't fall for our tricks. He wasn't interested in our distractions. *Nothing* could convince Atticus to let Simon dry his ears.

Although the rest of him was a picture to behold, Atticus went back to the house with wet ears. I'm wondering if a bit of dryer therapy with my old hair dryer might make the *next* mobile hydrobath experience easier and *complete*.

All things considered, I am pleased with the outcome of Bath #3. Atticus is our fourth Newfoundland, and each has had his own distinctive way of making his personal likes and dislikes known.

Atticus's bath behaviour illustrates his intelligence and personality as he adjusts to one of the essential hygiene routines necessary for being a family pet. Although he may never *thrill* to Simon's arrival, even as a puppy he shows his innate dignity and willingness to accept the rules of his human pack. Since Atticus knows I already love him, wet ears or dry, I appreciate this acceptance.

Jane Foot
Geelong, Victoria, Australia

About the Illustrator

Kathee Kiesselbach studied printmaking and painting at Indiana University, and is now studying wood engraving. She works at the University of Notre Dame and lives in Michigan with her husband, Wilhelm, and their three Newfoundlands, Brocka, Uma, and little Bismarck. The Newfs appear regularly in her work. Kathee created the cover for this book and the wood engraving, *Bismarck In Japan*, which appears at the end of the list, The Ninety-nine Newfies. You can see more of Kathee's creations at www.biggieboy.com.

This photo of Kathee and Brocka was taken in the spring of 2000. The photographer was her husband, Wilhelm.

About the Editor

Pat Seawell lives in San Antonio, Texas, with her husband, John P. Seawell, and their four kitties. She gardens for hummingbirds and butterflies, reads books, practices Tae Kwon Do, and volunteers with the Delta Society of San Antonio. She is looking forward to raising another Newfy puppy and editing another Newfy book.

Printed in the United States
16849LVS00004B/280-285